ENGLISH

VOCABULARY
ORGANISER

100 topics for self-study

CHRIS GOUGH

Language Teaching Publications

114a Church Rd, Hove, BN3 2EB, England
E-mail: ltp@ltpwebsite.com

ISBN   1 899396 36 5
© LTP 2001

The Author

Chris Gough has taught in London, Valencia and Granada and is currently working in Brighton teaching and training both native-speaking and non-native speaking teachers. He would like to thank Michael Lewis and Jimmie Hill for their guidance, expertise and patience, and Morgan Lewis for all his help, encouragement and enthusiasm. A special thanks to Gerri for putting up with it all.

Acknowledgements

Cover design by Anna Macleod.
Cartoons by Pantelis Palios.
Illustrations by Anna Macleod and Guy Passey.
Printed in the UK by Commercial Colour Press plc, London E7 0EW.

Vocabulary is important

What is the purpose of this book?

This book is designed to help you increase the number of words you know and help you to use them. It gives you thousands of words connected with 100 different topics. One of the main things you will learn is that a new word is useless unless you know how to use it.

What is vocabulary?

Vocabulary is not just words. When we talk about our vocabulary, we mean the words we know and our ability to use them. Here are four different ways to think about words:

Meaning

When we meet a new word, the first thing we want to know is what it means. In this book, for example, you will find the word for a type of fish – salmon. Only one kind of fish is called salmon, so that is easy.

Pronunciation

When you learn a new word, make sure you can say it. Make sure you know which syllable is stressed. If you are unsure, ask a teacher or use a dictionary with a CD-ROM which gives the pronunciation.

Collocation

Collocation is the way words combine with other words. There is little point in knowing the word risk, unless you also know the verb which goes with it – take a risk. We say that take collocates with risk. In the same way deep and shallow are adjectives which collocate with water. In this book you will find lots of collocation exercises.

Expressions

Expressions are groups of two, three, four or more words which always go together. For example, if you are in a shop and an assistant approaches you, you can say, "I'm just looking." If you are interested in finding out more about someone, you can ask them, "What do you do for a living?"

Should I translate words?

There is nothing wrong with translation. It is often the quickest way to check the meaning of a word. You will find exercises in this book which encourage you to write in translations of basic vocabulary. Remember that you often need to translate whole expressions, not just individual words. Check words in your bi-lingual dictionary, but then check in a good English-English dictionary which will give you good, natural examples of the word in context.

Why is vocabulary important?

Vocabulary is important because it is words which carry the content of what we want to say. Grammar joins groups of words together, but most of the meaning is in the words. The more words you know, the more you will be able to communicate. You can say a lot with words. There is not much you can say with grammar alone!

How many words are there in English?

Compared with other languages, English grammar is quite simple: there are no cases and nouns don't have gender. However, English contains more words than any other world language – hundreds of thousands. Very often English has two words when other languages only have one. For example, we can talk about two things being the same or identical. Questions can be hard or difficult.

How do we learn vocabulary?

The main way we increase our personal vocabularies is by reading a lot of natural English regularly. As a student, you can also learn by studying and doing vocabulary exercises like those in this book. This book brings words of similar meaning together into 100 units. We have organised vocabulary for you. If you study page 7, it will help you get the most out of this book.

Is grammar also important?

Vocabulary and grammar are both important. With a bigger vocabulary you will be able to talk about more things. With better grammar, you will be able to talk about them more fluently and more accurately.

Contents

Section 7: Food and drink

Section 8: Leisure time

Section 9: Sport

Section 10: The media

Section 11: Technology

Section 12: Money matters

Section 13: Travel and transport

Section 14: Education and work

Section 15: Society

Section 16: Our world

Section 17: Abstract concepts

Before you start

General guidance on studying

1. Before you start working through the units of *English Vocabulary Organiser,* do the exercises on this page. They are typical of the kinds of exercises in the units. Check your answers in the Answer Key.

2. Don't feel you have to work through the units starting at Unit 1. You can do them in any order.

3. Try to do a little every day. Don't work for 4 hours one day and then nothing for the next week.

4. Use the answer key wisely. The answers are not secret. They are there to help you. Try to do an exercise first, then check the answers when you have finished. If there is one example in an exercise which you do not understand, don't try to guess the answer, look it up in the key and in your dictionary.

1 Verb / noun collocations

Collocation is the way words combine with other words. Match the verbs on the left with the nouns on the right:

1. make	a. your arm
2. show	b. your alarm for 6 o'clock
3. set	c. a business
4. break	d. a mistake
5. set up	e. your exam
6. pass	f. interest in something

The important thing about this kind of exercise is that the answers should be very obvious. There are only a small number of things you can set up *or* pass.

2 Adjective / noun collocations

Now match the adjectives on the left with the nouns on the right:

1. heavy	a. lifestyle
2. strong	b. rain
3. tiring	c. childhood
4. happy	d. idea
5. healthy	e. smell
6. brilliant	f. journey

You can try to use the adjectives with different nouns, but there is always one which sounds best.

3 Adverb / verb collocations

Complete the sentences with the correct adverb:

deeply   clearly   strongly   freely

1. I . . . . . . recommend that you think again.
2. I . . . . . . remember putting the money here.
3. I . . . . . . regret what I said to you yesterday.
4. He . . . . admits taking drugs at university.

4 Fixed expressions

Here are six common expressions. Match each expression with a situation below:

1. Can we have the bill, please?
2. I'll have the same again, please.
3. I'm feeling a bit better, thank you.
4. We haven't got much in common.
5. I've been on my feet all day.
6. I can't afford it.

a. Two people discussing their relationship.
b. Someone talking about their health.
c. A person talking about money.
d. Asking for a drink in a bar or pub.
e. Someone complaining about their work.
f. The end of a meal in a restaurant.

5 Fill-in exercises

Use the correct form of the verbs below:

put   need   take   have

1. I'm going into hospital next month. I . . . . an operation on my knee.
2. They'll probably want to . . . . some X-rays to see if you've broken anything.
3. Your ankle's badly sprained, so I'm going to . . . . a bandage on it.
4. It's quite a deep wound. I'm afraid it . . . . stitches.

This is one of the most common kinds of exercise in this book. When you have filled in all the words, it is important that you go back and underline <u>the complete expressions</u> in which the words occur. In this exercise you should underline the following:

I'm having an operation   take some X-rays
put a bandage on it   it needs stitches

1 Age

1 Basic vocabulary

Translate these words into your own language:

baby   . . . .   generation   . . . .
young   . . . .   adult   . . . .
child   . . . .   middle-aged   . . . .
teenager   . . . .   old   . . . .

2 Ages

Match the expressions on the left with those on the right:

1. She's 3 days old.   a. She's still a child.
2. She's 18 months.   b. She's a newborn baby.
3. She's 8.   c. She's a teenager.
4. She's 14.   d. She's an adult.
5. She's 20.   e. She's a toddler.

Do the same with the following:

6. He's 28.   f. He's in his early forties.
7. He's 35.   g. He's fairly elderly.
8. He's 48.   h. He's in his mid-thirties.
9. He's 42.   i. He's middle-aged.
10. He's 85.   j. He's in his late twenties.

The expression elderly people *is a more polite way of talking about old people.*

3 A two-year-old boy

Look at this example:

He's two years old.
> I've got a two-year-old son.

Re-write these examples in a similar way:

1. My son is eleven.
   I've got an . . . .
2. We've got a daughter of six.
   We've got a . . . .
3. Their baby's only two months old.
   They've got a . . . .

Look at this example:

They are all 10 years old.
> They're all ten-year-olds.

Now re-write these examples in a similar way:

4. I teach kids of seven and eight.
   I teach . . . .
5. Most of them were only sixteen.
   They were mostly . . . .
6. The boy the police arrested was only nine!
   He was only a . . . .

4 Expressions with 'age'

Use these words to complete these expressions with 'age':

of   look   your   same
get   at   all   child

1. the . . . . age as (me)
2. when I was . . . . age
3. people of . . . . ages
4. when you . . . . to my age
5. at the age 43
6 you don't . . . . your age
7. a . . . . of his age
8. . . . . your age

Now use the expressions in the sentences below:

a. Do you think you should be smoking . . . . . .
   . . . . ? I mean, you're only 15.
b. You're lucky to have the chance to go to
   university. , I had
   to get a job and start earning some money.
c. John F. Kennedy became one of the youngest
   Presidents of the United States . . . .
d. Isn't Peter home yet? A . . . .
   should be in bed by 10 – at the latest!
e. The great thing about roller-blading is that
   . . . . seem to be doing
   it – young and old.
f. Our son is . . . . the boy
   next door. They're in the same class.
g. You're not really 50, are you? I don't believe
   it. . . . .
h. . . . .,
   you'll realise there's more to life than going
   clubbing and riding motorbikes.

5 The generation gap

Use the following expressions in the sentences below:

the age difference   the generation gap
the younger generation   of my generation

1. Many older people think that . . . . are only interested in money.
2. My wife is ten years older than me, but . . . . has never been a problem.
3. You can't expect me to use the internet! People . . . . grew up without telephones!
4. My husband and I can't stand the music our children play or their taste in clothes. I suppose it's just . . . . !

6 He's very mature for his age

Use the following words in the dialogues below:

great   grown-up   bright
fit   remarkable   tall

1. Jane's only two years old, but she can count up to ten.
   > Really? She sounds very . . . . . for her age.

2. Peter's only 14, but he's nearly as tall as me.
   > Yes, he's quite . . . . . . for his age, isn't he?

3. Grand-dad plays tennis three times a week.
   > I know. He's very . . . . for his age.

4. You know, Ruth's 50, but she's still a very attractive woman.
   > I know. She looks really . . . . . for her age.

5. Laura's only 14, but when she puts make-up on, you'd think she was 17.
   > Yes, she's very . . . . . for her age, isn't she?

6. My grandmother's 100, but she lives alone and looks after herself. She's amazing!
   > Yes, she's quite . . . . for her age.

7 Age idioms

The following idioms are all about getting old. Complete them using these words:

getting   dog   over   wrong

1. You can't teach an old . . . . new tricks.
2. She's the . . . . side of 40.
3. He's . . . . the hill.
4. He's . . . . on a bit now.

Now use these idioms, changing the grammar if necessary to complete these sentences:

a. John will never change the way he does things. You . . . .
b. In professional football, you're . . . . at 35.
c. I think I'll have to start taking life a bit easier. I am . . . . , you know!
d. Sheila looks great for her age. You'd never guess she's . . . . of 50!

8 Famous quotes

Complete these quotes with the following words:

age   feel   income   forty

1. You're only as old as you . . . .
2. Life begins at . . . .
3. Women lie about their . . . . . . ; men lie about their . . . .

Do you think the last one is true?
Have you ever lied about your age?

Add your own words and expressions

2 Stages of life

1 Basic vocabulary

Put these words into the following sentences:

childhood   adolescence   birth   puberty

1. Was he present at the . . . . . . of his son?
2. I think I had a very happy . . . .
3. Girls usually reach . . . . about a year before most boys.
4. . . . . can be the best or the worst years of your life.

Now use these words, which relate to the later years of life:

old age   retirement   marriage   middle age

5. My first . . . . . . unfortunately only lasted a couple of years.
6. Now that I'm over 40, I can feel . . . . approaching.
7. I want to stop work when I'm 60 and have a long and happy . . . .
8. In his . . . . my father wrote a book about his wartime experiences.

2 In my childhood

Use these words in the patterns below:

growing up   at school   teens   kid
at university   child   twenties   single
childhood   teenager   student   young

a. in my   . . . .
b. when I was a   . . . .
c. when I was   . . . .

Now use the correct form of these verbs:

have   spend   bring up   grow up

1. I . . . . . . my childhood in the country. I loved walking home from school across the fields.
2. I was . . . . . . in the country so it took a long time to get used to living in London.
3. I . . . . . . in the country so when I moved to London it was quite a shock.
4. I . . . . . . a very strict upbringing. I had to study for two hours after school and had to be in bed by 9.

3 When I get old

Match the beginnings of these sentences with the endings below:

1. I don't want to go to university
2. I'm going to spend more time with my grandchildren
3. Will you still love me
4. We won't be able to go out as much
5. At least we'll have some peace and quiet

a. when the kids grow up and leave home.
b. when I'm old and grey?
c. when I leave school.
d. when I retire.
e. when we have children.

4 Important events in people's lives

Match the verbs with the words on the right:

1. leave   a. your wife / your father
2. get   b. schools / jobs / your career
3. change   c. a baby / children
4. have   d. engaged / married / divorced
5. move   e. school / home
6. lose   f. house

Now use some of the expressions in the sentences below. You might need to change the form of the verb or the pronoun.

7. I'm not sure what I'll do when I . . . . It depends on my exam results.
8. I wasn't surprised when I heard that they'd decided to . . . . I never really understood why they got married.
9. When we move to Bristol the children will have to . . . . I'm worried that it might affect their studies.
10. Bill's never really recovered from . . . . in a car accident two years ago. They'd been married for twenty years.
11. I want to find my own flat but my parents think I'm too young to . . . .
12. The place we're in now has only got two bedrooms. We'll have to think about . . . . soon.

5 The best day of my life

Complete the following sentences with the expressions below:

my lucky break   the best day of my life   turning-point   the lowest point

1. I'll never forget the day I got married. It was . . . .
2. The day I decided to change my career was the big . . . . in my life.
3. Being offered that job in Las Vegas was . . . . I've never looked back!
4. I've had some bad times, but . . . . in my life was probably when I lost my job at IBM.

6 Expressions with 'life'

Complete the following expressions with the words below:

my	way	whole
new	all	full

a. . . . . my life
b. start a . . . . life
c. it's a . . . . of life
d. spent his . . . . life
e. in all . . . . life
f. a very . . . . life

Now use the expressions in the sentences below:

1. My grandfather . . . . in the navy. He travelled all over the world.

2. I've worked hard . . . . Now I'm looking forward to retiring.

3. I was in India last month. The Taj Mahal is incredible. I've never seen anything like it . . . .

4. My grandmother's nearly 90 now. She's been married three times and lived in six different countries. She's had . . . .

5. My best friend's had enough of Britain. He's going off to America to . . . .

6. When I first started this job, I didn't like travelling up and down to London on the train every day but now . . . .

7 Decisions and choices

Use these words to complete the sentences below:

bad   right   wrong   wise   difficult

1. I had to decide if I wanted to get a job or go to university. It was a very . . . . . . choice.

2. I'm going to give this job up and go back to college. I hope I'm making the . . . . . . decision.

3. I'm pleased you're going to study at Oxford. I think you've made a very . . . . . . choice.

4. It was definitely the . . . . . . decision to come here in October. It's freezing.

5. I hear you're thinking of becoming self-employed. Personally, I think that would be a . . . . . . move.

What was the best / happiest day of your life so far? Have there been any major turning-points in your life?

Add your own words and expressions

3   Babies and children

1   Basic vocabulary

Complete the following sentences with these words:

pregnant   feed   born   newborn
healthy   toys   birth   pregnancy

1. I'm going to stop work when the baby is
. . . .
2. Women shouldn't smoke during . . . .
3. Julie's staying in hospital for a few more
days. It was quite a difficult . . . .
4. Have you heard? Jane's . . . . again.
5. Looking after a . . . . baby is more
difficult than you think.
6. I'm exhausted. I have to get up three times
every night to . . . . the baby.
7. I don't mind whether it's a boy or a girl as
long as it's . . . .
8. Don't forget to bring some . . . . for
the children to play with.

2   Expecting a baby

Complete the following sentences with the correct form of the verbs below:

plan   expect   lose   get

1. One of the girls at my school . . . .
pregnant when she was only 14.
2. We only . . . . to have two children,
so Jane was a bit of surprise – to both of us!
3. Have you heard? Lisa's . . . . another
baby. It's due in November.
4. A friend of mine crashed her car when she
was pregnant and . . . . the baby.

3   Having a baby

Put the following in the most logical order 1 – 7:

a. She gave birth to a beautiful baby girl.

b. She got pregnant.

c. She went into labour.

d. They called her Helen.

e. She was in labour for eight hours.

f. She was rushed to the maternity ward.

g. She had a scan to see if the baby was OK.

4   We've just had a baby

Match the words with the pictures:

dummy   pram   cot   buggy

Complete the following sentences with the words and phrases below:

nappy   sleepless nights   child-minder
twins   baby-sitter   nursery school
crawling   breast-feeding   maternity leave

1. We've had quite a few . . . . since
the baby was born. I'm absolutely exhausted
most of the time.
2. The baby's crying again. I think her . . . .
needs changing.
3. I can't drink any alcohol at the moment. I'm
. . . .
4. I wish we could go out a bit more in the
evening, but getting a . . . . is very
expensive.
5. I've still got two months of my . . . .
left but I'm not sure what to do then. I'd
quite like to go back to work but employing
a . . . . to look after the baby will
be so expensive.
6. Justin's six months now. He's just started
. . . . He'll be walking in no time.
7. Jenny's nearly three now. She'll soon be able
to go to . . . . and I'll be able to go
back to work.
8. If you think having one baby to look after is
difficult, imagine what it's like if you have
. . . . or even triplets.

5 Childhood memories

Match the sentences below with the pictures on the right:

I remember .... .

1. playing with toy cars.

2. playing with dolls.

3. collecting stamps.

4. playing board games with the family.

5. learning to ride a bike.

6. skipping in the playground at school.

7. flying my kite.

8. skate-boarding.

6 Good or bad behaviour

Read this text and then put the coloured expressions into the correct group below:

I wish our children were more like my brother's children. His children are so well-behaved – they're so polite and they always seem to do what they're told. Our children are so naughty all the time. Tommy's always getting into trouble at school – last week he broke a window in one of the classrooms. And my daughter Jenny's no better – last week she got told off by her teacher for drawing on the desk in the classroom. I do love my children very much – I just wish they could learn to behave themselves a bit better.

being good: . . . .
not being good: . . . .

7 Rules

Match the beginnings of the sentences on the left with the endings on the right. Some of the beginnings match with more than one ending.

1. My parents made me
2. They didn't let me
3. I had to
4. I couldn't
5. I wasn't allowed to

a. brush my teeth before I went to bed.
b. wear make-up till I was 14.
c. do my homework before I could watch TV.
d. watch TV after 9 o'clock.

Now complete the first part of each sentence so that it is true for you.

In some countries it's against the law to smack your children. What do you think?

Add your own words and expressions

4 Death

1 Basic vocabulary

Use these words in the sentences below:

died   dead   death   deaths   dying

1. The ambulance was too late. The boy was
   . . . . . by the time it arrived at the
   hospital.
2. I'm a bit upset. My grandmother . . . . . .
   last week.
3. My best friend is very upset. Her father is
   . . . . . . of cancer.
4. My brother never really recovered after his
   wife's sudden . . . .
5. The number of . . . . . in road accidents
   has increased again this year.

If you say that somebody has passed away *or
that somebody has just* lost his wife *or* lost her
husband, *it is kinder and less shocking than
saying that somebody has 'died'.*

**Now match the words on the left with the
definitions on the right:**

6. widow	a. the document which says what will happen to your possessions when you die
7. widower	b. the person whose job it is to arrange funerals
8. will	c. the ceremony for burying or cremating someone
9. undertaker	d. a woman whose husband is dead
10. funeral	e. a man whose wife is dead

2 When someone dies

Complete each of the following sentences with the phrases below:

made a will   left me £2,000 in her will   inherited the family business
was widowed   came to her funeral   died of cancer

1. As soon as Mrs Johnson knew she was dying, she . . . . , leaving all her money
   to The Red Cross. She . . . . a few months later.
2. When my aunt died, she . . . .
3. When her father died, Sally . . . .
4. Helen was very popular. When she died, more than two hundred people . . . .
   . . . .
5. Poor Sheila! She . . . . only a year after she got married. Her husband had
   a heart attack and died very suddenly while they were on holiday in New Zealand.

3 How did he die?

**Which of these expressions go with the two
structures below?**

a road accident   the war   cancer
a heart attack   old age   a car crash

a. He died of . . . .
b. He was killed in . . . .

Now use the correct form of these verbs:

freeze   starve   bleed
burn   drown   choke

1. Ten people . . . . to death in a fire in
   Birmingham last night.
2. Aid workers have warned that unless food is
   sent soon, thousands of people will . . . .
   to death.
3. The victim of the attack was stabbed in the
   chest and . . . . to death.
4. The baby swallowed a coin and . . . . to
   death.
5. It is believed that the two climbers . . . .
   to death in temperatures of minus 30°.
6. A man . . . . today after jumping into
   the River Thames to save his dog.

**Now match the verbs and nouns to make three
expressions which fit in the sentence below:**

committed   his own life
killed   suicide
took   himself

7. Police believe the young man . . . .
   . . . . after his wife left him.

4 Funerals

Match these words with the picture:

grave   coffin
gravestone   cemetery
hearse   mourners
crematorium   wreath

Now use the correct form of these verbs:

bury   cremate   scatter   visit

I've only ever been to two funerals. My mother died five years ago and she was (9) . . . . in a little churchyard near where she lived. I still try to (10) . . . . . . her grave every month if I can. A few months ago one of my best friends was killed in an accident. He was (11) . . . . and his ashes were (12) . . . . in the sea near Bournemouth, where he grew up.

5 Death idioms

The idea of death is often used in a metaphorical sense. Match the following sentences 1-5 to the ideas a-e:

1. What a boring place! It's completely dead after 10 o'clock at night.
2. My Walkman isn't working. I think the batteries must be dead.
3. Latin is a dead language.
4. I'm dying for a drink.
5. The break-up of the Soviet Union signalled the death of communism.

a. I really need one.
b. They are not working any more.
c. The end of something.
d. Nothing happens.
e. It is not used any more.

A tomb is different from a grave. Graves, always below the ground, are where ordinary people are buried. Tombs, often above the ground, are grand memorials to very important or rich people. We talk about my grandfather's grave, but the Tomb of Tutankhamun.

Here is an amusing little poem which some native speakers say when they hear someone coughing:

It's not the cough that'll carry you off.
It's the coffin they'll carry you off in!

This headline appeared in a British newspaper in 1997. What was the story?

NATION FILLED WITH GRIEF

Add your own words and expressions

5   Family

1   Basic vocabulary

Your immediate family: your mother, father, brothers and sisters, or, if you are married, your husband, wife and your sons and daughters.

Your relatives or your relations: all your immediate family plus your grandparents, great-grandparents, uncles, aunts and cousins.

Use these words below:

aunt	grandfather	grandsons
uncle	grandmother	nephew
niece	granddaughters	cousins

1. Your parents' parents are your . . . . and your . . . .
2. Your father's brother and sister are your . . . . and your . . . .
3. Your aunt's and uncle's children are your . . . .
4. Your brother's son and daughter are your . . . . and your . . . .
5. Your children's children are your . . . . and your . . . .

Relations and relatives are two words for the same people.

2   In-laws

Your in-laws are your husband's or wife's family or your children's husbands and wives. Look at this family tree and put names to the relations:

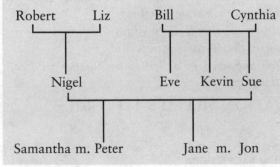

Robert — Liz	Bill	Cynthia

Nigel   Eve   Kevin   Sue

Samantha m. Peter   Jane m. Jon

1. Nigel's mother-in-law _____
2. his father-in-law _____
3. his brother-in-law _____
4. his sister-in-law _____
5. his son-in-law _____
6. his daughter-in-law _____

3   Different types of family

Look at the following short texts and find an example of:

  a. a nuclear family
  b. an extended family
  c. a single-parent family
  d. a couple who adopted a child
  e. a couple with no children

1. We're married with three kids. Our eldest son, Simon, has just started secondary school, our daughter, Lisa, is eight and our youngest son, Luke, is only five.

2. We've only been married for a year. We're not planning to start a family just yet.

3. I'm a single mum. I bring up my son Josh on my own. Josh doesn't mind being an only child but I think he'd like a brother or sister one day.

4. We share the house with my mother and father and my wife's sister and her kids. Everyone helps to look after all the children.

5. We couldn't have children of our own so we decided that adoption was the only answer. Lily came to live with us two years ago. She seems very happy at the moment but we realise that she might want to find her real mother one day.

You can say single mother, single father, single mum, single dad or a single-parent family.

Match the beginnings and endings of the sentences below:

1. We're not planning to start
2. They help us take care of
3. We adopted
4. We share
5. She might want to find

a. the house with my wife's family.
b. a baby from China.
c. her real mother one day.
d. the children.
e. a family just yet.

4 Expressions with 'family'

Complete the following sentences with the words and phrases below:

> the whole family
> a very close family
> a big family
> family tree
> a big family reunion

1. I come from . . . .
   I've got four brothers and two sisters.
2. We're . . . . We see each
   other almost every day and if ever I'm in
   trouble, I know I can turn to one of them for
   help.
3. It's my son's eighteenth birthday next week.
   We're hoping to get . . . . together.
4. My wife and I are celebrating our 40th
   wedding anniversary soon. We're planning to
   have . . . .
5. When I was researching my . . . . , I
   found out that my great-great-grandfather
   came over to England from Ireland 120 years
   ago.

5 It runs in the family

Complete the following expressions with the verbs below in their correct form:

> tell   look   run   get   take

a. She . . . . . . just like her mother.
b. She's . . . . . . her father's nose.
c. He . . . . . . after his father.
d. It . . . . . . in the family.
e. You can't . . . . . . them apart.

Now use the expressions to complete the following sentences:

1. John's got a terrible temper. He . . . .
   . . . .
2. You can see that Jane is Mary's daughter.
   She . . . .
3. All my brothers and sisters are good at
   sport. It . . . .
4. You can see that little Rebecca is a Smith.
   . . . .
5. We've got identical twins in my class at
   school. . . . .

Who do you look like in your family? Who do
you take after? Is your family very close?

Add your own words and expressions

6 Friends

1 He's my best friend

Use the following words to complete the sentences below:

> lifelong   mine   old
> acquaintance   close   best

1. I hear you work with Peter. Did you know he was a friend of . . . . ?
2. I suppose Sandra is my . . . . friend. We ring each other most evenings.
3. I'm going up to see some . . . . friends in Scotland next week. I haven't seen them for over 30 years!
4. I wouldn't say he was a . . . . friend. We used to work together and we go for a drink now and again.
5. I met Martin at university. It was the start of a . . . . friendship.
6. I wouldn't really call Sam a friend. He's just an . . . . I know him through Kirsty and Paul.

In informal British English young men often call their friends mates. *You can say somebody is your* best mate. *In the United States men sometimes call their male friends* buddies.

2 Other words for *friend*

Match the words on the left with the ideas on the right:

1. workmate   a. We study together.
2. partner   b. We work for the same firm.
3. classmate   c. We write every month.
4. pen-friend   d. We share a flat.
5. flatmate   e. We live together, but aren't married.

3 Making friends

Complete the following sentences with the words and phrases below:

> a. made
> b. true friends
> c. made friends with
> d. met him through
> e. pleased
> f. friendly with
> g. got to know
> h. introduced

1. How do you know Susan?
   > Rachel and Peter . . . . me to her.
2. How do you know Paul?
   > I . . . . Steve and Peter.
3. I really enjoyed my time at university. I . . . . so many new friends.
4. People say that Philip is a bit reserved but I . . . . him quite well when we had to work on that report together.
5. We had a great time on holiday in Spain. We . . . . a nice couple who were staying in the apartment next to ours.
6. I didn't know you were . . . . the people next door to us. I saw you there last night.
7. It's when you are having a difficult time that you know who your . . . . really are.
8. Anna, can I introduce you to an old friend of mine? This is Zoe. We were at college together.
   > Hi, Anna, ... to meet you.

4 Why people are friends

Match the beginnings and endings of the sentences below:

1. I didn't like Jenny at first but now we get on
2. We live in different towns now but we still try to see
3. Mark and I get on very well. We've got so much
4. Lucy's my best friend. I know I can always rely on
5. Even if we move to different countries, we'd always stay
6. Mike and I do everything together. We really enjoy
7. I think we're friends because we come from
8. I've known Susan since we were at school. We go back

a. similar backgrounds.
b. in common.
c. in touch.
d. each other's company.
e. a long way.
f. very well.
g. her.
h. each other whenever we can.

5 Problems in a friendship

Complete the following letters to a magazine problem page with these words and phrases:

lose   go our separate ways
fell out   drifted apart
isn't speaking   row

Dear Sally,
I've been really good friends with Emma since we started in the same class two years ago but recently we (1) . . . . over a boy that we both like. I knew Emma liked him but when Steve asked me out I accepted. Emma was really angry and we had a terrible (2) . . . . Now she (3) . . . . to me. I like Steve but I don't want to (4) . . . . . my best friend. What should I do?

Dear Sally,
All the time we were at school Lucy and I were really close friends. We really enjoyed each other's company and did everything together. But since she went to university we seem to have (5) . . . . She's made lots of new friends and doesn't have time for me. Do you think there is anything I can do to keep her as a friend or should I just accept it's time to (6) . . . . ?

Use the words friends and family to complete this famous saying:

You can choose your . . . . , but not your . . . . !

Is there a similar saying in your language? Have you got a best friend?

Add your own words and expressions

7 Love and romance

1 Basic vocabulary

Complete the following text with the words and phrases below:

in love	going out
boyfriend	kissed
girlfriend	romantic
relationship	date

Peter had never had a (1) . . . . Anna had never had a (2) . . . . When they started (3) . . . . together, they were both very nervous. For their first (4) . . . . Peter wanted to take her somewhere (5) . . . . . , so he booked a table at an Italian restaurant. He walked her home. When he left, they (6) . . . . goodnight. The next day Anna told her best friend that she was (7) . . . . with Peter and that this was the first really serious (8) . . . . in her life.

If a girl has a boyfriend, and a boy has a girlfriend, they are romantically involved. Girls also often refer to their female friends as girlfriends.

2 Crazy about you

Match the beginnings and endings of the expressions below. Use one of the endings twice.

1. She fancies	a. with him.
2. She's not really interested	b. about him.
3. She's absolutely crazy	c. in him.
4. I don't know what she sees	d. you.
5. She's always flirting	

Now use the expressions to complete the following sentences:

6. Julie seems to really like Ian, but personally, ... He must be at least ten years older than her.
7. John isn't very happy at the moment. He really likes this girl at college but . . . . at all.
8. Debbie goes bright red every time she talks to you. I'm sure . . . .
9. Tina spends almost every evening with this new guy she's seeing. . . . .
10. I'm sure Liz fancies that guy in the accounts department. . . . .

3 Starting a relationship

Match the beginnings and endings of the sentences below:

1. Sarah's very happy at the moment. She's seeing
2. Have you heard about Mark? He's going out
3. Have you heard about Laura and Joe? They've started
4. Apparently, Phil and Liz have been seeing
5. Did Sally tell you about Mike? He asked

a. going out together.
b. her for a date.
c. with Susie Jones, the singer.
d. some guy she met on holiday.
e. a lot of each other recently.

In American English you say that you are dating somebody instead of seeing or going out with them.

4 Falling in love

Read the following sentences and put the words and phrases in colour into the correct column below:

1. It started out as just a casual relationship but one day I realised we had fallen in love.
2. Tina and Mike spend every minute together. They're obviously madly in love.
3. I met a guy when I was in Greece, but I knew it was just a holiday romance. I never saw him again after we got back.
4. John's been with Linda for ages. He absolutely adores her.
5. I haven't had a girlfriend for a while now. I had a brief relationship with someone a few months ago, but it didn't really work out.

Serious	Not serious
. . . .	. . . .
. . . .	. . . .
. . . .	. . . .

5 The relationship

Match the beginnings of the phrases on the left with the endings on the right:

1. She loves
2. She's in love
3. She fell in love   a. with him.
4. She kissed   b. him.
5. She lives
6. She married

Now decide if each of the following sentences can end in together. If not, put a line through it.

a. They're going out together.
b. They're sleeping together.
c. They're in love together.
d. They've moved in together.
e. They're always kissing together.
f. They live together.
g. They're always holding hands together.
h. They're married together.

6 The end of a relationship

Use these expressions in the situations below:

finished with
never stop fighting
split up
had a huge row
weren't right for

1. Do you think I should invite Jeff and Sue to the party?
   > Haven't you heard? They've finally decided to . . . .
2. Didn't you know I'm not seeing James any more? I . . . . him last week. It was fine while it lasted, but I think we both knew we . . . . each other.
3. We invited Dave and Kate over for dinner last Saturday. It was really embarrassing. They . . . . and Kate went home in the middle of the main course.
4. Julie and Dave . . . . I'm surprised they stay together.

Very often if two people split up, they tell their friends that "we're just good friends now".

If you want to deny that you are "having a relationship" with someone, you can say "We're just good friends."

7 He's been seeing somebody else

Complete the response in four different ways:

I hear Mark and Lucy have split up. What happened?
> She found out that he was . . .

1. being   a. somebody else.
2. seeing   b. unfaithful.
3. having   c. on her.
4. cheating   d. an affair.

Are you romantic?
Do you believe in love at first sight?

Add your own words and expressions

8 Marriage

1 Basic vocabulary

Translate the following words into your language:

1. engaged . . . .   5. wife   . . . .
2. wedding . . . .   6. husband . . . .
3. married . . . .   7. divorce   . . . .
4. marriage . . . .   8. divorced . . . .

2 Getting engaged

Use the correct form of these words and expressions:

get engaged   propose to   set a date
arrange   ask

1. I've got some news. I'm really excited. Mark . . . . me to marry him last night. I said yes!
2. I remember the day my husband . . . . me. We were on holiday in Greece. It was very romantic.
3. Have you heard? Martin and Lisa have just . . . . They're planning to get married next year.
   > Really? That's fantastic. Have they . . . . ?
4. In some countries parents . . . . their children's marriages. They look for a suitable partner for their son or daughter to marry.

The man you are engaged to is your fiancé. The woman you are engaged to is your fiancée. Nowadays these words are less common.

3 Before the wedding

Julie and Dave are getting married next month. Match the beginnings of the phrases on the left with the endings on the right:

1. Julie has sent out   a. her wedding dress.
2. Dave has asked   b. a stag night on the Friday before the wedding.
3. They've booked   c. a wedding list.
4. Julie has bought   d. a hen night on the Friday before the wedding.
5. They've bought each other   e. invitations to all the wedding guests.
6. They've made   f. wedding rings.
7. Julie's going to have   g. the hotel for the reception.
8. Dave's going to have   h. his brother to be best man.

A wedding list is a list of the wedding presents you want, usually from one big department store.

4 People at the wedding

Use these words to describe the picture:

bride   groom   best man
clergyman guests   bridesmaids

The two people getting married are the . . . . . . and the . . . . They are being married by the . . . . The two little girls are the . . . . The man standing on the groom's right is his . . . . The wedding . . . . . . are watching the ceremony.

5 The vows

Here are the marriage vows a man says in Britain. Complete them using these words:

health   death   worse   poorer

I (*John Smith*) take thee (*Jane Brown*) to be my wedded wife, to have and to hold from this day forward, for better, for (1) . . . . . ., for richer, for (2) . . . . . ., in sickness and in (3) . . . . . ., to love and to cherish, till (4) . . . . . . us do part.

6 The wedding

The following events describe a traditional wedding. Put them in the correct order:

a. Their friends throw confetti at them.

b. They cut the cake and make speeches.

c. Her father walks down the aisle with her.

d. They leave for their honeymoon.

e. They spend ages taking photographs!

f. The bride arrives at the church late.

g. The couple make their wedding vows.

h. They go to a hotel for the wedding reception.

i. The happy couple walk back up the aisle, man and wife!

The correct order is: . . . .

In Britain people either have a church wedding or they have a civil ceremony in a registry office. They don't have both as in some countries. If people get married in church they usually have a white wedding – the bride wears a traditional white dress.

7 They're happily married

Use these words and expressions in the text below:

> silver wedding
> get married
> happily married
> golden wedding

I'm Keith Barratt. I'm 21 and a student. I'm still single and probably won't (1) . . . . till I'm nearer 30.

My parents are very (2) . . . . They were married for 3 years before I was born, so next year they're celebrating their (3) . . . . anniversary.

Last year my grandparents celebrated their (4) . . . . – 50 years with the same person! That's quite an achievement!

8 When things go wrong

Complete the following sentences with the words and phrases below:

a. destroyed our marriage

b. broke up

c. get a divorce

d. left him

e. got custody of the children

f. saved our marriage

g. didn't work out

h. separated

1. His wife . . . . two years ago for another man.

2. I was so happy when I got married but things . . . . and we split up three years ago.

3. Our marriage . . . . after my wife discovered I'd been seeing somebody else.

4. My wife and I . . . . last year. We hadn't been very happy for a while. We've now decided that the best thing is to . . . .

5. A few years ago my husband started seeing another woman. I tried to forgive him but it was impossible. In the end it . . . .

6. Things started to go wrong after about three years. I guess we just got bored of each other. Then I had a baby and things got much better. I think that's what . . . .

7. I got divorced five years ago. Unfortunately, my ex-wife . . . . and now I only see them at the weekend and for a few weeks during the summer.

Your ex-wife or ex-husband is the person you were married to before your divorce. When people are speaking, they often just say ex – "I got divorced last year but I still see my ex sometimes".

Add your own words and expressions

9 General appearance

1 He's quite a big guy

Match the pairs of sentences with the pictures on the right:

1. He isn't very tall.
   He's short and stocky.

2. She's tall and slim.
   She's got a lovely figure.

3. He's quite a big guy.
   He's quite well-built.

4. She's a bit overweight.
   She's quite plump, isn't she?

5. He's very fat.
   He's absolutely enormous.

6. He's very thin.
   He's so skinny.

a.

b.

c.

d.

e.

f.

Slim is more positive and attractive than thin. Skinny is negative. If somebody is skinny, they are too thin. Saying that somebody is overweight or plump is more polite than saying they're fat.

2 A small, slim, blue-eyed blonde

Look at the following extracts of written language and match them to their sources below:

a.
> Small, slim, blue-eyed blonde, GSH, early 30's WLTM hunky male 28-38 for fun and friendship. Call me on 09765-567892.

b.
> The first man was small and wiry, with sharp, strong features. Behind him walked his opposite, a huge man, with wide shoulders; and he walked heavily, dragging his feet a little, the way a bear drags his paws.

c.
> The police are looking for a man of average height and medium build in his mid-twenties. He was last seen wearing a dark green or grey anorak.

d.
> The tallest man in medical history is Robert Pershing Wadlow who was born on 22nd February 1918 in Illinois, USA, and who died on 15th July 1940 in Michigan. He was last measured on 27th June 1940 and was found to be 272cm tall.

1. An extract from a novel.
2. An extract from a newspaper report.
3. An extract from the Guinness Book of Records.
4. An advertisement in a lonely hearts section of a newspaper.

What do you think WLTM and GSH mean?

3 Adjective + noun collocations

Use these collocations in the sentences below:

long nails   bad skin

big feet   deep voice

lovely complexion   long legs

hairy chest   thin legs

1. Size 12! Are these your shoes? You've got really . . . . , haven't you?
2. You've got such . . . . Would you like to move the seat back a bit?
3. I've never seen you in shorts before. You've got such . . . . You should go running and try to build up them up a bit!
4. My boyfriend's got a really . . . . It's like being with a gorilla.
5. You've got such lovely . . . . Are they real?
6. He's got such a . . . . I find it very sexy when he speaks to me on the phone.
7. Keith's new girlfriend must spend a fortune on face cream to have such a . . . .
. . . .
8. Poor Tim. He's had really . . . . ever since he was 13.

4 Order of adjectives

Put these descriptions in the correct order:

1. He's a . . . . man with . . . . hair. *(short, tall, fair, good-looking)*
2. She's a . . . . woman with . . . . hair. *(tall, long, thin)*
3. I've got . . . . hair and I'm tall and very . . . . *(thin, straight, black)*
4. She's very . . . . with a . . . . tan and . . . . hair. *(blonde, lovely, good-looking, long)*
5. I wouldn't describe my husband as . . . . and . . . . ! Short, overweight, and going thin on top is more accurate! *(handsome, dark, tall)*

5 Distinguishing features

Match the sentences with the pictures:

1. The accident left a scar on his forehead.
2. He's got a birthmark on his head.
3. I've just had a tattoo done.
4. He's got a mole on his back.

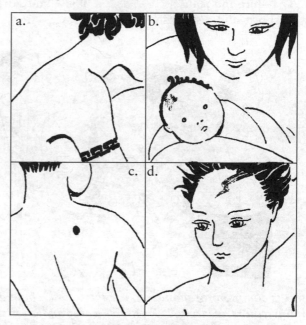

How tall are you?
Do you have any distinguishing features?
Try to think of a famous person who is:

tall and thin
short and stocky
absolutely enormous.

Add your own words and expressions

10   Clothes

1   Basic vocabulary

Which person is wearing:

1. T-shirt and jeans	2. a blouse and skirt	3. a bow tie	4. a shirt and tie
5. shorts and a sweatshirt	6. a dress	7. a waistcoat	8. a jacket and tie

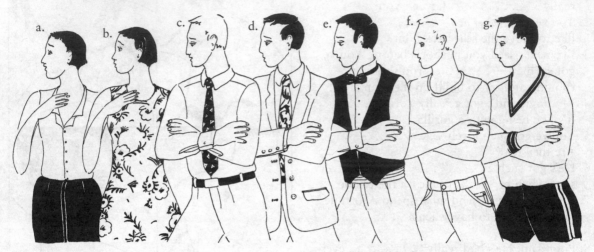

It is common for women to use top to talk about any shirt, T-shirt, blouse or jumper – "That's a nice top you're wearing." Trousers, jeans, and shorts are plural words and take a plural verb form – "Those are nice trousers" or "These shorts are very comfortable". You can also say a pair of trousers, a pair of jeans or a pair of shorts. In American English trousers are called pants.

2   Outdoor clothes

Match the words with the pictures:

coat   anorak   hat   cap   gloves   scarf

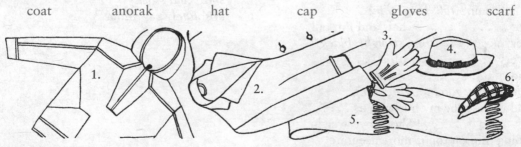

3   Shoes

Match the words and phrases with the pictures:

boots   trainers   sandals   slippers   high heels   clogs   flip-flops

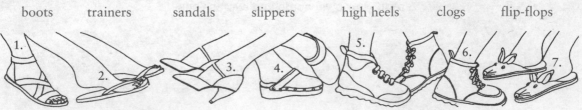

4 Underwear

Match the words with the pictures:

knickers   underpants   bra
vest   tights   boxer shorts

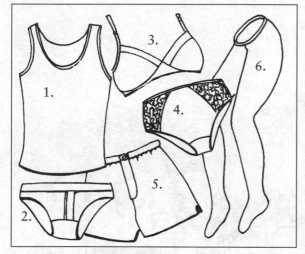

5 Parts of clothes

Match the words with the pictures:

pocket   button   zip
sleeve   collar   cuff
hood   heel   laces

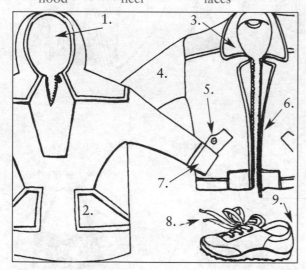

6 Jewellery and accessories

Match the words with the pictures:

necklace   ring   belt
scarf   earring   brooch
handbag   watch   umbrella

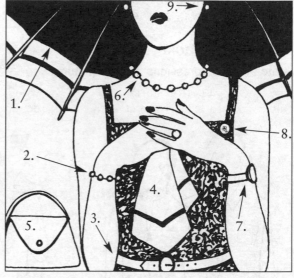

7 What size are you?

Match the following sizes to the clothes below:

1. small, medium, large, extra-large
2. UK 12 / European 40
3. UK size 15 / European size 38
4. UK size 4 / European size 37
5. 32 waist, 32 inside leg
6. Size 34C / European 75C / French 90C
7. UK size 9 / European 44

a. ladies' shoes   e. men's shirt
b. men's trousers   f. bra
c. tights, T-shirts etc   g. men's shoes
d. ladies dress/blouse/skirt/trousers/knickers

Add your own words and expressions

11 Talking about clothes

1 Basic vocabulary

Translate the following words into your language:

1. cotton . . . .
3. linen . . . .
5. denim . . . .
7. suede . . . .

2. wool . . . .
4. silk . . . .
6. leather . . . .
8. fur . . . .

2 A leather jacket

Match these expressions with the pictures:

a cotton shirt a woolly jumper a silk blouse
a leather jacket a denim skirt a fur coat

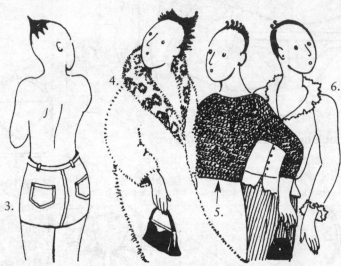

3 Patterns

Match these adjectives with the pictures:

striped floral plain (or self-coloured) checked

   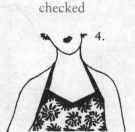

4 Shape and style

Write the following words with the correct group of words below:

	shirt	skirt	shoes	trousers
	tight	long	flat	long-sleeved
	1. baggy	2. knee-length	3. platform	4. short-sleeved . . . . . .
	flared	short	running	collarless

28

5 Describing clothes

Complete the following dialogues with these words:

fashionable	smart	casual
worn-out	scruffy	dress well

1. You're looking very . . . . today.
   > Yes, I'm on my way to a job interview.
2. You must spend a fortune on clothes.
   > I don't really, but I must admit I do like to
   . . . .
3. Will I have to wear a suit to the meeting?
   > No, I expect most people will be wearing
   fairly . . . . clothes.
4. I need a new dress for this party but I don't
   know what colour to go for.
   > Well, pink's supposed to be . . . . at
   the moment, isn't it? It's this season's colour.
5. Why are you throwing that jacket out?
   > It's . . . . Look, it's got a hole
   under the arm and most of the buttons are
   missing!
6. I like your new trousers. They're very smart.
   > Well, I start my new job tomorrow and I
   can't turn up wearing . . . . old jeans.
   Everyone there is very well-dressed.

6 It doesn't really suit me

Use these words in the sentences below:

wrong	go with	tight
match	suit	fit

1. It doesn't . . . . me. It's too tight.
2. It doesn't . . . . me. I'm too old for it.
3. It's the . . . . size. It's too small.
4. Do you think this top goes with my skirt?
   > Well, no. They don't . . . . at all,
   actually.
5. It's a bit . . . . for me.
6. This skirt doesn't . . . . this jacket.

7 Get

Add the following verbs in the sentences after the verb get:

changed	on
dressed	dressed up

1. That's a nice jumper you've got . . . . . .
   Is it new?
2. I don't usually get . . . . until after
   I've had my breakfast.
3. I'm going to wash the car. I think I'll just get
   . . . . into some old clothes.
4. Do we have to get . . . . for this dinner
   party tonight or can I just wear jeans?

Now underline the complete expressions with get.

If you get dressed, you put your clothes on.
If you dress up, you put on special clothes – for example, for a party.

Which one of these don't you do up: your jacket / your coat / your buttons / your zip / your socks / your belt? The opposite of 'do up' is undo.

8 Taking your clothes off

Match the beginnings and endings of these sentences:

1. He took   a. feet.
2. She got   b. no clothes on.
3. They had bare   c. undressed.
4. He was completely d. his clothes off.
5. She had   e. naked.

Have you ever bought second-hand clothes?
Would you wear a fur coat?

Add your own words and expressions

12 Describing character

1 Positive or negative comments

Mark the following P (positive) or N (negative):

1. She's got so much personality.
2. She's a bit difficult at times.
3. She isn't easy to get on with.
4. She's got a great sense of humour.
5. She's a bit of a pain sometimes.
6. She's great fun.
7. She can be a pain in the neck.
8. She's my kind of person.

Can you think of people you know who fit these descriptions?

2 He's always doing that

Match the first part of these descriptions with the second parts below:

1. Tony isn't very sensitive.
2. Mark's so aggressive.
3. Simon's very thoughtful.
4. He's so absent-minded.
5. Joe isn't very self-confident.
6. He's so vain.

a. He's always buying me little presents.
b. He's always looking in the mirror.
c. He's always worrying about what people think of him.
d. He's always saying the wrong thing.
e. He keeps forgetting where he's put things.
f. He keeps getting into fights.

3 He's far too modest

Complete the following dialogues with the following expressions:

far too modest   far too sensible
much too shy   much too proud
much too loyal   far too honest

1. I think Mark took some money from my bag while we were out.
   > No, he's . . . . to do a thing like that.
2. I'm still waiting for Lisa to say sorry for sending that fax to the wrong address.
   > You'll wait a long time! Lisa's . . . . to admit anything's her fault.
3. Jenny left a window open when she went out this morning. Anybody could've got in.
   > Are you sure it was Jenny. She's . . . . to do anything like that.
4. Apparently, Amy asked Tom if he'd like to go out tomorrow night.
   > I don't believe you. She's . . . . to ask a boy out!
5. Julie got the highest mark in the class, but she didn't say a word.
   > No, she wouldn't. She's . . . . to say anything about it.
6. I thought Martin was a good friend but he's been telling everybody that I'm boring.
   > Are you sure? Martin's . . . . to say something like that behind your back.

4 Opposites

Match the adjectives in sentences 1 – 5 with the opposites in sentences a – e:

1. Tom's really generous. He bought everyone in the pub a drink last night.
2. Claire's very hard-working. She never leaves the office until after six o'clock.
3. Tina's very outgoing. She's made friends with everybody else in the class already.
4. Brian's a very easy-going sort of guy. Nothing seems to worry him.
5. Jack's such a cheerful little boy. I've never seen him in a bad mood.

a. Bruno's so shy. I don't think he's spoken to any of the other students yet.
b. I don't understand why he's so miserable. He never stops complaining.
c. Lucy's very tense. She's always worrying about something or other.
d. Don't expect Tom to put any money in the collection. He's much too mean.
e. I can't believe Emma's husband's so lazy. He just sits and watches TV all evening.

In British English informal words for men are: guy, bloke and lad; lad is only used for young men.

5 She can be a bit moody

Complete the following dialogues with the words and phrases below:

> moody   amusing   stubborn
> arrogant   selfish   silly

1. Lucy never thinks about anyone but herself.
   > Yes, she can be a bit . . . . sometimes.
2. Oh, Laura's impossible. One minute life is wonderful and the next minute she's in her room crying.
   > Yes, she can be a bit . . . . , can't she?
3. I really don't like Bob. He seems to think that he's more important than anybody else.
   > He certainly can be very . . . .
4. Martin's such good fun. He's got a great sense of humour.
   > Yes, he can be very . . . . at times.
5. I wish Joe would stop playing practical jokes all the time. It gets very tiring.
   > Yes, he can be really . . . . . . at times. I wish he'd grow up and behave like an adult.
6. I told Emma that she shouldn't leave university but she never listens to me.
   > No, she really can be very . . . . when she wants, can't she?

6 Don't be so nosey

Complete the dialogues below with these adjectives:

> bossy   sensitive   fussy   nosey

1. How much do you earn in your new job?
   > That's a bit . . . . . of you!
2. You can do the washing up while I'm out.
   > You can be so . . . . . at times!
3. Jenny's really upset about what you said.
   > She's too . . . .
4. I can't eat these vegetables. They've been cooked in oil.
   > Oh, don't be so . . . . . .

Now go back and add these expressions to the end of the responses:

a. I was only joking!
b. I'm not your slave!
c. It's none of your business, actually.
d. All you ever do is complain!

7 Types of people

Here are 8 different kinds of people. Use them in the sentences below:

a gossip	a big-head
an extrovert	a laugh
a couch potato	a snob
a coward	a liar

1. You shouldn't believe a word Justin says. He's a terrible . . . .
2. Maria's a terrible . . . . She's always talking about everybody else in the office.
3. Roberto's quite an . . . . , isn't he? He's got hundreds of friends!
4. Martin's such a . . . . He never stops telling people how wonderful he is.
5. You can't keep running away from your responsibilities. You're such a . . . .
6. Just because Dave didn't go to university doesn't mean he's any less intelligent than you. Don't be such a . . . .
7. Emma's husband's such a . . . . He just sits around all day watching TV.
8. Billy knows hundreds of jokes. He's such a . . . . . . !

8 Negative prefixes

Change these words into their opposites by adding un, dis, in, or im:

. . . reliable	. . . honest	. . . sensitive
. . . pleasant	. . . loyal	. . . tolerant
. . . patient	. . . mature	. . . friendly
. . . decisive	. . . ambitious	. . . selfish

Add your own words and expressions

31

13 Adjectives to describe people

1 That was a silly thing to do

Use these pairs of adjectives in the sentences:

wise / sensible	careless / silly
horrible / nasty	strange / funny

1. I locked my keys in the house this morning.
   >That was a very . . . . . / . . . . thing to do.
2. I gave my neighbours' little boy some money for his holidays and his parents took it from him!
   > Really? What a . . . . . / . . . . thing to do.
3. I'm thinking of getting myself a private pension.
   > Good idea. That's a very . . . . . / . . . . thing to do.
4. They've been married for 25 years and then one day she just walked out and never came back.
   > Really? What a . . . . . / . . . . thing to do!

2 It's very brave of you

Match the beginnings and endings of the following sentences:

1. It was a bit cheeky of you
2. It's very brave of you
3. It was very generous of you
4. It was very clever of you
5. It was a bit dishonest of you

a. to finish this crossword so quickly.
b. not to tell them they'd given you too much change.
c. to go to India on your own.
d. to ask the teacher how old she is.
e. to pay for all the drinks.

Now complete the following dialogues with the phrases below:

very kind	very tactful
a bit clumsy	very rude

6. I invited Sue and Gerry for dinner. They turned up an hour and a half late and didn't even apologise!
   > Really, that was . . . . of them, wasn't it?

7. Sarah spilt coffee all over the carpet. It made a terrible mess.
   > Oh dear. That was . . . . of her, wasn't it?
8. Mary knew how busy I was, so she offered to collect the kids from school for me.
   > That was . . . . of her.
9. Sue said she had a headache, but she knew that Chris, her first husband, was going to be at the party.
   > That was . . . . of her. It would have been very embarrassing if she'd turned up.

3 Aren't you being a bit selfish?

Complete the following dialogues with the words below:

fussy	pushy	selfish
pessimistic	intolerant	optimistic

1. I know I'm going to get this job – the interview went so well.
   > I think you're being a bit . . . . Hundreds of people have applied for it.
2. I'm trying to persuade Liz to give up her job and come and live with me in Scotland.
   > Aren't you being a bit . . . . ? You know how important her career is.
3. I've looked at fifteen flats and I haven't seen one I really like.
   > Don't you think you're being a bit . . . . ? You'll never find one that's perfect.
4. Why haven't they phoned me back? I know I'm not going to get this job.
   > Aren't you being a bit . . . . ? You only had the interview yesterday.
5. Do you think Ann will come on holiday with me?
   > Slow down! You've only just met her! Aren't you being a bit . . . . ?
6. I hope Bob doesn't become manager. I don't like his accent.
   > Don't you think you're being a bit . . . . ? You can't dislike him just because of the way he speaks!

4 Wordbuilding

Complete the following sentences with a noun formed from the adjective at the end of each sentence:

1. Thousands would have died in last year's famine in Ethiopia, if it wasn't for the . . . . of ordinary people.
(generous)

2. They've always shown me great . . . .
(kind)

3. The theatre's sent me tickets for the wrong day again. I can't believe their . . . .
(careless)

4. Considering how ill I've been, I thought my boss would show a bit more . . . .
(sympathetic)

5. She handled the situation very well. She showed great . . . .
(sensitive)

6. You've been such a great help. I'd like to buy you dinner as an expression of my
. . . .
(grateful)

7. I do wish those children would show a little more . . . . sometimes.
(patient)

8. He just told me to shut up and walked off. I've never known such . . . .
(rude)

9. You don't like him because of his accent? You could show a bit more . . . .
sometimes.
(tolerant)

10. I think one day we might doubt the . . . . of this decision.
(wise)

Did you notice how many of these words were used with the verb show? Go back and underline the show + noun expressions.

5 What a nasty thing to say

Which words fit in the two examples below?

nice	nasty
mean	lovely
sweet	unkind
kind	rude
spiteful	horrible

1. He said I was fat.
 > Really? What a(n) . . . . . thing to say.
2. I can't believe you're forty-five. You look much younger than that.
 > What a . . . . . thing to say. Thank you.

6 Don't be so impatient

Complete the following sentences with the words below. Then add the comments at the end.

nosey	pessimistic
impatient	childish

1. Haven't you finished? Come on! Hurry up! I've got to go out in ten minutes.
 > Oh, don't be so . . . . !
2. How much do you earn?
 > Don't be so . . . . !
3. Well, if you won't let me watch what I want to watch, I'm not doing the washing up.
 > Oh, don't be so . . . . !
4. I know I won't get this job. I don't know why I bothered applying.
 > Don't be so . . . . !

a. Why don't you grow up?
b. I've only got one pair of hands!
c. Why not look on the bright side?
d. It's none of your business!

Add your own words and expressions

14 Feelings and emotions

1 Basic vocabulary 1

Match the situations with the feelings below:

1. I didn't understand any of the questions.
2. A huge dog came running towards me.
3. We're taking the kids to the zoo on Saturday.
4. I've got my driving test tomorrow.
5. I've been up since half past five.
6. I forgot my Dad's birthday again.
7. My Mum and Dad arrived at the club and started dancing!
8. You only say you don't like Steve because you haven't got a boyfriend.

a. I'm starting to feel really tired.
b. You're just jealous.
c. I was really scared.
d. I was really confused.
e. I feel so guilty.
f. I'm really nervous.
g. They're really excited.
h. I was so embarrassed.

2 Basic vocabulary 2

Now do the same with these situations:

1. I can't believe I got so drunk.
2. I didn't expect the film to be so violent.
3. Why didn't you phone to say you'd be late?
4. There's a huge spider in the bath!
5. They talked about computers all evening.
6. I got the results back from the hospital today. They're negative, thank goodness!
7. When my daughter became a doctor, I was really pleased.
8. She came home to find we'd organised a big party for her.

a. I'm really frightened of them.
b. I felt so proud.
c. We were very worried.
d. I was so bored.
e. I'm so relieved.
f. She was so surprised.
g. I feel so ashamed.
h. I was quite shocked by it.

3 Moods and feelings

Use the correct form of these verbs in the situations below:

show   hide   get   be (2)

1. If you love Kay, you've got to tell her. Don't . . . . . . your feelings from her.
2. Why . . . . . . you in such a bad mood today? Have I upset you?
3. Ann's a very emotional person. She isn't afraid to . . . . . her feelings in public.
4. I've . . . . . mixed feelings about leaving. I'll be glad to say goodbye to this place, but I'll miss all my friends.
5. You seem to . . . . . in a good mood this morning! Have you won the lottery?

Now go back and underline the complete expressions.

If someone is a bit moody or in a funny mood, they are not very happy.

4 'Get' + feeling

'Get' is a common verb to use with emotions. Use the correct form of these expressions:

get a bit tired   get a bit worried
get really excited   get bored
get nervous   get a bit confused
get really jealous   get embarrassed

1. My boyfriend doesn't like it if I speak to other boys when we're out. He . . . .
2. Lisa said she'd be home by eleven. I'm beginning to . . . .
3. Can't we go out and do something? I'm . . . . just watching TV.
4. Shall we stop and have a rest soon? I'm . . . .
5. We're taking the children camping next weekend. They're . . . . about it.
6. Don't keep asking him about his girlfriend. Can't you see he's . . . . ?
7. These instructions aren't easy to follow. I'm . . . .
8. I've got my driving test next month. I'm already . . . . about it.

5 Extreme feelings

Complete the following dialogues with these words:

amazed	disgusted
exhausted	horrified
stunned	terrified

1. You must have been quite frightened when the pilot announced that he was going to land in Kuwait.
   > I was absolutely . . . .

2. Did you say you saw people in the sea?
   > Yes! In the middle of winter! I was absolutely . . . .

3. What a long day! You must be tired.
   > I'm absolutely . . . .

4. Did you see the news last night? English football fans in trouble again! I don't know what they're thinking about.
   > Yes, I was absolutely . . . . I just don't understand why they have to do it.

5. I hear Tony's just lost his job. How's he taking it?
   > He was absolutely . . . . He thought he had a job for life.

6. Did you read about the murder of that little girl?
   > Yes, I think the whole country is . . . . that that sort of thing can happen.

6 Dependent prepositions

Complete the following sentences with these prepositions:

by	about	of

1. I'm afraid . . . . dogs.
2. I'm really nervous . . . . the test tomorrow.
3. You should be ashamed . . . . yourself.
4. There's nothing to worry . . . . .
5. It took me . . . . surprise.

6. Well done! We're so proud . . . . you.
7. I'm tired . . . . doing the same thing day after day. I need a change.
8. I was quite shocked . . . . the way he reacted.
9. I wish I hadn't been so horrible to Ruth now. I feel really guilty . . . . it.

7 I couldn't believe my eyes

Use these expressions in the situations below:

> a. I can't be bothered.
> b. I went bright red.
> c. I was scared stiff.
> d. I can't wait.
> e. I couldn't believe my eyes.

1. You're off to the Caribbean tomorrow, aren't you?
   > Yes, I'm so excited. . . . .

2. I hear you spilled your coffee all over the table at the meeting yesterday.
   > Yeah! I was so embarrassed. . . . .

3. Are you going to fill in that job application this evening?
   > No, ... I'm too tired.

4. A cow in the garden! You must have been a bit surprised.
   > I was. . . . .

5. The snake you're holding in this photo is enormous. Weren't you frightened?
   > Yes, I was. . . . .

Add your own words and expressions

15   Happy or sad

1 Basic vocabulary

Match the groups of sentences with the pictures:

1. I'm a bit disappointed.
   I'm not very happy.
   I could've done better.

2. We're absolutely delighted.
   We're absolutely ecstatic.
   We're absolutely thrilled.

3. I'm very pleased with it.
   It's just what I wanted.
   I'm glad you like it.

4. She's very upset.
   She's very unhappy.
   She's absolutely heartbroken.

5. He's depressed.
   He's miserable.
   He's really fed up.

2 She broke my heart

We use a lot of idiomatic expressions when we are talking about people's moods. Complete the expressions in green with these nouns:

heart   world   tears
joy   moon

1. We won 3–0 today. It was a great result.
   We're over the . . . .
2. My Dad was killed in a car accident when he was 30. It broke my mother's . . . .
3. When we heard we'd managed to get tickets for their only UK concert, we were jumping for . . . . .
4. I knew she was upset, but it took me by surprise when she suddenly burst into . . . . .
5. I can't believe how lucky I am. I'm so happy. I'm on top of the . . . .

3 Give me a smile

Use the correct form of these verbs in the sentences below:

laugh   frown   cry   smile   moan

1. Come on, everybody! . . . . I'm trying to take a picture.
2. When Keith told that story about the time he was stuck in a lift, it was so funny, I couldn't stop . . . .
3. Diana's very upset. I can hear her upstairs . . . . in her room.
4. It wasn't a very relaxing holiday. My husband . . . . . . about everything! First it was the hotel, and then it was the rain. Then, when the sun did come out, it was too hot! I wish we'd stayed at home!
5. Why do you keep . . . . . ? Is something the matter? Are you unhappy about something?

4 Feeling homesick

Look at this letter that a foreign student has written home to his girlfriend. Complete the letter with the words and phrases below:

missing	lonely	on my own
homesick	myself	looking

Dear Donna

Life here in England is very different from Brazil. The food is nothing like ours and all the pubs close at eleven o'clock. I haven't made many friends yet. Sometimes I feel a bit (1) . . . . . If I think about Rio for too long, I start to feel quite (2) . . . .

It really is all quite interesting. Now and again, I go out with the other students in my class, but I spend most of my free time by (3) . . . . I went to the cinema (4) . . . . on Friday night – I've never done that before!

I'm really (5) . . . . you and I'm (6) . . . . forward to coming home next month.

Yours

Paulo

5 More formal comments

Match up the halves of these more formal sentences. Notice the nouns in colour.

1. It gives me great pleasure
2. He was overcome with grief
3. We wish you great joy and happiness
4. It was with great sadness
5. Martin was a huge disappointment
6. One can see the misery

a. to his father.
b. this war has caused on every street corner.
c. in your future life together.
d. to announce that the winner is Mr C. Gough.
e. that I left my home town after so many years.
f. when his wife passed away.

6 Supporting a friend

Look at the following expressions and decide if you say them when somebody is happy (H) or sad (S):

1. Congratulations!   . . .
2. What's the matter?   . . .
3. I feel a bit sorry for her. . . .
4. Cheer up!   . . .
5. Well done!   . . .
6. I'm really sorry to hear that. . . .
7. That's a pity.   . . .

Here are 7 situations. Try to decide which of the above expressions fits best in each one:

a. Your friend's mother has just died.
b. Your friend is getting married.
c. Your friend needs encouraging.
d. Your friend has just won a golf tournament.
e. Your friend has been crying.
f. Your sister has just lost her job.
g. Your friend can't come to your party.

Here are 3 more expressions. They are similar in meaning to 3 expressions above. Match them up:

8. I'm SO sorry.
9. What's up?
10. What a shame!

They say it's no use crying over spilt milk. What does it mean? Do you agree?

Add your own words and expressions

16 Getting angry

1 Basic vocabulary

Mark these words and expressions in the following way:

    1 = angry
    2 = less angry

a. in a rage   d. cross
b. livid   e. irritated
c. annoyed   f. furious

2 He was absolutely furious

Match words of similar meaning from the two columns:

cross	livid
annoying	calm
furious	irritating
OK	annoyed

Now use the pairs in the situations below:

1. I bet Julie was angry when she found out you'd lost the tickets.
   > No, she was quite . . . . . . / . . . . . . about it, actually.

2. How did your boss react when you told her you'd forgotten to send off that order?
   > She was quite . . . . . . / . . . . I had to phone the clients in America and apologise.

3. What did your Dad do when you told him you'd crashed the car?
   > He was absolutely . . . . . . / . . . .

4. Can you turn your Walkman down? I can hear every word. It's really . . . . . . / . . . .
   > Oh, sorry. I didn't realise.

3 He hit the roof

Match the beginnings and endings of the sentences below:

1. It doesn't take much to make him angry. He's always losing
2. When Sarah finds out I've broken her camera, she's going to go
3. He's very bad-tempered. He's always shouting
4. I know you're angry but that's no reason to raise
5. I've never seen him so angry. He was shaking
6. When my dad found out I'd crashed the car, he hit

a. and swearing.
b. with rage.
c. the roof.
d. mad.
e. his temper.
f. your voice.

4 Angry idioms

Use the following words to complete the idioms in the sentences below:

nerves   enough   crazy   death   straw

1. Will you please stop interrupting? You're driving me . . . .
2. Will you shut up? You're really getting on my . . . .
3. I've had just about . . . . . . of this. My train has been late every day this week.
4. Right, that's the last . . . . The food was cold, the wine was warm and now they've got the bill wrong. I'm going to call the manager and complain.
5. I'm sick to . . . . . . of this. If they ask me to work on Saturday morning again, I'm quitting the job.

5 Excuses and apologies

Complete the expressions below with these words:

blame	mean
fault	realise
more	help

a. What . . . . . . can I say?
b. I didn't . . . . . to do it.
c. I couldn't . . . . . . it.
d. It wasn't my . . . .
e. Don't . . . . . me.
f. I didn't . . . .

Now use the expressions in these situations:

1. Hey, what do you think you're doing? I was before you.
   > I'm sorry. I . . . . there was a queue.

2. I hear you had an accident in your car last week.
   > Yes, but . . . . Somebody came out of a side road without looking.

3. That's the third glass you've broken this week.
   > I'm really sorry. . . . . It was an accident.

4. We wouldn't have missed the train if you hadn't taken so long to get ready.
   > . . . . ! It was you that didn't want to pay for a taxi to the station.

5. Did you eat all that chocolate that was in the fridge?
   > Yes, I'm sorry. I saw it there and . . . . You should've hidden it somewhere.

6. I'll never forgive you. How could you have done something like that?
   > Look, I've said I'm sorry. . . . . ?

6 Angry and calm responses

Look at the following situation:

> Peter broke an expensive vase playing with a ball in the living room. His father is absolutely furious but his mother is quite calm about it.

Look at the following lines from their conversation. Decide who is speaking – Peter's father (F) or his mother (M):

1. Don't worry. We can buy a new one.
2. I've told you a thousand times before.
3. It doesn't really matter, does it?
4. It's not the end of the world.
5. You never listen to a word I say.
6. It was an accident. He didn't mean to do it.
7. I could kill him.
8. Calm down! Don't you think you're over-reacting?

7 Yourself

Look at the following pairs of sentences and underline the one that's true for you:

1. I'm fairly calm and easy-going.
   I often lose my temper.

2. There are lots of things that really annoy me.
   I don't let too many things bother me.

3. I often notice other people's annoying habits.
   Other people's habits don't bother me.

Road rage is when a driver gets very angry with another driver. Have you ever experienced it?

Add your own words and expressions

17   Liking and disliking

1 Liking something a lot

Which of the two choices in colour expresses a stronger feeling?

1. What's this CD? I really like / quite like it.
2. I like / do like your coat. Where did you get it?
3. You should go to New York one day. You'd love / like it.
4. I'm going to have a dessert. I love / absolutely adore strawberries.
5. Why don't you get Claire a CD? She's very keen on / absolutely mad about Blur.
6. I quite enjoy / really look forward to going to the gym after a hard day in the office.

A *modern and informal way of saying that you like doing something is* I'm into it. *For example:*

I'm really into that kind of music.
He's into everything alternative – vegetarian food, alternative medicine, that kind of thing.

2 Positive, neutral or negative?

It is very common to talk about liking or disliking something by saying, for example: "it's fantastic" or "it's terrible". Put the words and phrases below into the correct box:

wonderful	fantastic	excellent	great
appalling	terrible	not bad	all right
brilliant	awful	dreadful	OK

very positive	neutral	very negative

3 Saying you like something

Match the beginnings and endings of the sentences below:

1. I really enjoy
2. I'm really looking forward
3. I'm very keen
4. I'm very fond
5. My little girl's absolutely crazy
6. I get a lot of enjoyment

a. on jazz. I've got about 200 CDs.
b. of Paris. I've been there five times.
c. about horses.
d. from gardening.
e. my work.
f. to seeing all my friends again.

4 When you are asked what you like

Match up the questions and answers to make two-line conversations:

1. Shall we get a bottle of red wine?
2. Do you fancy going to the cinema?
3. Do you like fish?
4. Do you eat here often?
5. Do you like whisky and things like that?
6. Have you been to that new club?

a. Not much, really. I prefer meat.
b. I wouldn't be seen dead in it! It's for kids!
c. Well, actually, I'd prefer white.
d. I can take it or leave it, actually.
e. I'd rather stay at home, if you don't mind.
f. Yes, it's one of my favourite restaurants.

5 Prepositions

Complete the text below with the following prepositions:

on   about   to   into   of   from

Although I'm keen (1) . . . . leading a healthy life, I'm not mad (2) . . . . health food shops and I'm certainly not (3) . . . . alternative medicine. I'm too fond (4) . . . . sweet things and good wine! I get a lot of enjoyment (5) . . . . sport, but after a game of football, I do look forward (6) . . . . going out for a really nice meal with a good bottle of Spanish wine, followed by coffee and chocolates!

6 Saying you don't like something

Match the beginnings of each sentence on the left with the pairs of endings on the right:

1. I don't   a. stand that song.
                    bear him.

2. I'm not   b. like it much.
                    really like it.

3. It doesn't   c. hate it.
                    loathe the idea.

4. I can't   d. very keen on sport.
                    really interested in art.

5. I absolutely   e. interest me.
                    appeal to me.

Which four phrases express very strong dislike?

. . . .

. . . .

. . . .

. . . .

Now complete each of the sentences below so that they are true for you:

1. I don't like . . . . very much.
2. I'm not really very keen on . . . .
3. I'm not very interested in . . . .
4. . . . . doesn't really appeal to me.
5. I can't stand . . . .
6. I can't bear it when people . . . .
7. I absolutely loathe . . . .

7 Adding a comment

Add the correct ending to these sentences:

1. I don't think you'll like the film much. It's nothing . . . .
2. Why do so many people like jazz? I don't know . . . .
3. I don't really understand why people like champagne so much. It does . . . .
4. I don't think I'll come to the opera with you. I'm not really . . . .
5. I've never been to watch rugby. It's not really . . . .
6. I suppose techno music's OK, but I could . . . .

a. into that sort of thing.
b. special.
c. live without it.
d. nothing for me.
e. my cup of tea.
f. what they see in it.

8 Word order

Put the adverbs at the end of each sentence into the correct place in the sentence:

1. I like Maria's husband.   very much
2. I don't like this pub.   at all
3. I thought it was brilliant.   absolutely
4. I hate people telling me what to do.   really

If you go off something, do you start to like it or start to dislike it?

Add your own words and expressions

18   Head and face

1 Basic vocabulary

Match the words below to the parts of the head and face in the pictures:

hair	. . . .	forehead	. . . .
eyebrow	. . . .	eyelashes	. . . .
eyelid	. . . .	nose	. . . .
cheek	. . . .	mouth	. . . .
lips	. . . .	tongue	. . . .
teeth	. . . .	chin	. . . .
neck	. . . .	beard	. . . .
moustache	. . . .	ear	. . . .

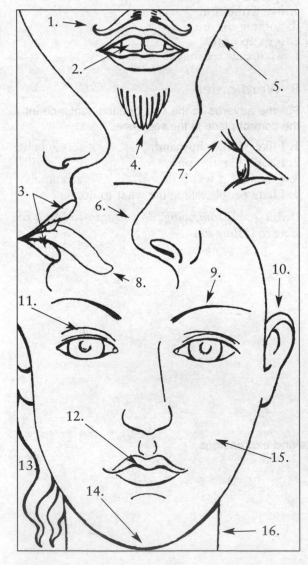

2 Close your eyes

Use the correct noun with the verbs in the boxes:

eyes   head   teeth   nose   hair

a.	turn shake nod hit scratch	your . . . . . .
b.	comb brush wash dye lose	your . . . . . .
c.	clean brush	your . . . . . .
d.	blow	your . . . . . .
e.	open close rub ruin	your . . . . . .

Now use the correct form of some of the expressions in the sentences below:

1. I need a new image. I'm thinking of . . . . . .
. . . . blonde.

2. I'm sure I'll be bald by the time I'm thirty.
My dad . . . . . all . . . . in his twenties.

3. My dentist keeps telling me . . . .
up and down as well as from side to side.

4. When I came off my motorbike, I . . . .
hard on the road even though I was wearing
my crash helmet.

5. You'll . . . . if you never
take a break from that computer screen!

6. In our culture . . . . means
you agree while . . . . usually
means 'no'. This isn't the same in all cultures.

7. Have you got a paper hankie? I need to . . . .
. . . . I hate having a cold!

8. Are you . . . . because
you're not sure what to do or because it's
itchy?

3 I can't stop yawning

Complete the following sentences with the correct form of the verbs below:

wink   frown   yawn   grin   smile   go red

1. Come on everybody, ... I'm trying to take your picture.
2. I should have gone to bed earlier last night. I can't stop . . . . today.
3. I knew Peter was only joking because he . . . . at me – but Jim believed him!
4. What are you . . . . for? I don't think it's funny at all.
5. When I asked Mark if he knew about the missing money, he . . . . . . bright . . . . . . I'm sure he knows something about it.
6. Is something wrong? You keep . . . . !

4 Chewing, kissing and spitting

Add these verbs to the correct group of nouns:

kiss   chew   blow out
lick   suck   spit out

1. . . . . . . a stamp / an ice-cream
2. . . . . . . a lollipop / a cough sweet
3. . . . . . . a candle / a burning match
4. . . . . . . gum / your food properly
5. . . . . . . a friend goodbye / your girlfriend
6. . . . . . . something that tastes nasty

Now complete the following sentences with the correct form of these verbs:

blow   spit   swallow   bite

1. I don't understand why footballers have to keep . . . . . . on the pitch all the time. It's disgusting.
2. Don't let the baby play with that coin. She'll only put it in her mouth and . . . . . . it.
3. Stop annoying the dog. One of these days he's going to . . . . . . you.
4. I wish you wouldn't keep . . . . . . cigarette smoke across the table while I'm eating.

5 Head and face idioms

Parts of the head and face are often used metaphorically or in idiomatic expressions. Complete the following sentences with the words below:

mouth   face   eye   nose
eyes   ear   ears   tongue

1. I hear you're going to live in China. I couldn't believe my . . . . . . when Tom told me.
2. I saw Louise kissing Mark outside the cinema last night. I couldn't believe my . . . . . . !
3. Why did you have to tell Sandra about me dancing with Liz at the party last night? You've got a big . . . .
4. Excuse me. Could you keep an . . . . . . on my bag while I go for a swim?
5. I'm not going to work today. I just can't . . . . . . another day of sitting in front of that computer.
6. Don't tell me the answer. It's on the tip of my . . . .
7. He never listens to anything anybody says. It just goes in one . . . . . . and out the other.
8. I've told you before. Keep your . . . . . . out of my business.

6 Dandruff and spots!

Where would you see the following examples of written language?

1. Brushing with Ultramint will help fight the plaque that causes gum disease.
2. Apply to wet hair and gently massage into hair and scalp. If dandruff persists, consult your doctor.
3. Regular use helps prevent acne.
4. Get rid of your wrinkles by using Oil of Olay moisturising cream night and morning.

Add your own words and expressions

19 Hair and face

1 Basic vocabulary

Match the descriptions to the pictures:

short hair   long hair   bald
wavy hair   curly hair   shoulder-length hair

Make sure you know these hair colours: light / dark brown, auburn, red, fair, blonde, black, grey, silver, white.
Note that you can say 'She's a redhead' but you can't say 'She's a blackhead' or a 'blondehead' etc.
If you want to make your hair curly, *you go to the hairdresser's and have* a perm.

2 Hairstyles

Match these hairstyles to the pictures:

a ponytail   a centre parting   tied back   spiky
a fringe   a side parting   dreadlocks   shaved

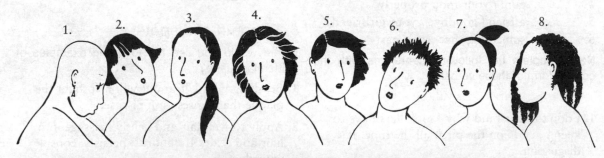

Note: If you have highlights, *you have* dyed *some parts of your hair a different colour. Of course, you can dye all your hair a different colour – 'She's got dyed blonde hair.'*

3 Looking after your hair

Use these words to complete the text below:

anti-dandruff   implants   dandruff   wig
conditioner   extensions   shampoo   greasy

I wash my hair three times a week using a regular (1) . . . . and once a week I also use a
(2) . . . . I'm a bit bored with my hairstyle. I'd like to have much longer hair so I'm thinking
about getting hair (3) . . . . My boyfriend needs help with his hair. It's a bit (4) . . . .
and he gets (5) . . . . so I bought him some (6) . . . . shampoo. He's also going a
bit thin on top. In fact, he's going bald. He's thinking about having hair (7) . . . . I don't
mind – as long as he doesn't start wearing a (8) . . . . !

4 Face – distinguishing features

Use these words to complete the sentences below:

complexion	mole	scar
make-up	cheekbones	pierced
wrinkles	beards	false teeth
teeth	unshaven	spots

1. Sarah wears a lot of . . . . She looks better without it, if you ask me.
2. I'm getting old. I'm starting to get . . . . round my eyes.
3. My sister's had her nose and eyebrow . . . . She looks quite good, actually.
4. I had terrible . . . . when I was a teenager. No wonder I was so shy with girls.
5. Fiona's got lovely high . . . . I find her very attractive.
6. Peter's got a beautiful smooth . . . . – like a baby's.
7. I don't like men with . . . . but I quite like the . . . . look – you know – one or two days without shaving.
8. My mum's got a small, brown . . . . on one of her cheeks.
9. I cut myself climbing a tree when I was ten and I've got this . . . . just below my ear.
10. My grandfather looks really funny when he smiles because he's got two . . . . missing and he refuses to wear . . . .

If a man always shaves, we say he is clean-shaven.

5 Skin colour

We say that people are black or white but not black-skinned or white-skinned. We can say people are dark-skinned or fair-skinned. We sometimes say that somebody has got a pale complexion or that they are pale-skinned but if we just say that somebody is pale or looks pale, it is because they aren't feeling very well.

6 Word order

Put the words in the following sentences into the correct order:

1. such skin she's clear lovely got.
. . . .
2. she's cheekbones beautiful such got high.
. . . .
3. got white teeth beautiful such he's.
. . . .
4. light she's curly hair brown got.
. . . .
5. blue got she's piercing eyes beautiful.
. . . .
6. got he's greasy long hair horrible.
. . . .

7 Adjectives

Match each of the following lines of adjectives with one of the following words:

nose	teeth	ears
eyes	hair	face

1. round, square, oval, fat, thin, tanned
2. brown, blue, green, big, small, piercing
3. big, long, thin, pointed, flat, broken
4. white, yellow, rotten, false
5. dry, dull, lifeless, shiny, silky
6. small, large, sticking out

Add your own words and expressions

20   Parts of the body

1 The body

Match the words and pictures:

waist	back	elbow	wrist	shoulder	neck
bottom	leg	breast	ear	chest	arm
armpit	stomach	foot	ankle	hip	head

1. . . . . . .

2. . . . . . .

3. . . . . . .

4. . . . . . .

5. . . . . . .

6. . . . . . .

7. . . . . . .

8. . . . . . .

9. . . . . . .

10. . . . . . .

11. . . . . . .

12. . . . . . .

13. . . . . . .

14. . . . . . .

15. . . . . . .

16. . . . . . .

17. . . . . . .

18. . . . . . .

Backside **and** *bum* **are very informal words for bottom –** *"Come on, get off your backside and help me with this."*
Belly **is a very informal word for stomach –** *"You'll get a fat belly if you keep eating so much."*

2 The hand
Match the words and pictures:

finger palm nail thumb

3 The leg and foot
Do the same with these words:

thigh

calf

big toe

knee

heel

toes

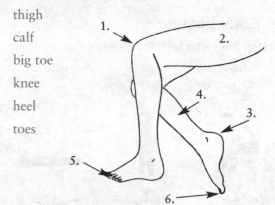

4 Inside the body
Decide whether the words below are bones (B) or organs (O):

1. spine . . .
2. heart . . .
3. skull . . .
4. ribs . . .

5. liver . . .
6. kidneys . . .
7. lungs . . .
8. pelvis . . .

5 What the organs do
Match the beginnings of the sentences on the left with the endings on the right:

1. The average heart
2. The heart
3. The air we breathe in
4. The skeleton
5. Muscles
6. Blood
7. The skin
8. The kidneys

a. passes through the windpipe and into the lungs.
b. circulates around the body supplying oxygen to the cells.
c. pumps blood around the body through the arteries.
d. helps to regulate body temperature.
e. separate waste liquid from the blood.
f. beats more than 100,000 times a day.
g. are attached to bones by tendons.
h. supports the body and protects the internal organs.

Now do the same with these:

9. The spine
10. Veins
11. Arteries
12. The womb
13. Joints
14. The liver
15. The bladder

i. supports the back and protects the spinal cord.
j. is a bag which collects urine before it is passed out of the body.
k. carry blood from the heart to all parts of the body.
l. carry blood from all parts of the body to the heart.
m. is the part of a woman's body where a baby grows and develops.
n. are where two bones are connected together by ligaments.
o. helps to clean the blood and produces bile.

Add your own words and expressions

21   Body movements

1   Body posture

Match the verbs with the pictures:

bow   kneel   lean
lie down   stand up   sit down

2   Moving your body

Match the words with the pictures:

run   dance   walk   jump
climb   dive   hop   crawl

3   Moving things

Use the correct form of these verbs in the sentences below:

lift   push   pull   drag

1. Excuse me, could you help me . . . . . . my car to the side of the road?
2. The best part of the film was when he . . . . . her towards him and kissed her passionately.
3. My suitcase is so heavy I can hardly . . . . it off the ground.
4. Two policeman . . . . one of the protesters from the crowd and threw him into the back of the police van.

4   Verbs in expressions

Complete the following boxes with these verbs:

jump   sit   lean   walk   lie   climb

1.	4.
down the road	onto the roof
to school	up the hill
for miles	a mountain
. . . through the park	. . . the ladder
to work	over a wall
out of the room	out of the window
around town	a tree
2.	**5.**
against the wall	in bed
out of the window	on the beach
. . . too far	. . . down
across the table	on your back
forward / back	awake
3.	**6.**
up and down	in an armchair
into the pool	on a stool
into the sea	back and relax
. . . over a wall	. . . upright
out of the window	around talking
off the roof	on the sofa

You need to learn these as whole expressions.

5   Losing your balance

Complete the following sentences with the correct form of the verbs below:

slip   fall off   fall down
collapse   trip over

1. I . . . . the dog last night and hit my head on the coffee table.
2. I . . . . the stairs and almost broke my neck!
3. I . . . . my bike and hurt my shoulder.
4. It's quite icy outside. Be careful not to . . . . and break something.
5. The old man . . . . in the street and was rushed to hospital.

*A **wet floor** or an **icy pavement** is slippery.*

6 Hand and leg movements

Match these verbs with the pictures:

hold (your head)	reach	punch
throw	kick	wave
clap (your hands)	point	catch

Now complete the following sentences with the correct form of these verbs:

shake	stamp	step	reach
hold on	slap	grab	wave

1. My feet are soaking wet! I've just . . . . in a huge puddle!
2. That guy must have said something very rude. The woman with him has just . . . . his face!
3. There was nothing I could do. The man just . . . . my handbag and ran off up the street.
4. You're taller than me. Could you . . . . . . up and get that book for me?
5. There was a huge spider on the bathroom floor. My Dad just . . . . . . on it and that was the end of the spider!

6. Everyone in the crowd was . . . . a flag as the Queen passed by. She . . . . back!
7. You're supposed to . . . . the bottle before you take the medicine.
8. It was so windy last night. I really had to . . . . to my umbrella to stop it blowing away.

7 Moving quickly or slowly

Look at the following sentences and then put the words and phrases in colour into the correct column below. Use a dictionary to help you.

1. Mary tiptoed along the corridor, trying not to wake the children.
2. I think Beckham's badly injured. He's limping over to the side of the pitch.
3. I saw that he'd come off his bike and I rushed over to see if I could help.
4. It was a pretty quiet weekend. On Sunday we just strolled round the park and then had lunch in the pub.
5. It started pouring with rain so we dashed into a shop doorway.
6. I leapt up to answer the phone and spilled my coffee down my trousers.
7. I thought I saw somebody creeping about in the garden last night. Did you see anything?
8. She marched into the office and demanded to speak to the manager.
9. I love wandering round town on Saturday, just looking in all the shop windows.
10. As soon as Helen heard she'd passed the exam, she raced home to tell her parents.

Quick movements	Slow movements
. . . .	. . . .
. . . .	. . . .
. . . .	. . . .
. . . .	. . . .
. . . .	. . . .

Add your own words and expressions

22   The senses

1 Basic vocabulary

Match the five senses with the pictures:

sight   hearing   smell   taste   touch

1.  2. 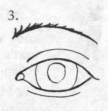 3. 4. 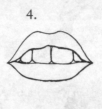 5.

2 Senses as nouns

Match the two parts of these sentences:

1. I love the sound of
2. I hate the smell of
3. I hate the taste of
4. I love the feel of
5. I love the sight of

a. cheap aftershave.
b. birds singing outside my window.
c. my own home when I'm back from holiday.
d. whisky. It's much too strong for me.
e. silk. It's so soft.

3 Senses as verbs

Match the beginning of each sentence on the left with two of the comments on the right:

1. Shall I open the window?
2. Do you have to wear that shirt?
3. Why don't you have a shave?
4. I've just spoken to Tina on the phone.
5. Where on earth did you get this wine?

a. It makes you look ridiculous.
b. She sounded very upset.
c. It smells disgusting in here.
d. It tastes revolting.
e. Your face feels so rough.
f. It sounded as if she'd been crying.
g. It makes you look like a clown.
h. It stinks in here.
i. It tastes like vinegar.
j. Your face feels like sandpaper.

4 Using our senses consciously

Match the two parts of these sentences:

1. Come and smell
2. Come and taste
3. I was just looking at
4. I always listen to
5. Feel

a. the radio in the morning.
b. these roses. Aren't they lovely?
c. this soup. It's delicious.
d. your photos of the wedding. They're fantastic.
e. this blouse. Do you think it's silk?

5 Using 'can' and 'can't'

Fill the gaps in the following sentences with can or can't together with one of the verbs below:

hear   see   smell   taste   feel

1. Could you move your head? I . . . . properly.
2. I think I . . . . gas.
3. Speak up a bit. I . . . . what you're saying.
4. I think it's going to be cold tonight. I . . . . it in my bones!
5. This dish is very spicy. I . . . . . really . . . . . the chilli in it.

6 Watch, see and look

Complete the following sentences with the correct form of these verbs:

watch   see   look

1. Did you . . . . Kate at the party last night?
2. I think I'll stay in and . . . . TV tonight.
3. Did you . . . . (or . . . .) that horror film on TV last night? It was brilliant!
4. I learned how to cook by . . . . my mother in the kitchen
5. If you . . . . carefully, you can see a green woodpecker at the top of that tree.
6. Come and . . . . at this old school book I've found.
7. Did you . . . . that car? It must have been doing about 130 kph.

We often use the expression have a look: *"Can I have a look at your camera?"*

7 Ways of looking

Choose the correct endings below:

1. Tina suddenly spotted
2. Penny gazed at
3. Liz glanced at
4. Lucy stared at
5. The old lady peeped through

a. the bill in disbelief. Surely, £2,000 wasn't the correct amount.
b. one of her friends on the other side of the bar. "Hi Fiona," she shouted.
c. the curtains. She enjoyed watching all the neighbours coming and going.
d. her watch nervously. He should be here by now, she said to herself.
e. the toys in the shop window, wishing it was her birthday.

These verbs are all more common in written English.

8 Using your ears

Use the correct form of these expressions:

pay attention   overhear
listen carefully   catch

1. If you . . . ., you can actually hear the sea from here.
2. Sorry, I didn't . . . . what you said.
   > That's because you weren't . . . .
3. How do you know Sam and Lisa are planning to get married?
   > I . . . . them talking about it in the kitchen last night.

9 Metaphorical uses

The verbs see, hear, feel, touch **and** smell **can all be used with non-literal meanings. Use the correct form of one of these verbs in the following situations:**

1. I know you're thinking of emigrating to Australia, but I . . . . . . you're making a big mistake.
2. I . . . . . . you're thinking of retiring early.
3. We went to a talk last night about life in Ethiopia. The speaker had just spent a year there, working as a nurse. Some of her experiences really . . . . us.
4. "I . . . . . . a rat!" is a common idiom, meaning that you are suspicious about something.
5. You must be making a lot of money! I . . . . . you've just bought a brand-new Mercedes.

A very common use of see is in the expression, I see what you mean. (= I understand.)

If something is very sad or emotional, it can touch you. You can also feel touched. For example: "My students bought me a birthday present. I was really touched."

When we speak of a sixth sense, what do we mean?

Add your own words and expressions

23   Feeling ill

1   Basic vocabulary

Translate the words in colour into your language:

1. I've got a cold.   . . . .
2. My neck aches.   . . . .
3. I think I've got flu.   . . . .
4. I've got a pain in my knee.   . . . .
5. I've got a sore back.   . . . .
6. My arm hurts.   . . . .
7. Have you got a temperature?   . . . .
8. What are the symptoms?   . . . .

2   Saying you don't feel very well

Match the beginnings of each sentence on the left with the pairs of endings on the right:

1. I'm   a. terrible / awful / dreadful.
                     a bit under the weather.

2. I've got   b. ill.
                     not very well.

3. I don't feel   c. a cold.
                     the flu.

4. I feel   d. very well.
                     too good.

3   Serious conditions

Match the condition on the left with the part of the body that it particularly affects on the right:

1. appendicitis   a. your stomach
2. tonsillitis   b. your lungs
3. hepatitis   c. your head
4. asthma   d. your appendix
5. an ulcer   e. your joints and bones
6. arthritis   f. your blood
7. migraine   g. your tonsils

Match the diseases with their possible causes:

8. AIDS   h. stress
9. typhoid   i. the sun
10. heart disease j. smoking
11. skin cancer   k. a mosquito bite
12. malaria   l. dirty water
13. lung cancer   m. unprotected sex

4   Causes and symptoms

Match the symptom on the left with the cause on the right:

1. I've got a blister.   a. I think I've been working too much.
2. I've got a headache.   b. Our bed is too soft. We need to get a firmer one.
3. I've got jetlag.   c. I had too much to drink at dinner last night.
4. I've got a bad back.   d. I've just been chopping some wood.
5. I'm feeling really run down. e. It must have been that take-away last night.
6. I've got a splinter in my hand. f. I wore the wrong shoes to go hill-walking!
7. My nose is blocked up.   g. I always get hay fever at this time of year.
8. I've got diarrhoea.   h. It was an 18-hour flight and a 10-hour time difference.

Now match the following pieces of advice to the situations above:

9.   Make sure you drink plenty of water. Otherwise, you'll get dehydrated.
10. Go straight to bed for a couple of hours, then get back to your normal sleeping pattern tonight.
11. Why not take some time off and go somewhere warm? That's what you need!
12. There's a special kind of plaster you can use on blisters. I had one and it helped a lot.
13. Get one of those nasal sprays from the chemist. They always work for me.
14. Have you tried an osteopath or a chiropractor?
15. Let me see. Have you got a pair of tweezers?
16. Stick to orange juice in future!

5 Health problems

Complete the following dialogues with the sentences below:

a. I've got a bit of a hangover.
b. I feel dizzy.
c. I've caught a cold.
d. You'll make yourself ill.
e. I always get seasick.
f. I've got indigestion.

1. What's the matter?
   > I think I ate my dinner too quickly. . . . . .
   . . . .

2. Maybe we should take the boat. It's much cheaper than flying.
   > Oh no, I'd rather not. . . . .
   . . . .

3. I think . . . .
   > Well, why don't you have a glass of hot lemon and honey and get an early night?

4. . . . .
   > Well, it's your own fault. You shouldn't have opened that second bottle of wine!

5. You look exhausted. You've been working too hard recently. If you don't slow down a bit, ...

6. Are you all right? You've gone as white as a sheet!
   > No, I need to sit down. I . . . .

6 Illnesses and symptoms

Match these illnesses with the symptoms below:

hay fever   food poisoning   flu
an allergy   bronchitis   measles

1. I've got a terrible cough and pains in my chest, and I seem to be constantly short of breath.

2. I feel absolutely awful. My temperature is 41°, and I've got a headache and a runny nose. I've got a sore throat – it's agony every time I swallow.

3. I can't go near cats. I come out in a horrible red rash.

4. She's been off school for two weeks now. She's got a temperature and she's covered in little red spots. She's completely lost her appetite – she hasn't eaten a thing for the last three days.

5. I think it must be something I ate. I was sick all night. I still feel sick now and I've got a terrible stomach-ache.

6. It's the same every summer. My eyes get really itchy and I can't stop sneezing.

In British English be sick means vomit (bring food back up from the stomach).

If you have an allergy, you are allergic to something. Are you allergic to anything?

7 She's feeling a bit better

Complete the following dialogue with the correct form of the verbs below:

recover   feel   get   make

A: The office is empty. Where is everybody this morning?

B: Well, Jane phoned to say she's got an upset tummy, but she said she'll come in as soon as she's . . . . a bit better – probably this afternoon. Dave's got the flu and he says it'll take him a few days to . . . . over it – and Sarah's plane was delayed at the airport for seven hours and she wants an extra day to . . . . from the journey. At least Mark's here – he'd been in bed with tonsillitis all weekend, but he's . . . . a speedy recovery and he's upstairs working at his computer at this very moment.

A: I'm glad somebody's here!

There are several different ways of talking about stomach problems. An upset stomach, an upset tummy or indigestion are not very serious. If it is serious, you might talk about stomach trouble.

Add your own words and expressions

24   Injuries

1 Basic vocabulary

Translate the words in colour:

1. There was blood all over the place.   . . . .
2. Do you bleed easily?   . . . .
3. The operation only left a small scar.   . . . .
4. The bruise will disappear in a few days. . . . .
5. Are you in pain?   . . . .
6. Look where the cat scratched me.   . . . .
7. His injuries are all fairly minor.   . . . .
8. This wound was caused by flying glass. . . . .
9. My ankle is very swollen.   . . . .
10. I've got a horrible blister on my foot.   . . . .
11. I've sprained my wrist.   . . . .
12. Be careful or that wasp will sting you.   . . . .

2 Accidents

Match the following expressions with the pictures below:

1. I've broken my arm.
2. I've sprained my wrist.
3. I've cut my thumb.
4. I've burnt my hand.
5. I've got a nosebleed.
6. I hit my head.
7. I got an electric shock.
8. I got stung by a bee.
9. I twisted my ankle.

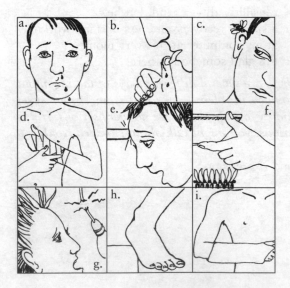

3 Wounds and injuries

Match the phrases with the pictures:

He's been injured.   He's been wounded.

Now complete the following sentences with the words below:

injured   injury   wound   wounded

1. It's quite a deep . . . . You'll probably need stitches. I'll take you to the hospital.
2. Venus Williams was unable to finish her match because of a shoulder . . . .
3. My grand-dad was . . . . in the war. He got shot in the leg.
4. There was a train crash in London this morning. Several people are seriously . . . .

Which of these words go with injury and which go with wound?

slight   knife   internal   deep
bullet   back   sports   stab

. . . .	. . . .
. . . .	. . . .
. . . . injury	. . . . wound
. . . .	. . . .

In spoken language it is common to use hurt instead of injured. For example, "Did you hear about the train crash this morning? Quite a lot of people have been hurt." In sport we always use injured. "Ronaldo is injured and will miss the next five matches."

4 Hurting yourself

Complete the following dialogues with the phrases below:

> a. burnt myself
> b. cut myself
> c. scratched myself
> d. injured myself

1. You've got blood on your face.
   > I know, I've just . . . . shaving.
2. What have you done to your hand?
   > I . . . . taking something out of the oven last night. I don't think it's too serious.
3. Have you ever been horse-riding?
   > Yes, once, but I fell off and . . . . quite badly. I've never done it since.
4. What's the matter?
   > I've just . . . . myself on that rose bush.

5 It's badly bruised

Match the phrases with the pictures:

1. He's unconscious.
2. It's bleeding.
3. It's bruised.
4. It's swollen.
5. He's got a black eye.
6. He's got a bad scar under his eye.

6 It was agony

Complete the sentences using these words:

agony	blood	black
pain	scratch	blisters

a. She's in a lot of . . . .
b. I'm . . . . and blue all over.
c. There was . . . . everywhere.
d. My feet are covered in . . . .
e. It's just a . . . .
f. It was absolute . . . . !

Now use the language above to complete the following sentences:

1. I ran in the London Marathon on Sunday. I'm in agony. My . . . . !
2. Don't worry. . . . . I'll get you a plaster.
3. I think we'd better call an ambulance. She's . . . .
4. My brother cut the top off his finger with a kitchen knife last night. . . . .
5. I shut my fingers in the car door this morning. I was in . . . .
6. I played rugby again yesterday. It was VERY physical. . . . . this morning.

Have you ever broken a bone, been knocked unconscious, cut yourself badly, or had a black eye?

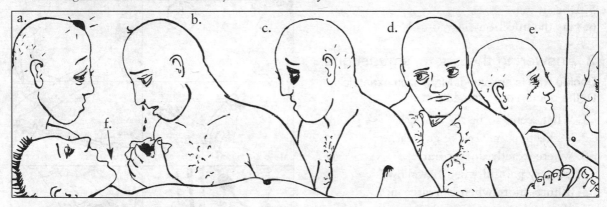

Add your own words and expressions

25   At the doctor's

1   Basic vocabulary

Complete the following sentences with the words below:

cough   symptom   appointment
virus   rash   infection
medicine   chemist's   prescription

1. Could I come in late tomorrow? My wife and I have an . . . . with the doctor.
2. That's a nasty . . . . . . you've got. You've really got to stop smoking.
3. The main . . . . . . of measles is little red spots all over your body.
4. I sometimes get a . . . . . . on my face after I've shaved.
5. I'm taking antibiotics for this ear . . . .
6. Last winter there was a really nasty . . . . going round.
7. Very often, rest is the best . . . . !
8. Did you take that . . . . to the . . . . ?

Now translate the words in colour:

1. Do you have any trouble swallowing?   . . . .
2. Does this hurt?   . . . .
3. Take a deep breath.   . . . .
4. Breathe deeply.   . . . .
5. Does it itch?   . . . .
6. Has the infection cleared up?   . . . .

2   Answering the doctor's questions

Decide who is speaking. Mark each example D (the doctor) or P (the patient):

1. What seems to be the matter?
2. It's keeping me awake at night.
3. Where exactly does it hurt?
4. It's very painful when I swallow.
5. It hurts more when I breathe in.
6. Now, take a deep breath.
7. Is there anything I can take for it?
8. Have you had any other symptoms?
9. It's nothing to worry about.
10. I'll give you something to relieve the pain.
11. I've got very bad wind.
12. I had it when I was a child.

3   Going to the doctor's

Put these events in the most logical order:

a. I went to see the doctor.
b. I went to the chemist's to get the medicine.
c. He said I had a chest infection.
d. He examined me.
e. I didn't feel very well.
f. He gave me a prescription for antibiotics.
g. I made an appointment to see the doctor.

1 . . .   2 . . .   3 . . .   4 . . .   5 . . .   6 . . .   7 . . .

4   Verb collocations

Use the verbs below to complete the following phrases. Then match the phrases with the pictures.

take   give   listen to

1. . . . . . . you an injection
2. . . . . . . your blood pressure
3. . . . . . . your chest
4. . . . . . . your temperature
5. . . . . . . your pulse
6. . . . . . . you a prescription
7. . . . . . . you a check-up
8. . . . . . . a blood sample

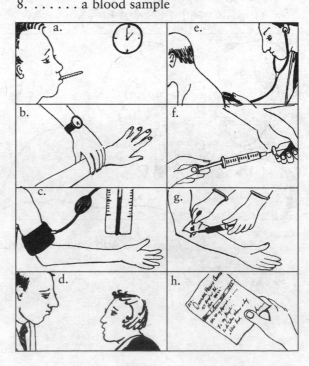

5 Medicines

Here is a list of common medicines. Match them up with the problems below:

a. sleeping pills / tablets
b. antibiotics
c. painkillers
d. eye drops
e. cough mixture

1. You can't sleep.
2. You have a dry cough.
3. You have a chest infection.
4. You have very bad backache.
5. You have an eye infection.

Americans talk about drugs instead of tablets or pills. In Britain drugs usually mean heroin, cocaine etc. In the United States a chemist's is called a drugstore.

6 Specialists

Your doctor might refer you to another professional to treat a particular problem. First mark the strong stress in each word. The first one is done for you. Then match them up with their speciality.

1. dietician
2. optician
3. physiotherapist
4. psychiatrist
5. chiropodist
6. paediatrician
7. gynaecologist
8. rheumatologist

a. You need glasses.
b. You are overweight.
c. You have ingrown toenails.
d. You are trying to have a baby.
e. You have arthritis.
f. You are very depressed.
g. Your two-year-old son is not well.
h. You hurt your shoulder playing tennis.

7 Alternative medicine

Here are seven words associated with alternative medicine. First mark the strong stress in each word. The first one is done for you. Then match the words and their descriptions.

hypnotism   herbal remedies
massage   aromatherapy
reflexology   homeopathy
acupuncture

1. Treating people with special oils, which are used in a bath or rubbed into the skin.
2. Treating somebody by putting them into a deep sleep and controlling what they think.
3. Treating people by rubbing various parts of their body to relieve pain.
4. Treating people with medicines made from special herbs and plants.
5. Treating people with needles to stimulate nerve impulses.
6. Treating people by pressing parts of their feet in order to treat problems in other parts of their body.
7. Giving people very very small amounts of drugs.

Have you ever used any of the above alternative therapies?

Add your own words and expressions

57

26   In hospital

1   Basic vocabulary

Translate the words in colour into your language:

1. Has he had the results of his X-ray? . . . . . .
2. He gave me an injection. . . . . . .
3. I needed four stitches. . . . . . .
4. I'll just put a bandage on it. . . . . . .
5. It won't leave much of a scar. . . . . . .
6. You'll need an anaesthetic. . . . . . .
7. They were all suffering from shock. . . . . . .
8. We were in the same ward. . . . . . .
9. The treatment will last for a month. . . . . . .

2   Hospital departments

Match the departments with the ideas a-f below:

1. casualty   4. intensive care
2. children's ward   5. maternity ward
3. operating theatre   6. outpatients' department

a. She's just had her first baby.
b. She cut her arm badly.
c. He's having his operation.
d. Our ten-year-old has a very high temperature.
e. I had to go for a check-up.
f. She's very ill. She needs constant attention.

Another name for the Casualty Department is A and E (accident and emergency).

3   When you come out of hospital

Match these descriptions with the pictures:

1. His leg's in plaster.
2. His arm's in a sling.
3. He's walking on crutches.
4. He needs a walking stick.
5. His ankle's bandaged up.
6. He had to have stitches.
7. He's in a wheelchair.
8. He can't walk without a zimmer.

4   In and around a hospital

Match these words with the pictures:

ambulance   nurse   surgeon
paramedic   patient   stretcher

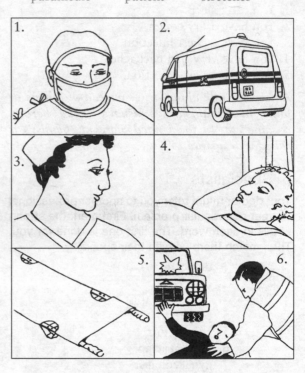

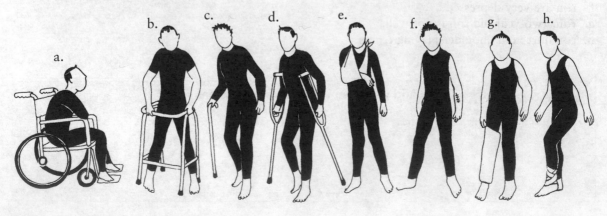

5 Treatment

Use the correct form of the verbs below. You will need to use some of them more than once.

put	need	do
have	leave	give

1. I'm going into hospital next month. I've got to . . . . an operation on my knee.
2. I couldn't feel a thing. They . . . . me an injection first.
3. It's quite a long operation so we'll have to . . . . you a general anaesthetic.
4. They'll probably want to . . . . some X-rays to see if you've broken anything.
5. Your ankle's badly sprained, so I'm going to . . . . a bandage on it.
6. It's quite a deep wound. I think it's going to . . . . stitches.
7. I'm a bit worried about having stitches. Do you think it'll . . . . a scar?
8. I injured my knee skiing a few months ago. I was hoping that resting it would be enough, but it looks as if it might . . . . surgery.

6 An emergency

Complete the following newspaper report with the correct form of these verbs:

rush	treat	injure	fight

Serious incident

A zoo keeper was very seriously . . . . today when he was attacked by a tiger at Whitesnade zoo in Yorkshire. Martin Kelly was attacked as he fed the animal in front of several visitors. He was . . . . to hospital in York where doctors are . . . . to save his life. Two elderly women who witnessed the whole attack were . . . . for shock.

Go back and underline the whole expressions.

7 Good and bad news

Look at the following sentences about people's medical condition and decide whether the news is good (G) or bad (B):

1. It's nothing serious.
2. The victim is in a critical condition.
3. She's in a stable condition.
4. We expect him to a make a full recovery.
5. I'm afraid there's nothing more we can do.
6. Her condition has deteriorated overnight.
7. She suffered only minor injuries.
8. She's in a coma.

If you are gravely ill, it is very serious.

8 Treat, cure or heal

Use the correct form of these words in the report below:

heal	treatment	treat	cure

Doctors in America claim to have found a cure for the common cold. A hundred people suffering from the usual symptoms were (1) . . . . for two days with a new drug at their laboratory in California.

They found that after forty-eight hours, half of the patients had been completely (2) . . . . They hope that the new (3) . . . . will be on the market within the next three years.

Meanwhile, doctors in Switzerland have announced that applying maggots to wounds will help them to (4) . . . . more quickly. The larvae speed up the process by eating the bacteria in and around the wound.

Cure can be used both as a noun and as a verb:

> *They're trying to find a cure for cancer.*
> *She was completely cured.*

Is hospital treatment free in your country? Are there long waiting lists to have operations?

Add your own words and expressions

27 A healthy lifestyle

1 Healthy or unhealthy

Put the following phrases into the correct box below:

fresh fruit   a lot of stress at work
smoking   regular exercise
plenty of fresh air   too much alcohol
lots of sugar   salad
fish   too much salt

```
. . . . . . . . . . .
. . . . . . . . . .
. . . . . . . . . .      is good for you.
. . . . . . . . . .
. . . . . . . . . .

. . . . . . . . . .
. . . . . . . . . .
. . . . . . . . . .      is bad for you.
. . . . . . . . . .
. . . . . . . . . .
```

Now use the correct form of the following verbs. Use each one twice.

avoid   keep   stay   give up   cut down

1. Playing tennis twice a week is what . . . . . . me fit.
2. Lots of fresh fruit and vegetables will help you to . . . . . . healthy.
3. My doctor keeps telling me I should . . . . . . smoking completely.
4. You don't have to stop drinking completely. Just try to . . . . . . a little.
5. If you can, try to . . . . . stressful situations.
6. It's easy to start a diet. It's much harder to . . . . . . to it!
7. You'll see a big difference if you . . . . the amount of sugar you take in tea or coffee.
8. It's not essential to . . . . alcohol completely. Some doctors think a little a day is actually good for you.
9. Eat small meals regularly. This means you should do your best to . . . . . . eating big meals – especially late at night.
10. My weight has . . . . . . the same for the last ten years.

2 Watching your weight

Which two nouns go with each of these verbs?

1. join   a. weight
2. lose   b. a gym
3. put on   c. a diet
4. go on   d. a few kilos
5. resist   e. chocolates
6. cut out   f. a health club
                 g. a crash diet
                 h. anything sweet

Now use four of the verbs above to fill the gaps in the following dialogue:

A: I don't know what to do. I seem to . . . . weight so easily. Every time I weigh myself, I'm a kilo heavier!
B: Well, you do eat a lot of fatty food – perhaps you should . . . . it . . . . of your diet.
A: Oh, I don't know. I find it very difficult to stick to a diet. I just can't . . . . chocolates.
B: At least you should try to cut down on all those burgers you eat. Perhaps you could . . . . a gym or a health club.

3 She's in really good shape

Look at the following text and put the phrases in colour into the correct list below:

My Mum's in really good shape. She goes to the gym twice a week and plays tennis on Sunday. My Dad, on the other hand, is really unfit. He spends all day in front of the TV – he gets out of breath if he has to get up to answer the phone! My sister's a swimming instructor. As you can imagine, she's as fit as a fiddle, but my brother, who used to play rugby every weekend, has let himself get really out of condition – he must have put on twenty kilos in the last two years. Finally, there's my grand-dad. He's nearly eighty but he's got loads of energy. He plays golf three times a week and jogs round the park on the other days!

fit and healthy	not fit
. . . .	. . . .
. . . .	. . . .
. . . .	. . . .

4 Personal questionnaire

Tick the statements which are true for you. Then look at the key to see how healthy you really are!

1. a. I walk to work.
    b. I drive to work.
2. a. I have muesli for breakfast.
    b. I never eat muesli.
3. a. I never eat between meals.
    b. I eat sweets between meals.
4. a. I play sport at least once a week.
    b. I gave up sport years ago.
5. a. My waist size is the same as 5 years ago.
    b. My waist is bigger than 5 years ago.
6. a. I do the housework in the evening.
    b. I sit and watch TV in the evening.
7. a. I drink in moderation.
    b. I drink a lot at weekends.
8. a. I occasionally eat a few chocolates.
    b. I eat sweets on a regular basis.
9. a. I don't eat chips.
    b. I have chips more than once a week.
10. a. In shops I always walk upstairs.
    b. In shops I always take the lift.
11. a. I eat fish at least once a week.
    b. I never eat fish.
12. a. I go dancing when I get the chance.
    b. You'd never catch me dancing!
13. a. I always refuse puddings.
    b. I never refuse puddings.
14. a. I go out into the country a lot.
    b. The countryside is for animals!
15. a. I like to relax by reading a book.
    b. I relax by going to the pub.

6 Collocations

Complete these collocations from the two exercises above:

1. eat . . . . meals
2. my waist . . . .
3. drink in . . . .
4. on a regular . . . .
5. get . . . . . of spots
6. look carefully at your . . . . .
7. eat more . . . .
8. try . . . . out all sugar and butter

5 Problems

Match these lifestyle problems with the pieces of advice below:

The problems:

1. My hair always feels lifeless and oily. If I wash it in the morning, I need to wash it again when I come home from work. And I can't seem to get rid of the spots on my face.

2. If I buy a new pair of trousers, they don't fit me after a couple of months. So now I buy all my trousers one size too big. That way they last twice as long.

3. I get really breathless if I have to go upstairs nowadays. I used to be able to run up stairs. Now I have to stop halfway up and have a rest.

4. When I come home from work, the first thing I do every evening is pour myself a large gin and tonic. It's the only way I can relax.

The advice:

a. Look carefully at your diet. Are you eating too many oily foods, like chips or potato crisps?

b. You'd be far better playing squash or tennis after work. That would help you relax far better. You need less stress in your life.

c. You're smoking too much. At the moment you are breathless. What will you do when the doctor tells you it's cancer?

d. You are simply eating too much. If you are putting weight on so quickly, you must simply eat less and eat more healthily. Try cutting out all sugar and butter immediately, then start cutting out other things, like cream. Change to semi-skimmed milk.

Add your own words and expressions

28   Houses and homes

1   Different kinds of house

Match the definitions with the pictures:

1. You live in a detached house if it stands in its own grounds.
2. Your house is semi-detached if it is joined to another one. People talk about living in a semi.
3. You live in a terraced house if your house is in a terrace of houses.
4. A flat can be in a block of flats or part of an older house.
5. A cottage is usually a small house in the country.
6. A bungalow is a house with only one floor.

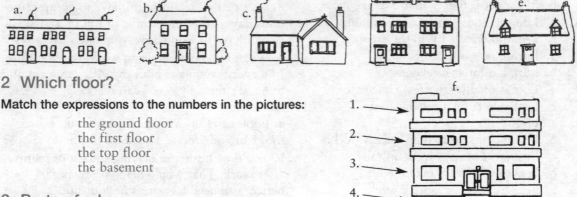

2   Which floor?

Match the expressions to the numbers in the pictures:

the ground floor
the first floor
the top floor
the basement

3   Parts of a house

Match the words with the numbers in the picture:

roof	steps	garage	chimneys	front door
gate	fence	balcony	hedge	lawn

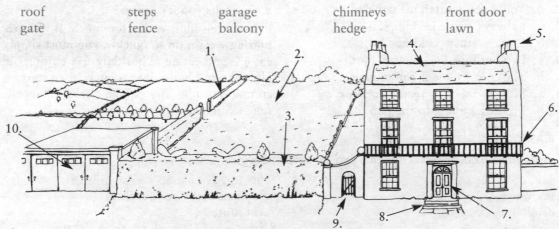

4   An empty room

Match the words with the numbers in the picture:

ceiling
power point
light switch
radiator
wall
floor

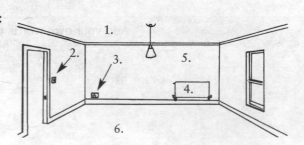

5 Rooms

Match the room with what you do in it:

1. You relax and watch TV
2. You cook
3. You eat your dinner
4. You sleep
5. You have a shower
6. You put up guests

a. in the bathroom
b. in your bedroom
c. in the living room / lounge
d. in the dining room
e. in the spare room
f. in the kitchen

6 Renting a flat

Complete the following text with these words:

tenants	deposit	furnished
advance	landlord	share

When I was a student, I decided to (1) . . . . a flat with a couple of good friends. We didn't have any stuff of our own, so we tried to find a nice (2) . . . . . . flat. We soon found somewhere that we all liked and we decided to take it.

We had to pay a (3) . . . . of £500 and one month's rent in (4) . . . . – a total of £1,000. We were lucky because the previous (5) . . . . had left the place really clean and tidy, so we moved in the next day.

Our (6) . . . . said we could paint the rooms if we wanted to, so I painted mine bright red!

Notice that you can rent or hire a car, and you can rent a flat but not hire a flat.

7 Features of a house

What makes you decide to rent or buy a house? Choose the correct ending for each sentence:

1. It's in a very nice   a. light.
2. It gets plenty of natural   b. space.
3. It's got central   c. neighbourhood.
4. It's got a fitted   d. kitchen.
5. It's got an open   e. glazing.
6. There's plenty of storage   f. fire.
7. It's got double   g. heating

8 Expressions with *house* and *home*

Use house or home in these sentences:

1. I don't fancy going out tonight. I'm going to stay at . . . . and watch TV.
2. When I'm 20 I'm going to leave . . . . and get my own flat
3. Is your . . . . a long way from the town centre?
4. What's your . . . . address?
5. Now that we're expecting another baby, we'll probably have to move . . . . This place is a bit small for four of us.
6. It's getting late. Let's go . . . . I'll call a taxi.
7. We're busy decorating our . . . . at the moment.
8. Don't make any dinner for me tonight. I won't be . . . . until late.
9. Does your . . . . town have an opera . . . . ?
10. My grandmother is in a really nice old folks' . . . .

You can also talk about an old people's home.

In your country do most people live in houses or flats? Do they own or rent their property?

Do you have similar expressions to these in your language?

There's no place like home.
Home is where the heart is.

Add your own words and expressions

29   The living room

1   In the living room

Match the words and phrases with the numbers in the picture:

carpet 18	fireplace 12	mantelpiece 9	sofa 14	dining chair 13
curtain 2	cushions 6	coffee table 15	television 5	picture 8
remote control 20	stereo system 4	lamp 7	rug 17	dining table 19
armchair 16	bookcase 3	blind 1	clock 10	ornament

2 At home

You are having friends round to your home. Match the beginnings and endings of these comments:

1. What a
2. Come in and
3. Would you like
4. Black
5. These cakes look
6. I'd rather
7. Where's
8. Make yourselves
9. Can I take

a. at home.
b. have tea, actually.
c. lovely house!
d. your jackets?
e. sit down.
f. delicious.
g. or white?
h. some coffee?
i. your loo?

3 Paying a compliment

Match the comments and follow-up questions:

1. I like your speakers.
2. What a fantastic view!
3. What an interesting picture!
4. You've got a lot of books.
5. I love your clock.
6. What a lovely carpet!
7. Your plants are wonderful.
8. I've never seen such a lovely house.

a. Can you see the sea?
b. Is it Turkish or Persian?
c. Have you read them all?
d. Have you lived here long?
e. Who is it?
f. What's this one called?
g. Does it work?
h. What do they sound like?

Now add the responses:

i. Oh, yes, it just needs winding up.
j. Yes, since we were married.
k. They're great – really great sound.
l. My great-great-grandfather, actually.
m. It's a kind of geranium.
n. On a clear day, yes.
o. It's Indian, actually.
p. Yes, every one. I love reading.

4 Things on the dinner table

Match these words with the pictures:

knife   coaster   fork
placemat   wine glass   plate
napkin   soup spoon   dessert spoon

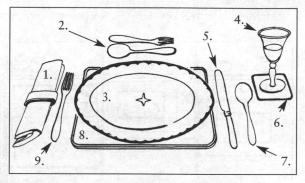

5 Dinner conversation

Complete these common expressions with the endings in colour below:

1. Could you pass . . . .
2. What about   . . . .
3. Can I give   . . . .
4. Help   . . . .
5. Are there any . . . .
6. What lovely   . . . .
7. Is there   . . . .
8. I'm allergic . . . .

a. the pepper, please.
b. to prawns, I'm afraid.
c. little fruit tarts!
d. you some more salad?
e. potatoes left?
f. any dressing on it?
g. some more wine for anyone?
h. yourself, everyone.

Is it common in your culture to comment on the food during a meal? For example: "This is lovely."

Add your own words and expressions

30   The kitchen

1   Kitchen appliances

Match these words with the pictures:

fridge   freezer   cooker   microwave   dishwasher   washing machine

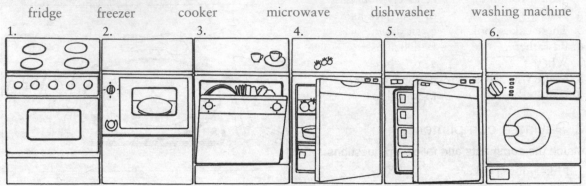

2   Sinks and things

Now do the same with these words:

work surface   sink   tap   cupboard   drawer   plug

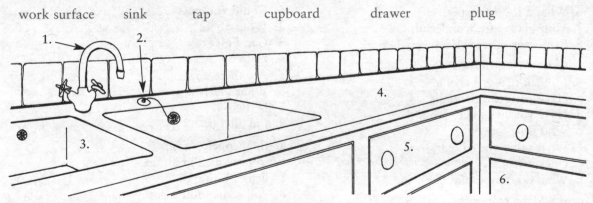

3   Plates and cutlery

Match these words with the pictures:

plate   dish   cup   saucer   glass   mug
knife   fork   spoon   teaspoon   bowl   jug

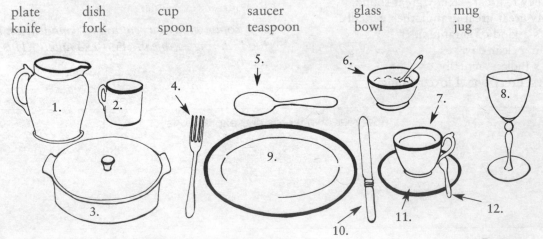

4 Kitchen equipment

Match the words and pictures below:

teapot	saucepan
wok	large cooking pot
kettle	frying pan
whisk	food processor
toaster	grater
scales	tin opener
corkscrew	casserole dish
mugs	oven glove

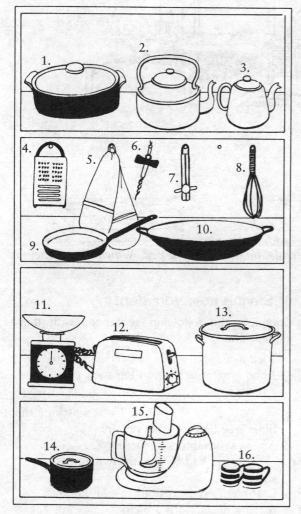

5 Common verbs in the kitchen

Use the correct form of these verbs to complete the sentences:

boil	do	set
heat	dry	open

1. Let's . . . . a bottle of wine. Can you get the corkscrew out of the drawer?
2. The kettle's just . . . . Would you like a cup of tea?
3. Here's the cutlery. Could you . . . . the table, please?
4. The problem with having a dinner party is that someone has to . . . . the dishes!
5. I'll . . . . the dishes if you like. Where do you keep the tea towels?
6. If the soup's a bit cold, why don't you . . . . it up in the microwave?

6 Test yourself

Use words from this unit to answer these questions:

1. What do you dry the dishes with?
2. What do you open a bottle of wine with?
3. What do you use to boil water in?
4. Where do you keep ice cream?
5. What do you beat eggs or cream with?
6. What do you open a tin with?
7. What do you make tea in?
8. Where do you wash the dishes?
9. What do you use to weigh food?
10. What do you grate carrots with?
11. What do you use to de-frost food which is frozen?
12. What do you use to carry something which is very hot?

Add your own words and expressions

31 The bedroom and bathroom

1 In the bedroom

Match the words and phrases with the pictures:

bed	wardrobe	rug	chest of drawers
lamp	alarm clock	bedside table	mirror

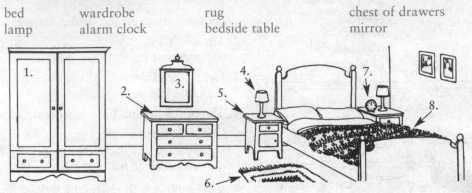

2 Parts of the bed

Match the words with the pictures:

sheet   mattress   pillow   blanket   duvet

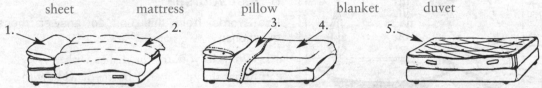

Don't forget these different types of bed: single, double, bunk-beds, sofa-bed. Which one of them is one bed on top of another?

3 What do you wear in bed?

Match these words with the pictures:

pyjamas	nightdress (nightie)
dressing gown	boxer shorts

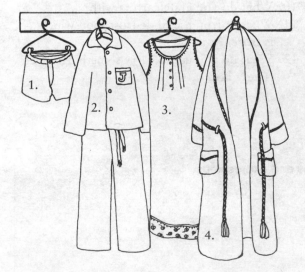

4 Saying how you slept

Complete the following sentences with these expressions:

I fell asleep	I overslept
I had a nightmare	I felt so sleepy
I woke up	I couldn't get to sleep

1. . . . . while I was watching the film. Jane had to wake me up.
2. After two chapters of the book, ... , I had to put it down and go to sleep.
3. Last night my next door neighbour was playing music until 3 o'clock. . . . . till 4! I was so annoyed.
4. . . . . in the middle of the night, and couldn't get back to sleep.
5. . . . . this morning. I didn't get to the office until nearly ten.
6. . . . . last night. I dreamt I came off my motorbike and broke my neck.

5 In the bathroom

Match the words and phrases with the numbers in the picture:

bath	shower	shower curtain	washbasin	toilet
mirror	towel	tiles	towel rail	toilet lid

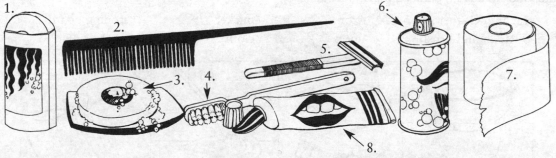

Now match these words and phrases with the pictures:

shampoo	soap	toilet roll	toothbrush
toothpaste	shaving foam	comb .	razor

6 Don't forget to brush your teeth

Add the following nouns to the verbs below. You will need to use one of the nouns twice.

your hair	a shower	a bath	your teeth
a shave	your face	your hands	a quick wash

have ....   wash ....   brush ....

....

....

....

In Britain you will often hear the bathroom or toilet informally called the loo – "I'm just going to the loo before we go."

Add your own words and expressions

32   Jobs around the house

1   Jobs you 'do'

Match the jobs with the pictures:

do the washing   do the washing up / dishes   do the ironing

do the dusting   **do the cooking**   **do some gardening**

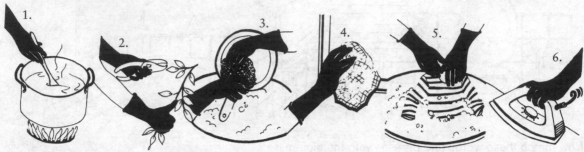

2   Equipment

Match the words and phrases with the pictures:

vacuum cleaner / hoover   iron   bucket   ironing board

dustpan and brush   mop   cloth   washing line

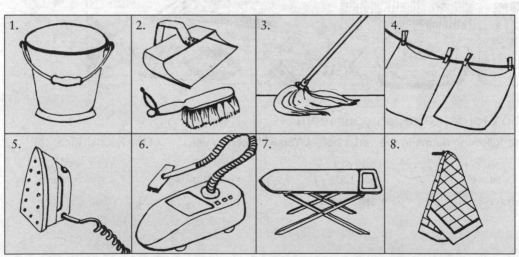

3   Verb collocations

Match the verbs on the left with the nouns:

1. make	a. the patio	5. hang out	e. the dishwasher
2. water	b. the sitting room	6. wipe	f. the washing
3. sweep	c. the bed	7. clean	g. the table
4. hoover	d. the plants	8. empty	h. the oven

Which one of these don't you polish: the table or the sofa?

What do you do first – clear the table or wipe the table?

4 Need / could do with

Match the sentences with the follow-up comments:

1. I must get the vacuum cleaner fixed.
2. The garden's in a bit of a state.
3. The plug on this iron is loose.
4. The front door looks terrible.
5. We've been here for ten years now.
6. Look at the state of this bath.

a. The screws need tightening.
b. The whole place needs re-decorating.
c. It really could do with a coat of paint.
d. It could do with a good scrub.
e. The grass needs cutting.
f. The carpets could do with a good clean.

Fix is more informal than mend or repair.

5 He should clean up a bit

Look at the picture below. John's parents are visiting him this afternoon and his kitchen is in a terrible mess. Fill the gaps in the sentences with the verbs below:

clear   throw out   empty   clean   put

1. He should . . . . the cooker.
2. He'll have to . . . . the table.
3. He ought to . . . . the waste bin.
4. He should . . . . his coat away.
5. He should . . . . all the empty bottles.

6 Complaining

Choose the correct ending for each sentence:

1. I really think we should tidy
2. I think we should give
3. The children are always making
4. I wish you'd put
5. I wish you'd stop leaving
6. The place looks like

a. things away after you.
b. a bomb's hit it.
c. the place up a bit.
d. things lying around.
e. a mess.
f. the whole house a good clean.

7 Asking for help

Complete the following sentences with these words:

hand   mind   something   favour

1. Could you do . . . . for me? Could you just run to the shop and get some more eggs?
2. Could you do me a . . . . ? Could you just peel these potatoes for me?
3. Could you give me a . . . . making the beds?
4. Would you . . . . helping me with the dinner?

Do you do much housework? Which jobs do you really hate doing? Which jobs don't you mind so much?

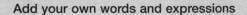

Add your own words and expressions

33 Problems around the house

1 Basic vocabulary

Translate the words in colour:

1. The window's broken.   . . . . . .
2. This radiator is leaking.   . . . . . .
3. The hot water tap is dripping.   . . . . . .
4. The drain is blocked.   . . . . . .
5. It has left a stain on the carpet. . . . . . .
6. All the carpets were ruined.   . . . . . .
7. The window won't open. It's stuck. . . . . . .
8. Have you had the lock fixed?   . . . . . .

2 Saying something doesn't work

Make complete expressions for describing problems:

1. It doesn't   a. making a funny noise.
2. There's   b. open it / close it properly.
3. It's   c. work.
4. I can't   d. something wrong with it.

3 Problems

Match each pair of beginnings on the left with one of the endings on the right:

1. My watch has   a. leaking.
   The clock has

2. The roof is   b. gone.
   The pipe is

3. The window is   c. stopped.
   The lock is

4. The light bulb has d. blocked.
   The fuse has

5. The handle has   e. come off.
   One of the buttons has

6. The sink is   f. stuck.
   The drain is

4 Accidents

Complete the following dialogues with the correct form of the verbs below. Be careful – one of them is irregular.

drop	ruin	smash
burst	knock	stain

1. Who broke my grandmother's vase?
   > I'm afraid it was me. I . . . . it off the table yesterday when I was cleaning.

2. Your Dad doesn't look very happy. What's happened?
   > I was kicking a ball about in the garden earlier and I . . . . the bathroom window.

3. How did this plate get broken?
   > I'm sorry. I . . . . it on the floor when I was washing up yesterday.

4. Did you have a good time round at Steve's last night?
   > No, not really. I spilled a glass of red wine. It's completely . . . . his carpet.

5. Oh, you've dyed your hair. I like the colour.
   > Thanks, but the problem is I've . . . . the bath a horrible brown colour and I can't get it off.

6. Where are you going?
   > Round to Mark's house. A pipe's . . . . in his kitchen and there's water all over the floor.

We also say that something leaves a stain – "the blood left a stain on my shirt."

5 Plumbers, builders, electricians

Match the six sentences below with the responses:

1. The bathroom tap's still dripping.
2. All of these power points need replacing.
3. That bathroom ceiling needs fixing.
4. Some of these cables look very old to me.
5. I don't know what's wrong with the central heating system.
6. This wall doesn't look safe at all.
7. This radiator's leaking again.
8. The damp on this wall is getting worse.
9. There's something wrong with this light switch.

a. > I know. We'd better find an electrician.
b. > Yes, I know. We'll have to get a builder in.
c. > Well, we'd better call a plumber.

6 Tools and things

Match the words and phrases with the pictures:

scissors	needle and thread
glue	nails
screws	hammer
spanner	torch
screwdriver	saw
paintbrush	ladder
mousetrap	pliers

Add your own words and expressions

34   Meat, fish and groceries

1 Meat

Put the different types of meat below into the correct place on the diagram:

beef	lamb	pork	chicken	ham	turkey
liver	veal	bacon	duck	kidney	guinea fowl

pig
. . . .
. . . .
. . . .

Different kinds of meat

cow
. . . .
. . . .

poultry
. . . .

sheep
. . . .

. . . .
. . . .
. . . .

inside an animal
. . . .
. . . .

Have you ever tried pheasant, rabbit, quail, venison or ostrich?

2 Meat collocations

Add the following words to their correct group below:

chicken	burger	steak	pork	chops

1. fillet / rump / sirloin / T-bone . . . . . .
2. pork / lamb . . . . . .
3. . . . . . . chops / sausages
4. chicken / beef / bacon . . . . . .
5. . . . . . . breast / wing / leg

The most common kind of meat of all is perhaps the hamburger, but of course, it isn't made of ham!

3 Fish and seafood

Match the words with the pictures:

salmon	sole	squid	lobster	crab	prawn
mussels	trout	tuna	plaice	snapper	clam

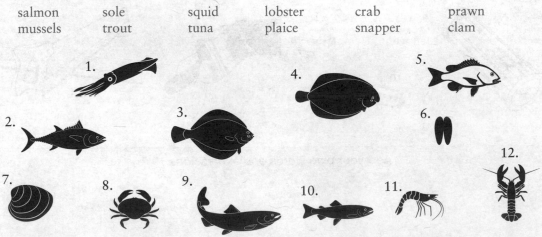

In Britain fish and chips is very popular. The fish is usually cod, haddock or plaice.

74

4 Do you take sugar?

Match these sentences with the responses. Check any words you don't know in your dictionary.

1. Do you take sugar?
2. Would you like some cereal for breakfast?
3. Why did you buy flour?
4. Can you get a loaf when you're out?
5. Would you like marmalade on your toast?
6. Do you want some mustard on your burger?
7. Do you want anything on this salad?
8. Shall we have rice with this stir-fry?

a. > I'd rather have noodles, actually.
b. > I'm going to make a few cakes.
c. > No thanks, ketchup is fine.
d. > Yes, two, please.
e. > Some cornflakes would be nice.
f. > I'll just have a little dressing, please.
g. > White or brown?
h. > No thanks, just butter.

5 Collocations 1

Match each of the following lines of words with one of the types of food below:

cheese   soup   bread   oil   rice   salad

1. green, mixed, potato, fruit   . . . .
2. white, brown, wholemeal, rye, sliced, garlic   . . . .
3. tomato, chicken, mushroom, home-made, tinned   . . . .
4. mild, mature, soft, cream, blue, goat's   . . . .
5. brown, long-grain, wild   . . . .
6. olive, vegetable, sunflower   . . . .

6 Collocations 2

Now do the same with the following:

yoghurt   ice cream   sauce   chocolate   pie   cake

1. chocolate, fruit, cheese, birthday, wedding   . . . .
2. natural, strawberry, black cherry, Greek, low fat   . . . .
3. tomato, pesto, soy, oyster, apple, mint   . . . .
4. milk, plain, white, dark, Belgian   . . . .
5. meat, chicken, apple, cherry, home-made   . . . .
6. vanilla, strawberry, chocolate, Italian   . . . .

7 Expressions with *and*

Match the words on the left with the words on the right:

1. salt and   a. biscuits
2. fish and   b. butter
3. bread and   c. cream
4. cheese and   d. pepper
5. strawberries and   e. chips

Add your own words and expressions

35   Fruit and vegetables

1 Different kinds of fruit

Match these words with the pictures:

apple	pear	bananas	lemon	orange
peach	pineapple	grapes	(black)currants	plums
cherries	strawberries	raspberry	pomegranate	melon

2 Collocation

Write the following words in the correct box below.
Some of them go with both words.

fresh	frozen
ripe	raw
citrus	tinned
tropical	stir-fried
rotten	organic

fruit   vegetables

3 Fruit words

Complete the sentences with the following words:

exotic	stones	skin	pips
varieties	seedless	bitter	bunches

1. Whatever you do, don't try to eat the
. . . . . . of a banana!
2. Plums and peaches have large . . . .
3. Grapes and bananas grow in . . . .
4. Grapes can be seeded or . . . .
5. Grapes have seeds, but lemons and limes
have . . . .
6. Mangoes, lychees and starfruit are sometimes
called tropical or . . . . . . fruit.
7. Golden Delicious, Cox's, and Granny Smith
are different . . . . . . of apple.
8. A grapefruit is part of the same family as
the orange, but much more . . . .

4 Different kinds of vegetable

Match these words with the pictures:

potato	mushroom	carrot	onion	cabbage
broccoli	turnip	leek	courgette	aubergine
cauliflower	Brussels sprouts	peas	beans	sweet corn

5 Salad vegetables

Match the words with the pictures:

lettuce	tomatoes	cucumber
celery	avocado	sweet peppers

6 Vegetable words

Complete the sentences using these words:

shell	paprika	egg plants	beans
potato	peel	gherkins	zucchini

1. Aubergines are sometimes also called . . . .
2. In English we sometimes use the Italian word . . . . for courgettes.
3. Sweet peppers are red, green or yellow and are sometimes called . . . .
4. Haricot, broad, green, are kinds of . . . .
5. Small cucumbers which are pickled are called . . . .
6. Maris Piper, King Edwards and Jersey Royals are three kinds of . . . .
7. Before eating peas, you have to . . . . . them.
8. You . . . . . potatoes before cooking them.

36   Talking about food

1 Basic vocabulary

Match the words in colour with the definitions below:

1. Have you had breakfast?
2. What time do you have lunch?
3. What are we having for dinner?
4. Do you want some supper?
5. We've only got time for a snack.
6. I hope you've got a good appetite.
7. I'm starving.
8. We had a barbecue in the back garden.

a. a small meal eaten just before you go to bed
b. the desire for food
c. the meal eaten around midday
d. very hungry
e. the first meal of the day
f. a quick and easy meal
g. when you grill food outside
h. the main evening meal

In British English we say have breakfast, lunch, dinner. In American English people often say eat breakfast, eat lunch and eat dinner.

In the United States people have brunch. What do you think it is?

2 A balanced diet

In each of the following groups, three words collocate with the word in colour. Which is the odd one out in each group?

1. fast
   junk   food
   easy
   frozen

2. simple
   plain   food
   rich
   fat

3. strong
   hard   flavour
   mild
   distinctive

4. healthy
   fit   food
   organic
   fresh

5. main
   light   meal
   heavy
   fast

6. thin
   healthy   diet
   balanced
   fat-free

3 Problems with food

Complete the following sentences with these words:

stale	burnt	ripe
sour	rotten	fresh

1. I'm afraid I've done it again! The toast's . . . . I'll make some more.
2. I wouldn't drink that milk if I were you. It doesn't smell very . . . .
3. This milk tastes a bit . . . . Did somebody forget to put it back in the fridge again?
4. I can't believe it. I only bought this bread yesterday. It's . . . . already!
5. Some of these apples are . . . . and I only bought them at the weekend.
6. I'd leave these bananas for another day. They're not . . . . yet.

You can also say that meat, fish, fruit or milk is off or has gone off – "This milk's off. This fish is starting to go off."

4 It's absolutely delicious

Complete the following dialogues with the pairs of words below:

tasty / delicious
flavour / bland
flavour / tender
wonderful / revolting
off / disgusting

1. Yuk! This salmon smells a bit . . . .
   > Yes, it's absolutely . . . .
2. Your chicken looks very . . . .
   > Mm, it's absolutely . . . .
3. This sauce hasn't got much . . . ., has it?
   > No, it's a bit . . . ., I'm afraid.
4. I've just discovered a . . . . blue cheese from Spain.
   > Oh, how . . . . ! I can't stand blue cheese.
5. I've never tasted lamb with so much . . . . . .
   > Yes, and it was so . . . ., wasn't it?

5 Negative comments

Match up the food on the left with the most suitable comments:

1. coffee or tea	a. too strong / weak / sweet
2. steak	b. too many bones
3. an Indian dish	c. too rich / thick / bland
4. a sauce	d. a bit overdone / underdone
5. fish	e. too hot / spicy
6. a cake	f. a bit dry / stale

6 Talking about what you don't like

Now use the comments in exercise 5 to complete these conversations:

1. Have I put too much sugar in your tea?
   > Yes, it IS a bit . . . ., actually.
2. I've put quite a few chillies in this stir-fry. Do you like it?
   > Actually, it's a bit . . . . for me.
3. How's your steak?
   > Well, I prefer it well done. This is a bit
   . . . . for my taste.
4. More sauce?
   > No thanks. It's a bit . . . . for me.
   Remember, I'm on a diet.

5. That cake looks delicious.
   > Well, it's not very fresh. I think it's at least a week old. It's very . . . . In fact, I would even say it's a bit . . . .
6. Why didn't you choose the fish?
   > There are always . . . .!
   I can't be bothered with them.

7 Are you hungry?

Match these sentences with the follow-up comments below:

1. Is dinner nearly ready?
2. I don't know what's wrong with me.
3. No more for me, thanks.
4. I'm glad we went for that walk.
5. I shouldn't really be eating this chocolate before dinner.

a. I've lost my appetite.
b. It's really given me an appetite.
c. It'll spoil my appetite.
d. I'm starving.
e. I'm full.

Add your own words and expressions

37 Cooking

Before starting this unit, look again at unit 30 – The kitchen.

1 Basic vocabulary

Match the verbs in the following cooking instructions to the pictures below:

1. Fry the onions in a little oil until they are brown.
2. Boil the pasta in a saucepan of salted water for 15 minutes.
3. Place the chicken in a pre-heated oven at 190° and roast for one and a half hours.
4. Place the pizza directly on the top shelf of the oven and bake for 10 minutes.
5. Grill the sausages under a medium heat, turning occasionally.
6. To steam asparagus, place it in a steamer above a saucepan of boiling water and cook until it is tender.

Now match the verbs on the left with the nouns on the right:

7. bake   g. an egg / bacon / hamburgers
8. roast   h. a leg of lamb / a chicken
9. boil   i. bread / a cake / a lasagne
10. fry   j. rice / carrots / green beans

2 Cooking at home

Complete the following text with these words:

> recipe   ingredients   helping
> sauce   delicious   cook

I wouldn't say I'm a great (1) . . . . , but I had some friends round for dinner recently and it went quite well. I'd seen a (2) . . . . for fish curry in a magazine the week before and it sounded (3) . . . . – so I thought I'd try it. I went to the market and bought all the (4) . . . . and then spent the day in the kitchen. Everybody said they really liked it, especially the (5) . . . . , and I think they were telling the truth because everyone wanted a second (6) . . . . !

3 Preparing food

Label the pictures below with these verbs:

> grate   squeeze   beat   slice   chop   peel

Now match the verbs on the left with the phrases on the right in the two lists below:

1. peel   a. the mixture with a wooden spoon
2. pour   b. the potatoes and boil in a pan
3. slice   c. the cheese and add to the sauce
4. grate   d. the sauce over the meat and serve
5. stir   e. the ham as thinly as possible

6. chop   f. the eggs until light and fluffy.
7. mix   g. a lemon over the fish
8. beat   h. a little butter in a frying pan
9. melt   i. the vegetables into small pieces
10. squeeze   j. all the ingredients together

4 Ways of cooking

Some types of food are usually cooked or prepared in a particular way. Complete the following sentences with the types of food below:

potato   steak   eggs
onions   salmon   rice

1. I think I'll have *fried / boiled / poached / scrambled* . . . . . . for breakfast.

2. Would you like your . . . . . . *rare, medium or well-done?*

3. I fancy a *baked / a jacket / some mashed* . . . . . . with these sausages.

4. Shall we give them *smoked* or *poached* . . . . . . as a starter?

5. Would you like a couple of *pickled* . . . . . . with your salad?

6. Do you prefer plain boiled . . . . or fried . . . . ?

A baked potato is the same as a jacket potato.

6 A simple recipe

Complete the following recipe with the words and phrases below:

5 Entertaining a guest for dinner

Look at the following sentences that come from a conversation at the dinner table. Decide who is speaking, the host (H) or the guest (G).

1. The food's ready. Would you like to come through now?
2. What can I get you to drink?
3. I've brought some wine. I hope red's OK.
4. Dressing?
5. Where do you want me to sit?
6. Help yourself to some salad.
7. This pie is delicious. You must give me the recipe.
8. I forgot to ask if you were vegetarian.
9. Did you make this yourself?
10. I don't seem to have a fork.
11. What do you call these? I've never had them before. They're delicious.
12. Would you like another helping?
13. Not for me, thanks. I'm full.
14. Thanks for a lovely evening. The food was really lovely.

Spicy Stir-fry Beef

Preparation: 30 minutes
Cooking: 5 minutes
Ingredients:

450 grams fillet of beef

1 tablespoon of soft brown sugar

1 tablespoon of dark soy sauce

2 cm piece of fresh ginger, grated

a pinch of salt

2 tablespoons of oil

6 spring onions

freshly ground black pepper

serve   heat the oil   stirring
slice   cook gently   add

1. . . . . the beef into thin strips about 3 cm long.
2. Mix the sugar, spices and soy sauce in a bowl. . . . . the beef, ginger and salt and stir well.
3. . . . . in a wok and stir-fry the onions for one minute.
4. Add the beef and fry, ... constantly, for four minutes, or until the meat is browned.
5. Stir in a little more soy sauce and black pepper and . . . . for a minute or two.
6. . . . . with plain boiled rice.

Add your own words and expressions

38 Eating out

1 Basic vocabulary

Translate the words in colour:

1. Could we see the menu, please?   . . . .
2. Dessert before cheese?   . . . .
3. No, I don't think I'll have a starter.   . . . .
4. Could we have the bill, please?   . . . .
5. What are you having as a main course? . . . .
6. Did you leave a tip?   . . . .
7. Waiter!   . . . .

2 Eat in or take away?

Mark the following sentences (F) if you would hear them in a fast food restaurant or (R) if you would hear them in an expensive restaurant:

1. I've booked the table for nine o'clock.
2. Regular fries?
3. Would you like to see the wine list, sir?
4. Oh, and a can of Coke as well, please.
5. We'll have a bottle of the house red.
6. All the main courses are served with a selection of vegetables.
7. How would you like your steak?
8. Have you got a table for two?
9. Salt and vinegar?
10. There's no service charge, so I suppose we should leave a tip.
11. You pay the bill while I go to the toilet.

Fast food is food like hamburgers or kebabs.

3 Collocations

Without looking at exercise 2, match the words on the left with the words on the right to form common phrases:

1. service   a. list
2. wine   b. of vegetables
3. house   c. two
4. main   d. red
5. selection   e. charge
6. a table for   f. course

Now do the same with these verbs and nouns:

7. pay   g. a table
8. book   h. a tip
9. leave   i. the bill

4 Different places to eat out

Where would you see the following examples of language? Match the extracts with the sources:

a. In a pizza restaurant   d. Outside a pub
b. In a café   e. In a sandwich bar
c. In a Chinese takeaway

1.
THE NELSON ARMS
HOT AND COLD
BAR MEALS & SNACKS
TRADITIONAL ALES

2.
Menu for two

£14.00

pancake roll
sweet and sour pork
spare ribs
special fried rice
prawn crackers

3.

Bacon, lettuce, tomato	£2.50
Cheese and tomato	£2.30
Ham and cream cheese	£2.55
Ham and salad	£2.40
Egg mayonnaise	£2.30

4.

Full breakfast	**£4.50**
Bacon, egg & chips	**£3.75**
Omelette & chips	**£3.25**
Beans on toast	**£2.60**

5.

15. Al Tonno - Mozzarella cheese, tomato, tuna, onion, capers, olives, oregano.

5 A night out at a restaurant

Put the following events in the most logical order:

a. pay the bill
b. have the main course
c. have a starter
d. book a table
e. order your food
f. have a dessert
g. leave a tip
h. look at the menu

1 . . . 2 . . . 3 . . . 4 . . . 5 . . . 6 . . . 7 . . . 8 . . .

6 Answering the waiter

Match the waiter's questions with the customer's responses:

1. What would you like to drink?
2. Are you ready to order?
3. How would you like your steak?
4. Would you like some more coffee?
5. Would you like to see the dessert menu?

a. A bottle of the house white, please.
b. No thanks, could you bring the bill, please?
c. Not quite – just give us a minute or two.
d. Medium rare, please.
e. No, thanks. I'll just have a coffee, I think.

7 Starters, main courses, desserts

Are the following dishes starters (S), main courses (M) or desserts (D)?

1. strawberry ice cream
2. rabbit in mustard sauce
3. mushroom soup
4. lamb kebab with rice
5. prawn cocktail
6. lemon cheesecake
7. poached salmon in dill sauce
8. chocolate gateau
9. paté and toast

8 Dishes from around the world

Do you know which countries the following dishes come from?

1. lasagne   . . . . . .   7. moussaka   . . . . . .
2. paella   . . . . . .   8. burritos   . . . . . .
3. chop suey . . . . . .   9. sushi   . . . . . .
4. vindaloo . . . . . .   10. kimchi   . . . . . .
5. haggis   . . . . . .   11. borscht   . . . . . .
6. sauerkraut . . . . . .   12. bouillabaisse . . . . . .

How many of the dishes in exercise 8 have you tried?
Is it usual to leave a tip for the waiter in your country?

Add your own words and expressions

39 Drinks

1 What's your favourite drink?

Put these drinks into the correct column below:

| coke | juice | beer | wine | cider | cava | tonic | ginger ale |
| lemonade | stout | soda | pepsi | lager | rum | sherry | champagne |

alcoholic drinks	soft drinks
. . . .	. . . .
. . . .	. . . .
. . . .	. . . .
. . . .	. . . .
. . . .	. . . .
. . . .	. . . .
. . . .	. . . .
. . . .	
. . . .	

2 British beer and cider

Use the following words in the definitions below:

cider   bitter   lager   stout   scrumpy

1. . . . . is a light-coloured beer common throughout the world.
2. . . . . is a darker beer and common in Britain.
3. . . . . is a very dark beer. The most famous kind is called Guinness.
4. . . . . is made from apples. Another word for it in England is . . . .

3 Scotch whisky

Use these words to complete this short text about whisky:

malt   barley   distilleries
hops   peat   water

All over the world beer is brewed in breweries, usually from (1) . . . . Whisky, on the other hand, is mostly made in Scotland in (2) . . . . . . Whisky is a spirit made from (3) . . . .
There are two kinds of Scotch – (4) . . . . . . whisky and blended whisky.

Some of the most famous distilleries are in the Scottish Highlands and Islands. Whisky varies in colour and taste. This depends on the (5) . . . . . . used in the production process. Water which runs through (6) . . . . . . gives the whisky a darker colour and a taste like smoke.

4 Collocations

Match each of the following lines of words with one of the words below:

coffee   wine   drink   water
juice   milk   beer   tea

1. fruit, orange, pineapple, tomato   . . . . .
2. semi-skimmed, full-cream   . . . . .
3. mineral, still, fizzy, sparkling   . . . . .
4. red, white, rosé, dry, sweet, sparkling . . . . .
5. strong, low-alcohol, bottled, draught   . . . . .
6. black, white, strong, real, instant   . . . . .
7. strong, weak, herbal, green, mint   . . . . .
8. non-alcoholic, soft, fizzy, strong   . . . . .

A *fizzy* or *sparkling* drink has bubbles in it.

5 Ordering a drink

Match the drinks with the common ways of ordering them:

lager   bitter   Becks   red wine

1. a glass of . . . .
2. a pint of . . . . or . . . .
3. a half of . . . . or . . . .
4. a bottle of . . . . or . . . .

In a British pub you do not ask for a beer. You ask for a particular kind or brand of beer. For example, A pint of Harveys, please.
If you order A whisky, you will be given a blended whisky. If you want a malt whisky, you must ask for it by name. For example, A Glenfiddich, please.

6 Common expressions

Complete the following short dialogues with these expressions:

> Half or a pint?
> Cheers!
> I'll have the same again.
> What can I get you?
> This is my round.
> Ice and lemon?
> Can I have a soft drink?
> I'm sorry, I'm driving.

1. **Offering someone a drink**

   . . . .

   > Just a Coke, please.

2. **Buying a second drink for someone**

   Can I get you another?

   > Yes, please. . . . . , thanks.

3. **Refusing an alcoholic drink**

   Can I get you a pint?

   > No, thanks, I don't drink. . . . .
   . . . . , please. A tonic water.

4. **When you are driving**

   Would you like something to drink?

   > . . . . A cup
   of coffee would be nice, though.

5. **Buying everyone else a drink**

   . . . . What's
   everyone having?

6. **What size of drink?**

   Um, Guinness please.

   > . . . . ?

7. **What do you want with it?**

   Gin and tonic, please.

   > . . . . ?

8. **Responding to cheers**

   Cheers!

   > . . . . !

Cheers can also mean thanks or goodbye: "See you tomorrow, then." "OK. Cheers!"

7 Drinking verbs

Use the correct form of these verbs to complete the sentences:

feel	put	have	stick
mix	open	go	pour

1. I don't feel very well. I think I . . . . . . too much to drink at dinner last night.

2. I don't usually drink vodka. It . . . . . . straight to my head.

3. This champagne's flat. Let's . . . . . . another bottle.

4. I never drink alcohol if I've got the car. I always . . . . . . to mineral water.

5. I'd better not have any more of this wine. I'm . . . . a bit light-headed already.

6. Could you . . . . . . me another glass of wine, please?

7. I can't understand people who . . . . orange juice and whisky!

8. . . . . . . the cork back in the bottle. We'll finish it tomorrow.

If a fizzy drink is flat, it has lost its fizz.
If you wake up with a hangover in the morning, what were you doing the night before?

Add your own words and expressions

40   Talking about your free time

1 What are you doing tonight?

Match each of the beginnings of the questions with two endings:

1. What are you	a. any plans for this evening?
2. Are you	b. doing tonight?
3. Have you got	c. anything on this weekend?
	d. going out tonight?
	e. up to at the weekend?
	f. doing anything later?

Number 1 goes with . . . and . . . .
Number 2 goes with . . . and . . . .
Number 3 goes with . . . and . . . .

What are you up to? is more informal and would only be used between people who knew each other fairly well.

2 Meeting up with friends

Use the correct form of these expressions to complete the dialogues:

meet up with	go round	get together
have a party	come along	bring

1. What are you doing at the weekend?
   > Some friends of mine have just moved into a new flat and they're . . . . on Saturday night. Why don't you . . . . too? You can . . . . Sally, if you like – I'm sure she'd like Tony and Jane.

2. Are you doing anything tonight?
   > Nothing special. I'm just . . . . a few friends for a drink.

3. What are you up to this evening?
   > Not much really. I might . . . . to see Steve and his wife later.

4. Have you got anything special on this weekend?
   > Yes, I have actually. I'm seeing some old school friends. We all try to . . . . every couple of years and have a big night out in London.

If you go round to some friends, you visit them for a short time.

3 Let's have a night out

Match these ideas with one of the activities below:

1. I haven't been to see a play for ages.
2. Let's go out for a meal at the weekend. We haven't eaten out for a long time.
3. Shall we go and see a band? I haven't seen any live music for ages.
4. Do you fancy going out for a drink later?
5. Do you fancy going clubbing tonight?
6. Shall we go and see a film later?

   a. going to the pub
   b. going to the cinema
   c. going to the theatre
   d. going to a restaurant
   e. going to a nightclub
   f. going to a concert

Now use the correct form of these expressions to complete the dialogues:

   g. have a quiet night in
   h. go to a party
   i. have a very active social life
   j. be stuck indoors
   k. have some fun

7. Is everything OK with your new flatmate?
   > Yes, he seems to . . . . He's been out every night this week.

8. Are you going out tonight, Alison? There's a new club opened in the High Street.
   > Not tonight. I've been out every night this week. I want to . . . . for a change.

9. How's the exam revision going? I bet you're getting a bit tired of it, aren't you?
   > Absolutely! I've . . . . all week. I want to go out and . . . .

10. Are you doing anything exciting this weekend, Mark?
    > Yes, I'm . . . . up in London. Some friends of mine have just moved into a new house.

A party when you have moved into a new house is called a house-warming party.

4 Let's go out for the day

Put these words with the correct group below:

	go	go for	go to

the park
1. . . . . . .   the beach
the zoo

a walk
2. . . . . . .   a drive in the country
a swim

shopping
3. . . . . . .   clubbing
fishing

Now use some of the phrases to complete the following text. You might need to change the form of the verb.

I had a really nice weekend. I got paid on Friday and I decided I needed some new clothes, so I got up early on Saturday morning and (4) . . . .

After lunch I (5) . . . . in the park and sat on a bench in the sun reading the newspaper. They've just opened a new pool near my house so later in the afternoon I decided to (6) . . . . and I had a sauna as well.

My brother's kids are doing a project at school about wild animals and on Sunday morning we all (7) . . . . We had a great time watching the lions and feeding the monkeys.

Then in the afternoon I picked my girlfriend up in the car and (8) . . . . We found a really pretty little village that neither of us had ever been to before. By the time I got home it was nearly ten o'clock. I just had something to eat and went straight to bed.

5 A quiet night in

Choose the correct endings for each sentence:

1. Let's just stay in and watch
2. My Mum and Dad came over to play
3. I'd rather just stay in and finish
4. A few friends came round
5. Let's just get
6. We had

a. for dinner.
b. my book.
c. TV / a video.
d. a video out.
e. a few friends round for dinner.
f. cards.

7. Which three sentences answer the question: *What did you do last night?*
8. Which two sentences answer the question: *What shall we do tonight?*

What do you like doing in your free time?
Do you prefer a wild night out or a quiet night in?

. FREE TIME .

Add your own words and expressions

41   Hobbies and interests

1   Doing, playing and collecting

Use do, play or collect with the following words:

1. . . . .   coins
2. . . . .   chess
3. . . . . . .   crosswords
4. . . . . . .   stamps
5. . . . . . .   antiques
6. . . . . . .   computer games
7. . . . . . .   jigsaws
8. . . . . . .   cards
9. . . . . . .   postcards
10. . . . . . .   old photographs
11. . . . . . .   a musical instrument
12. . . . . . .   an evening course

2   Different games

Use these words in the sentences below:

a pack of cards   dominoes
chess   draughts
dice   backgammon

1. . . . . is a very popular
   game, now often played on
   computer. King, queen,
   bishop and rook are the
   names of some of the pieces.

2. . . . . is played on a board
   similar to a . . . . board,
   but with flat round pieces. The
   pieces move only in very
   simple ways.

3. You use . . . . to play games
   such as bridge and poker.

4. . . . . is played with black pieces with
   white dots on them. You lay them end to
   end until you have none left.

5. . . . . is played by two
   people with a board, round flat
   pieces and a dice. It is very
   popular in Greece and Turkey.

6. . . . . . . have six sides. They are
   used in board games from many
   different countries.

3   Playing games

Choose the correct ending for each sentence:

1. Come on, it's your turn – throw/roll
2. You need to shuffle the cards
3. It's your go. Hurry up and move
4. Did you take

a. one of my pieces just then? I wasn't looking.
b. the dice.
c. before you deal them.
d. one of your pieces. You're taking too long.

Now answer the following questions:

5. Which of these isn't a board game?
   chess / draughts / dominoes / monopoly

6. Which of these isn't a card?
   ace / king / queen / prince / jack / joker

7. Which of these isn't a chess piece?
   king / queen / bishop / knight / soldier / pawn

8. Label the pictures:
   hearts / clubs / diamonds / spades

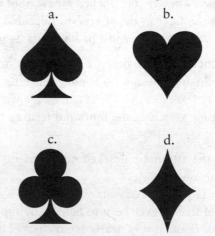

a.   b.

c.   d.

*Draughts is called checkers in American English
and on many computers. The general word for a
chess figure is piece – "One of the black pieces
is missing." We also use piece for draughts,
checkers and backgammon. In other board
games, the things we move are usually called
counters.*

*In modern English, dice is the singular and
plural form – one dice, two dice.*

4 Hobbies

Put the following words and phrases into the correct column below:

brushes	recipe
camera	sewing machine
cake decorating	pastry
material	tripod
develop a film	zoom lens
oil paints	needle and cotton
ingredients	watercolour
easel	pattern

photography	**painting**
. . . .	. . . .
. . . .	. . . .
. . . .	. . . .
. . . .	. . . .

making clothes	**cooking**
. . . .	. . . .
. . . .	. . . .
. . . .	. . . .

5 Prepositions

Complete the sentences below with these prepositions:

on   into   with   of   in (x 2)

1. I'm really interested . . . . photography.
2. I'm very keen . . . . gardening.
3. Claire's absolutely obsessed . . . . horses. She doesn't think about anything else.
4. I'm a big fan . . . . old black and white horror films.
5. I never thought I'd get . . . . computer games, but since my brother bought me one for Christmas I haven't stopped playing it.
6. I like looking round secondhand bookshops . . . . my spare time.

6 Interests

Use the correct form of these verbs to complete the sentences:

relax	take	give it up	learn
get	spend	join	take up

1. I'm . . . . to play the guitar.
2. I . . . . all my free time doing karate. I . . . . a club three years ago and I've just got my black belt.
3. I used to go windsurfing every week but I had to . . . . when I started university because I didn't have the time.
4. I paint most evenings and weekends. I find it relaxing and it . . . . my mind off work.
5. I go fishing quite a lot. It . . . . me out of the house and it helps me . . . . and forget all my worries.
6. I . . . . golf when I was about 40, when I had to stop playing rugby.

Have you got a particular interest? Make a list of the things you do and the things you need in the box at the bottom of the page.

· DRAUGHTS ·

Add your own words and expressions

89

42   Activities and interests

1 Outdoor activities

Match the words with the pictures:

hill-walking   skateboarding   rollerblading   surfing   windsurfing   fishing
hunting   orienteering   camping   skiing   gardening   riding

1.
2.
3.
4.

5.
6.
7.
8.

9.
10.
11.
12.

2 Related vocabulary

Match these sentences to the activities above. The words and expressions in green will help you.

1. I usually use three rods at the same time – you've got more chance of catching something.
2. We go to a park where there are some ramps and we practise different tricks.
3. This is a nice spot. You start putting the tent up and I'll get the sleeping bags.
4. People say it's cruel but I never shoot anything that I can't take home to eat.
5. I need to buy a bigger saddle and some new boots.
6. I prefer downhill to cross-country.
7. I cut the grass at least once a week.
8. You can usually get a pair of blades for around £40.
9. The waves are best on the west coast.
10. I use my smallest sail when it's really windy.
11. All you need is a good pair of walking boots, a rucksack and a waterproof jacket.
12. All you need is a map, a compass, and some luck!

We say do some gardening or do the garden. Use the verb go with all the other activities above – go hill-walking, go riding etc.

3 More extreme activities

Match the words and phrases with the pictures:

water skiing   climbing   scuba-diving   hang-gliding
paragliding   bungee jumping   parachute jumping   snowboarding

1.
2.
3.
4.

5.
6.
7.
8.

4 Social activities

Match the words and phrases with the pictures:

play pool   go ten-pin bowling   play darts   go folk dancing
go to a yoga class   play in a band   sing in a choir   play bingo

1.
2.
3.
4.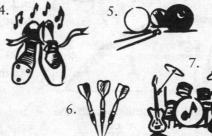
5.
6.
7.
8.

5 How often do you do it?

All the expressions below will help you to say how often you do a particular activity, for example, "I go swimming three times a week.**" Use these words to complete the expressions:**

time   often   twice   other   every   used   possible   times

1. As . . . . . as I can.
2. Not as often as I . . . . . to.
3. Three . . . . . a week.
4. All the . . . . . .

5. Every . . . . . Saturday.
6. . . . . . a week.
7. As often as . . . . . .
8. . . . . . Friday night.

Think of two activities you enjoy. How often do you do them?

Add your own words and expressions

43 Special occasions

1 Dates on the calendar

Match the words with the pictures:

Christmas   New Year's Eve   Easter
Hallowe'en   Valentine's Day

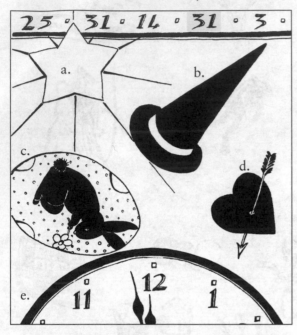

Now match the following descriptions with the occasions above:

1. Christians remember the death and resurrection of Christ but for many it is just a holiday. Children eat chocolate eggs.

2. At midnight on December 31st people welcome in the New Year.

3. Children dress up as witches and ghosts and go to fancy dress parties. They make lanterns, often from pumpkins.

4. People send cards to or buy presents for their lovers or people they fancy. Some people send an anonymous card so that it comes from a 'secret admirer'.

5. Christians remember the birth of Christ but for many people it is only a holiday and a time to decorate the house, give and receive presents, and eat and drink a lot.

If you fancy *someone, you find him / her attractive.*

2 Christmas

Match the days on the left with the dates on the right:

1. Christmas Eve   a. 25th December
2. Christmas Day   b. 26th December
3. Boxing Day   c. 24th December

Match the verbs with the nouns on the right:

4. wrap up   d. Christmas cards
5. decorate   e. carols
6. send   f. turkey
7. do   g. the Christmas tree
8. sing   h. crackers
9. eat   i. your Christmas shopping
10. pull   j. presents

Is Christmas important in your country? Tick the things above that you usually do at Christmas.

We say Happy Christmas *or* Merry Christmas! *and we say* Happy New Year *but* **not** *"Merry New Year."*

3 Anniversaries

Use these words to complete the sentences:

assassination   collapse   death   end
independence   discovery   birth   landing

1. The year 2005 is the 60th anniversary of the . . . . of the Second World War.

2. On August 19th every year, Elvis Presley fans commemorate the anniversary of his . . . .

3. 2009 marks the 20th anniversary of the beginning of the . . . . of Communism.

4. The new millennium was the anniversary of the . . . . of Christ.

5. The year 2008 is the 40th anniversary of man . . . . on the moon.

6. July 4th is the day the United States celebrate . . . .

7. 2003 is the 40th anniversary of the . . . . of John F. Kennedy.

8. 2029 marks the centenary of the . . . . of penicillin.

Notice the verbs mark *and* commemorate.

4 Carnivals

Complete the text below with these words:

firework   bands   parades
festivities   dancing   costumes

The biggest carnival in the world is 'Carnaval' in Brazil when the whole country stops for four days while everybody parties. There are lots of street (1) . . . . with amazingly decorated lorries (called *floats*) and people dressed in colourful (2) . . . . Everywhere you go there are samba (3) . . . . playing and people (4) . . . . Right through the night the (5) . . . . continue with more dancing and music and (6) . . . . displays which light up the night sky.

When people dress up, they might also wear a mask over their face.

A street parade is also called a street procession.

5 Births

Use these words and phrases to complete the short letter below:

was present   gave birth   fainted
are both fine delighted   weighing

Dear Marianne,

Just to let you know that Alice (1) . . . . to a beautiful baby girl on Wednesday – Kirsty Jane, (2) . . . . 6lbs 8oz.

Dan (3) . . . . at the birth and nearly (4) . . . . !

Anyway, we are all (5) . . . .

Mother and baby (6) . . . .

and should be home in a day or two.

Love

Christine

6 Birthdays

Complete the text below with these words:

blow   cake   cards   speech
present   candles party   dinner

The best birthday I've ever had was my 21st. My family said they were going to take me out to (1) . . . . but they had secretly planned a surprise (2) . . . . for me. As I opened the door to leave the house, there were about 30 friends standing outside. They all sang "Happy Birthday" and then we went back inside. I was given lots of (3) . . . . and then I was given a small (4) . . . . I opened it to find some car keys – my parents had bought me a car! My mother then brought out a (5) . . . . with 21 (6) . . . . on. I was so emotional I almost couldn't (7) . . . . them out! I then just managed to make a short (8) . . . . , thanking everyone for coming and then we partied into the night.

7 Congratulations!

We say 'Congratulations!' in different situations. Use these words to complete the sentences below:

passing   graduating reaching
having   winning   getting

You congratulate someone on ...

1. . . . . engaged.
2. . . . . their driving test.
3. . . . . from university.
4. . . . . an award or a sporting event.
5. . . . . a baby.
6. . . . . their 50th wedding anniversary.

Now match these wedding anniversaries to the correct number of years:

7. Ruby wedding   a. 50 years
8. Golden wedding   b. 25 years
9. Diamond wedding   c. 60 years
10. Silver wedding   d. 40 years

Add your own words and expressions

44   Film and cinema

1 Basic vocabulary

Match these words with their definitions below:

star   director   scene   critic   review

1. somebody who reviews new films
2. a very famous actor or actress
3. what a critic writes about a new film
4. the person who tells the actors and actresses what to do
5. one small part of a film

In Britain people go to the cinema. In the United States people go to the movies.

2 In the cinema

Put these words into the sentences below:

screen   subtitles   row   trailers   credits

1. Let's sit at the back. I don't like being too near the . . . .
2. I like to sit in the front . . . .
3. I find trying to read . . . . very annoying. I prefer dubbed films.
4. I like seeing all the . . . . for the new films that are coming out.
5. I usually stay at the end to read the . . . . because I like to know who some of the less important actors were.

3 Different kinds of film

Match the film titles with the short descriptions below:

a. Die Hard
b. The Bride of Dracula
c. The Magnificent Seven
d. The Sound of Music

1. Yul Brynner rides again in this *famous* western.

2. A *classic* horror film with Boris Karloff as the vampire.

3. Bruce Willis is the hero in this *predictable* action movie.

4. The popular but increasingly *dated* musical. Sing along with Julie Andrews.

Now do the same with these:

e. Witness
f. Spartacus
g. Saving Private Ryan
h. It Came from Outer Space
i. Four Weddings and a Funeral

5. A *ridiculous* science-fiction film as aliens attack a peaceful community in California.

6. Hugh Grant and Andie MacDowell star in this *hilarious* romantic comedy.

7. An *epic* historical drama with Kirk Douglas as the slave leading the revolt against Rome.

8. Harrison Ford protects an innocent boy who has witnessed a murder in this *gripping* thriller.

9. Steven Spielberg's *action-packed* war film provides Tom Hanks with one of his best roles.

Now decide whether the words in *italics* are positive or negative. Use a dictionary to help you.

Positive . . . .

. . . .

Negative . . . .

4 Making a film

Choose the correct ending for each sentence:

1. The Beach was set
2. Schindler's List was filmed in
3. Psycho was directed by
4. Titanic starred
5. Jurassic Park was based on

a. Leonardo DiCaprio and Kate Winslet.
b. a novel by Michael Crichton.
c. black and white.
d. in Thailand.
e. Alfred Hitchcock.

5 Talking about films

Delete the wrong word or expression in the following sentences:

1. *The Beach* was mainly filmed on location / on site in Thailand.
2. Jodie Foster won an Oscar for her performance / play in *Silence of the Lambs*.
3. Cat Woman was one of the characters / actresses in *Batman*.
4. Anthony Hopkins heads the cast / the players in this moving costume drama.
5. I got a bit confused. The plot / tale was too complicated for me.
6. I'll never forget the action / the scene where they drive over the cliff at the end of *Thelma and Louise*.
7. *The Age of Innocence* won an award for the best costumes / uniforms.
8. Most American films are translated / are dubbed when they're shown in Europe but some countries prefer to show them in English with subtitles.
9. Have you heard the soundtrack / the screenplay for *Trainspotting?* It's brilliant.
10. The special tricks / special effects in *Total Recall* are amazing!

6 It's won seven Oscars!

Match up the following verbs and nouns. Then use the expressions in the sentences below:

shoot	rave reviews
give	the scene
play	three Oscars
nominate	the role

1. Sean Connery . . . . of James Bond for many years.
2. The film has been . . . . . . for . . . . . . – best film, best actress and best original screenplay.
3. The director decided it would be better to . . . . in black and white.
4. I've heard it's a fantastic film. The critics have all . . . . . . it . . . .

7 Asking about a film

Match the questions and answers below:

1. Where's it on?
2. Who's in it?
3. What's it about?
4. Who directed it?
5. What's it like?

a. Steven Spielberg
b. A theme park terrorised by dinosaurs.
c. It's brilliant! / It's terrible!
d. Sam Neill and Laura Dern.
e. At the Odeon.

Do you know which film is referred to here?

What's the best film you've seen recently?

What's the best film you've ever seen?

Add your own words and expressions

45   Books and art

1 Basic vocabulary

Translate the following words into your language:

1. paperback . . . . . .   5. characters . . . . . .
2. novel   . . . . . .   6. chapter   . . . . . .
3. fiction   . . . . . .   7. poem   . . . . . .
4. non-fiction . . . . . .   8. poetry   . . . . . .

2 Kinds of books

1. Put the following into the correct column below:

encyclopedia   atlas   classic
ghost story   textbook   detective story
novel   dictionary   autobiography
biography   thriller   science fiction

fiction	non-fiction
. . . .	. . . .
. . . .	. . . .
. . . .	. . . .
. . . .	. . . .
. . . .	. . . .
. . . .	. . . .

2. In which of the non-fiction books would you:

a. look up the meaning of a word?
b. look up the height of Niagara Falls?
c. find a detailed map of China?

3. Which of the following books would you buy in the situations below?

a cookery book
a travel guide
a children's book
an autobiography

1. You don't like fiction. You prefer to read about the life stories of real people, written by the people themselves.
2. You are 20 years old and are leaving home to share a flat with some friends. You've never cooked for yourself before.
3. You don't know what to buy your seven-year-old nephew for his birthday.
4. You are going trekking in Nepal. You've never been there before.

Most biographies and reference books are hardbacks but most novels are paperbacks.

3 Writers

Match the writers with what they write:

1. Authors   a. write poetry.
2. Novelists   b. write about famous people.
3. Poets   c. write any kind of book.
4. Playwrights   d. write articles in newspapers.
5. Journalists   e. write fiction.
6. Biographers   f. write plays.

4 Novels

Mark each sentence P – if it expresses a positive idea – or N for a negative idea. The phrases in green will help you decide.

1. I've just finished a Stephen King novel. I couldn't put it down.
2. I just couldn't relate to any of the characters.
3. It's no masterpiece but it's very readable.
4. The main characters don't really develop and some of the minor characters are very one-dimensional.
5. The first few chapters were such heavy going that I gave up.
6. It's such a moving story. I couldn't stop thinking about it.
7. It's a very simple story but there's no real plot. Nobody seems to have a reason for doing what they do.

Novels are fictional stories invented by the writer although some are based on true stories.

A classic is a famous book which everyone agrees will last, for example, 'Pride and Prejudice' or 'The Three Musketeers'.

What kind of novels do you like?

5 Poetry

Use these words to complete the following:

poems   poetry   poet   verses   recite

When we did . . . . at school, we had to learn whole . . . . . . by heart and then . . . . . . them for the whole class. Philip Larkin was my favourite . . . . I remember the longest poem I had to learn had over 20 . . . . !

6 Painting

Use these words to complete the sentences below:

watercolours	portrait	landscapes
still life	abstract	oils

1. Probably the most famous . . . . in the world is the Mona Lisa in the Louvre.
2. Van Gogh was famous for his . . . . of the countryside around Arles in the south of France.
3. Picasso's early work was representational, but he soon developed an interest in . . . . art.
4. Many . . . . paintings contain a bowl of fruit and a bottle.
5. If you use . . . . . , it is easier to correct a mistake than if you use . . . .

An artist can also be called a painter. A painter can also be the person who paints your house. So, all artists are painters, but not all painters are artists!

7 Putting on an exhibition

Use these words to complete the text below:

exhibition	critics	gallery
collectors	paintings	artist

My sister's an (1) . . . . Her (2) . . . . are quite unusual but people seem to like them. Until recently she just exhibited her work in local bars and restaurants but last week a (3) . . . . in London contacted her to say they wanted to put on an (4) . . . . of her work. The art (5) . . . . from all the national newspapers will be there, so she's hoping she might get some publicity. There'll probably be quite a few private (6) . . . . there too, so she might make some money for a change!

Notice the difference between "It's a very interesting work" (one painting) and "I really like her work." (everything she does)

8 Other creative works

Match the following words with the pictures:

ceramics	mosaic	bust
statue	mural	sculpture

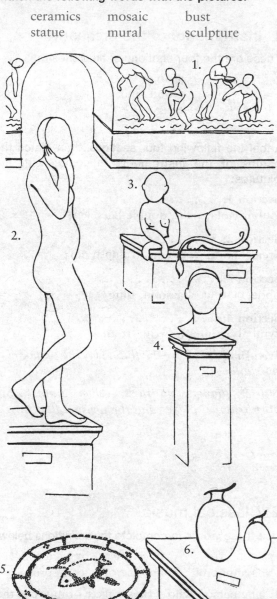

Add your own words and expressions

46   Music

1   Instruments of the orchestra

These are the four sections of an orchestra:

strings
woodwind
brass
percussion

Label the following four sections, then match the names of the instruments in colour with the pictures:

Section 1: . . . .
violin, viola, cello, double-bass, harp

Section 2: . . . .
French horn, trombone, trumpet, tuba

Section 3: . . . .
oboe, clarinet, bassoon, flute

Section 4: . . . .
cymbals, drum, timpani, triangle

We usually say play the flute, play the piano, play the violin etc.

Notice pianist, violinist, cellist, oboist, *but* horn/trumpet player *and the unusual* flautist.

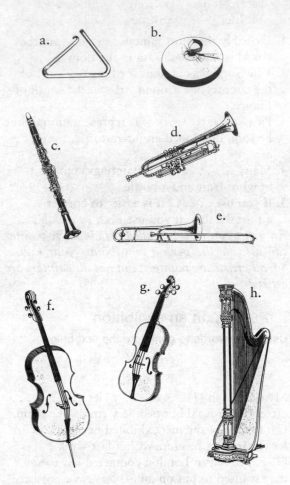

2   Classical music

Use these words to complete the definitions below:

concerto   overture   movements
symphony   conductor   composer

1. The person who writes a piece of music is the
. . . . – Beethoven, for example.
2. The person who directs the performance of
an orchestra is the . . . .
3. A long musical composition in several
. . . . for the full orchestra is a
. . . .
4. A . . . . is usually played by a solo
instrument such as the piano or violin and
the full orchestra.
5. An . . . . is a piece of music written as
an introduction to an opera or ballet.

3   Making music

Complete the sentences using these words:

music   voice   practice   solo
choir   ear   lessons   piece

1. Katy's got a beautiful . . . . She sings in
the local church . . . .
> Really? Does she ever sing . . . . ?
2. A friend of mine plays the piano really
well even though she can't read . . . .
She plays everything by . . . .
3. I'm having piano . . . . at the moment.
I try to do one hour's . . . . a day.
4. 'The Four Seasons' is my favourite . . . . . . of
music.

A choir *sings in church (The Vienna Boys Choir);*
a chorus *sings in an opera house.*

4 A rock band

Match these words with this picture of a rock band:

lead singer   guitarist   keyboard player
bass player   drummer   backing singers

5 Talking about bands

Complete the sentences below with these words:

gig   tour   chorus
verse   lyrics   venues

1. Have you heard that Radiohead are going on
   . . . . . . later this year? They're going to be
   playing at . . . . . . all round the country. I
   hope they do a . . . . . . somewhere
   near here. I'd love to see them.
2. Do you like Blur?
   > Well, I quite like the music but the . . . . . .
   are really silly. I don't know what they're
   singing about.
3. Why don't you like Oasis?
   > Their songs all sound the same. They sing
   one . . . . . . and then repeat the . . . . . .
   fifteen times.

6 Talking about recordings

Complete the sentences with these words:

track   album   songs
tune   solo   number one
charts   single   cover version

1. Have you heard Massive Attack's new
   . . . . ? It's fantastic.
   > Yes, the first . . . . is my favourite.
   I keep playing it over and over again.
2. I've just bought REM's latest album.
   > Yes, I've got that. It's great. There's a
   superb guitar . . . . right at the
   beginning. You'll love it.
3. Have you heard Billie's new single yet?
   > Yes, I don't like it much, but it's got such a
   catchy . . . . I can't get it out of my
   head.
4. Paul Weller normally writes all his own
   . . . . . . but on his new album he's done a
   . . . . of an old Bob Dylan number.
   It's absolutely brilliant – better than the
   original!
5. Britney Spears is releasing a new . . . . . . this
   week. I'm sure it'll go straight to . . . . . . in
   the . . . . . . like all her others.

7 What kind of music do you like?

Tick (✓) the types of music you listen to:

classical	. . .	techno	. . .
opera	. . .	rock and pop	. . .
jazz	. . .	heavy metal	. . .
soul	. . .	country	. . .
blues	. . .	folk	. . .
house	. . .	reggae	. . .
rap	. . .	world music	. . .

Add your own words and expressions

47   Ball and racquet sports

Note that racquet can also be spelled racket.

1 Team sports

Match the sports with the pictures:

football   rugby   American football
basketball   baseball   volleyball

In the United States football is called soccer.

2 Individual sports

Match the sports with the pictures:

tennis   table tennis   squash   badminton

Badminton is played with a shuttlecock. Badminton, tennis and squash are racquet sports. Table tennis is played with a bat.

3 Tennis and golf

If you play tennis or golf, and you do not know these words, check them in your dictionary:

Tennis: serve, ace, return, forehand, backhand, smash, topspin, slice, net, baseline, tramlines.
Do you know how to give the score in English? (See unit 50)

Golf: drive, chip, putt, tee (two meanings), fairway, bunker, green, bogey, par, birdie, eagle.
What do you do at the nineteenth hole?

If you are playing tennis or golf, you might want to say to your opponent: "Good shot!" or "Bad luck!"

4 Equipment

Match the words on the left with those on the right:

1. tennis
2. golf   a. bat
3. baseball   b. racquet
4. squash   c. club
5. table tennis   d. stick
6. hockey
7. badminton

5 Where you play

Match the words on the left with those on the right:

1. football
2. golf
3. tennis   a. court
4. basketball   b. pitch
5. badminton   c. course
6. volleyball
7. squash
8. rugby
9. hockey

In football, rugby, hockey, and basketball, if the ball goes off the pitch or court, it is out of play. In racquet sports and volleyball, if the ball lands outside the line, we say the ball is out – "I think that was just out." If it lands on or inside the line, we say it is in.

6 What you can do with a ball

Match these actions with the pictures:

hit it	throw it	catch it
head it	kick it	pass it

1.

2.

3.

4.

5.

6.

Now complete the following dialogues with the correct form of these expressions:

> pass the ball
> hit the ball so hard
> run with the ball

7. You played tennis with Greg last night, didn't you? I hear he's pretty good.
   > You're not joking! He . . . . that you spend most of the time trying to get out of the way!

8. Do you ever watch American football? It's pretty aggressive, isn't it?
   > Yes, when one of those guys . . . . I wouldn't like to get in his way!

9. I don't really understand rugby. Why do the players all stand in a line across the pitch?
   > Because they're not allowed to . . . . forward.

7 What's the sport?

Match each of the sports below with two of the following extracts from commentaries. The words in green will help you decide.

rugby	tennis	golf	basketball

1. She served five aces in the first set.
2. He took three putts on the eighteenth green to finish with a round of 72.
3. That's Johnson's third personal foul.
4. Another unforced error from Hingis who hit that forehand into the net when under no pressure at all.
5. Dalaglio ran from the halfway line to score a fantastic try.
6. He hit a poor drive at the fifth hole and ended up in a bunker.
7. That was a brilliant tackle by Metcalf as Jenkins burst through the middle.
8. The ball hits the ring and Connolly collects the rebound.

Note on cricket

If you visit England during the summer, you may see people playing cricket. It is commonly played on Saturday and Sunday afternoons. It has very complicated rules and you need very unusual words to talk about it. A game of cricket can last one day or as long as five days!

If you really want to know more about it, ask an English person to explain these terms: the batsman, the bowler, the umpire, fielders, runs, the wicket, the stumps, a four, a six, an over.

Add your own words and expressions

48 Football

1 Basic vocabulary

Complete the sentences below with these words:

match   pitch   away   team
goal   foul   pass   substitute
referee   red card   at home   offside

1. There's a big football . . . . on TV
   tonight – Barcelona and Chelsea.

2. Some of the fans ran onto the . . . . and
   the referee had to stop the game.

3. I was disappointed France won. I thought
   Brazil were the better . . . .

4. Beckham scored the . . . . but it was
   Fowler's brilliant . . . . that created the
   opportunity.

5. That was a deliberate . . . . He just
   blocked Zola as he tried to run past. The
   . . . . should have sent him off. That
   was definitely a . . . . offence.

6. It shouldn't have been a goal. Vieri was
   . . . . when the ball was played to him.

7. In the 65th minute Owen came on as a
   . . . . and scored almost immediately.

8. Arsenal should win when they play Benfica
   . . . . , but the second leg could be a
   different story. . . . . games are always
   much more difficult.

2 Players' positions

There are two ways to describe where somebody plays. Match the positions with the phrases below:

1. goalkeeper
2. defender
3. midfielder
4. striker / attacker
5. wide player

a. He plays in attack.
b. He plays in midfield.
c. He plays in goal.
d. He plays wide on the left.
e. He plays in defence.

*The goalkeeper is often just called the keeper.
Attacking wide players are sometimes called
wingers, or we say "He plays on the left wing."*

3 Around the pitch

Label this picture of the goal with these words:

goal-line   post   net   crossbar

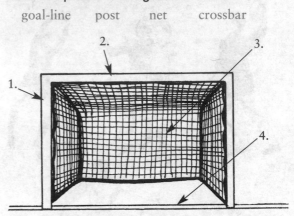

Write the correct number beside these expressions:

touch-line   . . .   corner flag   . . .
penalty area   . . .   six-yard box   . . .
penalty spot   . . .   halfway line
centre circle   . . .   goal   . . .

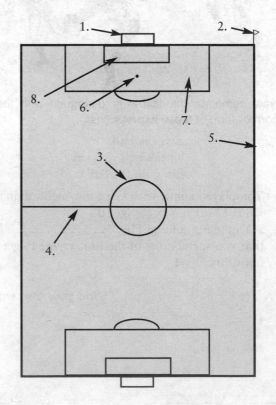

4 Talking about a game

Use the correct form of these verbs to complete the sentences below:

head	block	hit	save
score	have	commit	miss

1. Rivaldo . . . . . . an amazing goal from a free-kick in the last minute.
2. Germany would've won but the French goalkeeper . . . . . . a penalty in the 90th minute.
3. Brazil scored from a free kick when Maldini . . . . . . a foul just outside the penalty area.
4. He didn't need to pass. He should've . . . . . . a shot at goal.
5. Ronaldo was so unlucky. The ball . . . . . . the post and came back out.
6. It's 0-0 but Spain should be winning. Raul has just . . . . a penalty.
7. Giggs crossed the ball in from the left and Cole rose above two defenders to . . . . . . it into the net.
8. I thought it was a goal but a defender . . . . . . the shot on the line.

5 I'll take the penalty

Write the verb make or take with the words below:

1. . . . . . a save	5. . . . . . a corner
2. . . . . . a penalty	6. . . . . . a pass
3. . . . . . a run	7. . . . . . a free-kick
4. . . . . . a tackle	8. . . . . . a throw-in

6 A match report

Complete the match report below with the following expressions:

half-time	kick-off	extra time
stoppage time	first half	second half

"This is an absolutely fantastic match. We've played ninety minutes and there are three minutes of (1) . . . . to play. The score is France 3 – Spain 3. If it stays like this, there'll be (2) . . . . and if that doesn't produce a winner, it'll go to penalties.

Right from the (3) . . . . both teams attacked and with so many chances created it was incredible that there was only one goal in the (4) . . . . .That was scored by France – a brilliant shot by Thierry Henry. The Spanish coach must've said something to his players at (5) . . . . because in the (6) . . . . they were on fire. They scored three times in twenty minutes, two for Raul and one for Sergi. But France came back. Zidane made it 2-3 and then a fantastic goal by Pirés levelled the scores again."

If you want to know how to give a football score, see unit 50.

7 The referee

Below are things the referee does. Match the verbs with the phrases on the right:

1. give / award	a a player for a bad foul
2. disallow	b. his whistle to stop play
3. book	c. a free kick / a penalty
4. send	d. a goal for offside
5. blow	e. a player off

Which expression means the player is given a yellow card? Which expression means a red card?

Do you support a football team? Who is their coach / captain? Who is their star player? What's the name of their stadium?

Add your own words and expressions

49 Other sports

1 Basic vocabulary

Match the sports with the pictures:

swimming   cycling   skiing   ice-skating   ice hockey
horse racing   motor racing   show jumping   gymnastics   weightlifting

2 Sportsmen and women

Fill in the missing words in the table:

The sport	The person
1.	boxer
2. swimming	. . . .
3. skiing	. . . .
4.	skater
5.	gymnast
6. athletics	. . . .
7. motor racing	racing . . . .
8. cycling	. . . .
9.	jockey
10. the pentathlon	. . . .
11.	yachtsman
12. rowing	. . . .
13.	sky diver
14. weightlifting	. . . .
15.	climber

3 What's the sport?

Match the following commentary extracts with one of the sports from exercise 2. The words and phrases in green will help you to decide.

1. What an amazing fight! Lewis has won with a knock-out in the tenth round.
2. They're coming to the final fence now and the favourite Pink Gin is still in the lead.
3. Schumacher is off the track. He was trying to pass Hill, then he lost control of the car and that's the race over for him.
4. The next big race is the 800 metres, in which Sarah Gates represents Great Britain.
5. The women's downhill starts at ten and the men's slalom event follows at two o'clock.
6. And so Wescott wins the 100 metres freestyle to add to his victories in the breast-stroke, the backstroke and the butterfly.
7. After his performance on the rings, he'll be hoping for something better on the horse.
8. It looks like tomorrow's race is off. The forecast is for a force 8 gale!

4 Athletics

There are two types of athletics event: track events are all those which take place on the running track; all other events, except the marathon, are field events. Match these events with the pictures:

the hurdles   the javelin   the discus   the shot-put   the high jump   the long jump

1.

2.

3.

4.

5.

6.

The event when you have to hop, step and jump is called the triple jump.
A sprint is a short race – 100 metres, for example. The 800, 1500, and 3000 metre races are middle-distance events. A long-distance race is 5000 metres or more.

5 Boxing

Complete this newspaper report of a boxing match with these words and phrases:

first round	on points	heavyweight	bell
right hand	knock-out	corner	title

LEWIS RETAINS TITLE

The world . . . . champion, Lennox Lewis, successfully defended his . . . . against American Evander Hollyfield last night. Right from the very start Lewis had Hollyfield in trouble and at the end of the . . . ., Hollyfield was clearly very relieved to get back to his . . . . The . . . . went for the second round and Lewis immediately knocked his opponent down with a huge . . . . and it seemed only a matter of time before Lewis would win by a . . . . But Hollyfield recovered and as the fight went on he got increasingly stronger, causing the champion serious problems. In the end it went the full twelve rounds and Lewis was quite relieved to win . . . .

6 Fighting sports

Answer the questions below about these sports:

boxing   wrestling   judo
karate   kick boxing

1. Which three sports take place in a ring?
. . . .

2. In which of the sports do you use gloves?
. . . .

3. In which of the sports can you become a black-belt?
. . . .

4. In which of the sports do you throw your opponent?
. . . .

Do you know which sports the following sportsmen and women were famous for?

Carl Lewis   . . . .
Martina Navratilova   . . . .
Ayrton Senna   . . . .

Add your own words and expressions

50   Results and scores

1   Basic vocabulary

Translate the words in green into your language:

1. Who do you think will win? . . . .
2. I think he's going to lose. . . . .
3. Sweden beat Portugal 2-0. . . . .
4. He's a very difficult opponent. . . . .
5. It's a five-day tournament. . . . .
6. She lost in the semi-final. . . . .
7. I lost in the first round. . . . .
8. 3-2 is an excellent result. . . . .
9. It's his first trophy. . . . .
10. What was the final score? . . . .

2   Win or beat?

Complete each of the following phrases with either **win** or **beat**:

1. . . .   the final
2. . . .   on points
3. . . .   a medal
4. . . .   a point
5. . . .   a trophy
6. . . .   the cup
7. . . .   your rival
8. . . .   a race
9. . . .   the champion
10. . . .   your opponent
11. . . .   a competition
12. . . .   the championship
13. . . .   the favourite
14. . . .   the world record
15. . . .   the other team
16. . . .   by two seconds

Now use some of the nouns above to complete the sentences below:

17. Pierce has beaten the defending . . . .
18. Jackson holds the current . . . . which stands at 46.24 seconds.
19. Beatty is the hot . . . . in this race.
20. Warren is Black's closest . . . . in the 100 metres.

3   Tournaments

Below are six stages of a tennis tournament. Put the stages into a logical order. The first one has been done for you.

1e   2 . . .   3 . . .   4 . . .   5 . . .   6 . . .

a. Anna Kournikova was beaten in the quarter-finals.
b. Venus Williams won her semi-final against Monica Seles.
c. Lynsey Davenport was knocked out in the second round.
d. Venus Williams won the final to become champion for the second time.
e. Martina Hingis won her first round match.
f. Mary Pierce won a difficult third round match.

The same phrases are used in football competitions.

4   Races, records and medals

Choose the correct ending for the following:

1. Tessa Sanderson is absolutely delighted. She has won
2. It's every athlete's dream to represent
3. It's an incredible time – I think she's broken
4. As expected, the favourite from Kenya came
5. After so much preparation it was a big disappointment to finish
6. Runners from eight different countries will be competing
7. And with 200 metres to go, Samuels has taken

a. the world record.
b. in second place.
c. his or her country.
d. the gold medal.
e. in the next race.
f. the lead.
g. first.

Notice the complete expressions in this exercise, for example, break the world record.
What medals do you win if you come second or third?

5 Tennis scores

Look at the tennis scoreboard and complete the sentences below with these words:

losing   winning   beating   leading

	SETS				GAMES
SAMPRAS	6	6	—	—	4
AGASSI	4	3	—	—	3

1. Sampras is . . . . 4-3 in the third set.
2. Sampras seems to be . . . . Agassi easily.
3. At the moment Sampras is . . . . the match and Agassi is . . . .

When the score is:	You say:
15-0	*Fifteen-love*
15-15	*Fifteen-all*
30-15	*Thirty-fifteen*
40-40	*Deuce*

If the score is deuce *and Smith wins the next point, we say, "Advantage Smith".*

6 Football scores

Look at these football results:

Brazil	2	Italy	1
France	3	Spain	0
Germany	2	Holland	2

Use these verbs to fill the gaps below:

lost to   won   drew
conceded   beat   scored

1. Brazil . . . . . . 2-1.
2. Brazil . . . . . Italy 2-1.
3. Spain . . . . . . France.
4. Germany and Holland . . . . . . 2-2.
5. France . . . . . . three goals.
6. Spain . . . . . . three goals.

You say football scores like this:

2-1	*They won / lost two-one.*
2-0	*They won / lost two-nil.*
4-4	*They drew four-all.*
0-0	*They drew nil-nil. It was nil-nil.*

7   What makes a champion?

Match these sentences with the ideas in a-e below:

1. He's got so much talent.
2. He's got amazing stamina.
3. He's very competitive.
4. He's a very aggressive player.
5. He's got guts.
6. He's very dedicated.

a. He can keep running all day.
b. He sometimes gets into trouble with the referee.
c. He always wants to win.
d. He trains every day in wind, rain or snow!
e. He's not afraid of anything.
f. He makes it all look so easy.

Which three of the qualities above are important for the sports you play?

Add your own words and expressions

51   Television

1   Basic vocabulary

Use these words in the sentences below:

channel	widescreen	remote control
video	dish	portable TV
aerial	DVD recorder	cable
screen	subscription	pay-per-view

1. Although television was invented in 1924, television sets really only became widely available in the 1950's. When you see one of those early sets, the first thing you notice is how small the . . . . is.

2. One of the most recent developments is the . . . . which allows you to see films in a way which conventional sets didn't.

3. A . . . . is usually a small one which you can move from room to room or even take with you in your caravan.

4. . . . . developed using various different formats including VHS and PAL. With the advent of digital television, it won't be long before most people replace their old system with a state-of-the-art . . . .

5. You can't buy a television or video today without a . . . . You never need to move from your sofa.

6. If you've got . . . . television, you no longer need an . . . . on your roof, but if you want satellite television, then you need a . . . .

7. You have to pay a monthly . . . . charge if you've got cable or satellite.

8. . . . . is when you pay a one-off charge to watch a particular programme.

9. Every cable package comes with at least one shopping . . . .

In the UK there is still a distinction between Public Service Broadcasting – mostly the BBC – and the commercial stations such as ITV and Channel 4. The BBC is publicly funded. Everyone who owns a television set must pay an annual licence fee. Commercial TV is funded by the income from advertising.

2   Kinds of TV programme

Look at these different kinds of programme and the programme guide below. Write the time each kind of programme is on:

1. wildlife documentary   . . . .
2. soap opera   . . . .
3. cartoon   . . . .
4. comedy   . . . .
5. current affairs   . . . .
6. chat show   . . . .
7. costume drama   . . . .
8. game show   . . . .

4.30: Disneytime
More adventures with Mickey Mouse.

5.15: The Hidden Planet
Meet our closest living relatives – the chimpanzees.

6.15: Pride and Prejudice
The final episode of the Jane Austen novel.

7.30: Coronation Street
Joyce continues to search for her long-lost sister and Des gets a big surprise.

8.00: Who Wants to be a Millionaire?
The show in which hopeful contestants try to win the ultimate prize.

9.30: Michael Parkinson
Interviews with guests: singer Janet Jackson, footballer David Beckham and children's author JK Rowling.

11.00: Panorama
An investigation into why women are still paid less than men in many areas of business.

11.45: The Jack Dee show
More jokes and hilarious sketches with the northern comedian.

Which types of programme do you particularly like watching?

3 Talking about programmes

Use these words in the sentences below:

series   interview   programme   episode
serial   guests   repeats   highlights

1. What are you doing later?
   > I'm staying in tonight. There's a . . . .
   on that I really want to watch.

2. Is there anything worth watching on the telly
   tonight?
   > No, it's all . . . . again. Why can't they
   make some new programmes for a change?

3. So, why do you want to watch this
   programme so much?
   > They're going to do an . . . . with
   Brad Pitt about his new film.

4. I really don't like chat shows very much.
   > No, nor do I. The . . . . only come on
   to sell their latest film or their new book.

5. Is the Chelsea match on live tonight?
   > No, they're just showing the . . . .
   later in the evening.

6. I really miss 'Friends' now that it's not
   on. I used to watch it every week.
   > Well, you don't need to worry. There's a
   new . . . . starting next month.

7. Have you seen they've made Oliver Twist
   into a TV . . . . ?
   > Yes, it's on every Sunday for the next
   twelve weeks – the first . . . . is this
   Sunday.

A *series* has the same characters, but a different
story in each *episode*. A *serial* is one long story
divided into several episodes.

Telly is an informal word for television, used in
spoken English.

4 Talking about television

Complete the dialogues using these words:

contestants   adverts   presenter
channel   viewers   live

1. I want to record the MTV awards tonight.
   Could you set the video for me before we go
   out?
   > Yes, of course. Which . . . . is it on?

2. Did you see that film on TV last night? It
   was so violent.
   > Yes, apparently thousands of . . . .
   phoned in to complain.

3. Do you think the match will be on TV later?
   > Yes, of course. It's being shown . . . .
   on BBC1.

4. How many more times are they going to
   interrupt this film?
   > You're right. That's the fourth lot of
   . . . . already.

5. Did you see that new music show on TV last
   night? It was good, wasn't it?
   > Yes, it was OK but I didn't like the
   . . . . very much. They should've got
   someone younger.

6. Have you seen that new game show on
   Friday night? It's really funny.
   > Is that the one where they push the
   . . . . into a swimming pool if they
   give the wrong answers?

*Broadcast is a more formal verb than show –
"The Olympics are broadcast live by satellite all
over the world." It can also be used as a noun:
a news / live / outside broadcast.*

Add your own words and expressions

52   Newspapers

1   Kinds of newspaper

Match the newspapers with the definitions:

1. national paper
2. local paper
3. daily paper
4. broadsheet
5. tabloid

a. a paper that you can buy every morning
b. a paper that's sold throughout the country
c. a paper produced in one town
d. a serious paper that reports world events
e. a paper containing sensational stories about the private lives of rich and famous people

Tabloid and broadsheet refer to the size of the newspaper – tabloids are smaller than broadsheets. However, when we talk about tabloids and broadsheets, we are really talking about the content.

The Press means newspapers and journalists: "The Press seems to have turned against the Government recently."

2   Parts of the paper

If you were reading a newspaper in English, which part of the paper would you look in if you wanted to find out about the following?

1. the football results
   . . . .

2. what has been happening in the Middle East
   . . . .

3. a big fire in York
   . . . .

4. what readers think
   . . . .

5. the paper's opinion about something in the news
   . . . .

6. a new job
   . . . .

7. what is on at the theatre tonight
   . . . .

8. where to invest your money
   . . . .

9. the life of a famous actor who has just died
   . . . .

10. the temperature in Tenerife
    . . . .

11. finding a new partner
    . . . .

12. what a newly published book is like
    . . . .

3   People working for newspapers

Match the beginnings of the sentences with the endings below:

1. A reporter
2. The editor
3. A correspondent
4. A columnist
5. The proprietor

a. decides what goes in a newspaper or magazine.
b. finds interesting news stories and writes about them.
c. owns the newspaper.
d. writes a regular column in a newspaper or magazine.
e. sends reports from a particular part of the world or about a particular subject.

A journalist is anybody who writes or reports news either for a newspaper or television.

NEWS AND FEATURES

2-4	Home news
5-6	Foreign news
24-25	Business and money news
26-30	Sports news

REGULAR FEATURES

7-10	Health, Fashion, food
11-12	Reviews
13	Editorial and readers' letters
14-15	Obituaries
16-22	Classified
23	Personal
31	TV and entertainment guide
32	Weather forecast

4 Talking about newspapers

Use these words to complete the sentences below:

front page   headlines   privacy
circulations   supplement   article

1. Did you see that really interesting . . . .
   about India in the paper last Sunday?
2. Have you watched the news today?
   Somebody broke into the Queen's bedroom.
   > No, but I'm sure it'll be on the . . . .
   of all tomorrow's papers. I can see the
   . . . . already!
3. The tabloids are full of absolute rubbish.
   > I know. I'm amazed they have such big
   . . . .
4. I feel sorry for these film stars. Reporters
   seem to follow them everywhere.
   > No, they don't get much . . . . , do they?
5. I love the Sunday papers. There are so many
   sections and usually a colour . . . . too.

6 Verbs in newspaper reports

Use these common newspaper verbs below:

described   announced   demanded
claimed   appealed

1. Pensioner Sam Macdonald . . . . how his
   attackers laughed as they stole his money.
2. Police in Brighton have . . . . for
   witnesses after a man was attacked in the
   town centre late last night.
3. Angry friends and relatives have . . . .
   an inquiry after a man died in police custody
   yesterday.
4. 500 new jobs will be created in the Health
   Service, the Government . . . . yesterday.
5. Nobody has . . . . responsibility for the
   bomb which exploded in central London
   yesterday.

5 Headline words

Certain words are used frequently in headlines. Match the six words in green with their definitions. Then use them to complete the headlines.

1. hits   a. supports
2. quits   b. has a bad effect
3. backs   c. leaves a job

4. tragedy   d. a situation full of fear
5. scare   e. an argument or disagreement
6. row   f. a very sad situation

DIRECTOR . . . .
Philip Bosman has resigned
from his £150,000 job at
Presco Ltd after the company
announced a loss of £2 million
in its annual report.

PLANE . . . .
A pilot and his two passengers
were killed yesterday when the
plane they were flying in
crashed as it was landing.

FESTIVAL . . . .
There were angry scenes at a
meeting last night between
organisers of a music festival
and local residents who do not
want it to take place.

**PRIME MINISTER
. . . . PLAN**
The Prime Minister has given
his support to a plan which
aims to reduce the number of
young smokers.

**STRIKE . . . .
TRAVELLERS**
Thousands of travellers spent
the night at Heathrow Airport
after cabin crew and ground
staff went on strike over
working conditions.

BOMB . . . .
Police were called to a
department store in Oxford
Street after a caller claimed to
have planted a bomb.

Add your own words and expressions

53 Advertising

1 Basic vocabulary

Match the words with their meanings:

a commercial   a leaflet
a poster   classified ads

1. a large sheet of paper advertising something, for example, a play, a film or a concert.
2. a small piece of paper used for door-to-door advertising.
3. small adverts placed by private individuals in a newspaper.
4. a TV or radio advert.

2 Talking about advertising

Use these words to complete the sentences:

influence   publicity   agency
brand   sponsor   slogan
hype   competitors logo

1. Do people really buy things just because they've seen them advertised on TV?
   > Of course they do! Advertising has a huge . . . . on all the choices we make.
2. Advertisers like to think of a clever . . . . to make people remember their product. For example, Coca Cola's is 'It's the real thing.'
3. Nike are going to . . . . the next World Cup. All the players will have to wear the Nike . . . . on their shirts.
4. What . . . . of cigarette do you smoke?
5. Most companies spend a lot of money on advertising. It's the only way they can stay ahead of their . . . .
6. My sister's just got a job working for an advertising . . . . in London.
7. Did you see Jodie Foster on that chat show last night? She was really good.
   > She's been on all the shows this week. It's all just . . . . for her new film.
8. You went to see Spielberg's new film at the weekend, didn't you? What was it like?
   > Well, considering all the . . . . , I thought it was a bit disappointing.

We use hype when we think the advertising is exaggerated.

3 Advertising verbs

Choose the correct ending for each of the following:

1. Oasis are doing a tour to promote
2. I think it's a brilliant advert. It really grabs
3. Advertisers know that shoppers will always compare
4. Advertisers are experts at persuading people
5. They really want to sell this product. They've just launched
6. The tobacco industry has been trying very hard to improve
7. At the moment British Airways are advertising
8. We're trying to reach

a. to spend their money.
b. a huge advertising campaign.
c. the under-18 market.
d. two flights for the price of one.
e. their new album.
f. your attention.
g. one product with another.
h. its image.

4 Image adjectives

The adjectives below are often used to describe the image that advertisers try to create for a product. Match the adjectives on the left with the most likely product on the right in the two groups below:

1. macho   a. breakfast cereal
2. family   b. holiday
3. feminine   c. after shave
4. healthy   d. perfume

Now do the same with these:

5. trendy   e. tropical fruit juice
6. exotic   f. music system
7. hi-tech   g. car
8. reliable   h. clothes shop

Is there an advert on TV at the moment that you really like? What's it for?
What's the funniest advert you've ever seen?

5 Promoting products

Advertisers can promote products in different ways. Use these words to make compound nouns:

tour   offer   gifts   deal   loyalty

a. special   . . . .
b. sponsorship   . . . .
c. free   . . . .
d. brand   . . . .
e. promotional   . . . .

Now use the expressions in the following:

1. You don't normally buy this coffee.
   > No, but they had a . . . .
   . . . . at the supermarket – two jars for the price of one.

2. Did you see that Pulp are playing at the Odeon next month?
   > Yes, they're on a . . . .

3. David Beckham has just signed a new . . . . with Adidas. It's worth more than a million pounds a year.

4. The kids always want me to buy this cereal so they can get the . . . . inside!

5. Tobacco companies like to catch people young. They know the meaning of . . . .!

Make five more two-word phrases using these words:

magazines   shot   names   points   prices

f. competitive   . . . .
g. glossy   . . . .
h. brand   . . . .
i. selling   . . . .
j. mail   . . . .

Now use the expressions in the following:

6. Silk Cut and Johnnie Walker are common . . . . that everybody recognises.

7. I see that Audi have just launched a new model.
   > Yes, they've started a huge advertising campaign. There are ads in all the papers and . . . . – and TV commercials every five minutes!

8. We like to think that we offer quality products at . . . .

9. The fact that this car is so economical is one of its major . . . .

10. If you get a reply rate of 10% for a . . . ., that's good. 15% is thought to be excellent. 20% is brilliant.

WOULD YOU LIKE TO BUY – THIS GUN?

Add your own words and expressions

54   Telephones

1   Basic vocabulary

What are these words in your language?

receiver   mobile phone   answerphone
fax   public telephone   phone card

To make an international call, you need:

The international code	00
The country code	(44)
The area code	(1273)
The person's number	(736344)

In English we usually say phone numbers like this:

0	= oh (zero is sometimes also used)
63	= six three (not sixty-three)
66	= double six
666	= six double six

When you ring an organisation on a touch-tone phone, you might hear a menu of options; you might, for example be asked to press the star key (*) or the hash key (#).

2   Making a call

Use these words in the conversations below:

call back   no-one   wrong (x 2)
ring   that   this
take a message   there   it's

1. Hello.
   > Hi. Is . . . . . . Liz?
   Yes, who's that? I can hardly hear you.
   > . . . . . . Debbie. I'm on my mobile.

2. Hello.
   > Hello. Is Martin . . . . . . , please?
   I'm afraid he's out. Can I . . . . ?
   > No, don't worry. I'll . . . . later.

3. Hello.
   > Hi. . . . . . . is David Peaty. Could I speak to Chris, please?
   Oh, hello David. He's not in yet. Shall I ask him to . . . . you when he gets in?

4. Could I speak to Donald, please?
   > I think you must have the . . . . . . number.
   There's . . . . of that name here.

5. Hello, Peter Willis.
   > Sorry, ... number.

3   Talking about phone calls

Complete the following dialogues with the correct form of the verbs below. Use each verb once only.

make   look it up   give   answer
dial   call   leave   get

1. What time do you want me to pick you up this evening?
   > I'm not sure. I'll . . . . . . you on my mobile just before the train gets in.

2. Do you mind if I . . . . . . a phone call?
   > No, of course not. The phone's in the hall.

3. What time shall we meet?
   > I'm not sure yet. I'll . . . . . . you a call later this evening.

4. I'll phone later and give you Sally's new address.
   > I probably won't be in, but you can . . . . . . a message.

5. Do you know what Jim's number is?
   > Yes, ... 01273 for Brighton and then his number's 736344.

6. Do you know Sarah's number?
   > No, I'm afraid I don't. Why don't you . . . . in the phone book?

7. Shall I ring you later?
   > Yes, but I may be out. Have you . . . . . . my mobile number?

8. I'm in the bath. Can you . . . . that, please?

Notes

The verbs phone, call, and ring can all be used in these sentences:
   I'll . . . . you later.
   Why not . . . . me tomorrow?
   I'll . . . . you back.

Instead of answer, you can also say, "Can you get the phone, please?"

If you do not have a telephone directory, you can ring Directory Enquiries to find out someone's number.

If you want to know the time, you can ring the Speaking Clock.

4 Problems on the phone

Complete the text with the correct form of these expressions:

be engaged	get cut off
hang up	get through
call straight back	get the wrong number

I've had a terrible morning! I've been trying to
(1) . . . . to Mr Francis for the
last hour and a half. First I (2) . . . .
. . . . – an old lady answered the phone
and started telling me about her cats!
Then when I did dial the right number it (3) . . .
. . . . – he seems to spend most of
his day on the phone. Finally, after about
twenty attempts, his secretary answered the
phone. She was just about to put me through,
when we (4) . . . . – I don't
know what happened. Anyway, I (5) . . . .
. . . . and finally I got to speak to him. I was
just about to tell him about the meeting when
he suddenly told me that he had to speak to
somebody urgently on another line. I couldn't
believe it – he just (6) . . . . on me!

5 An answerphone message

Put the following answerphone message into the correct order:

a. but if you'd like   . . .
b. we'll get back   . . .
c. as we can. Thank you.   . . .
d. to the phone right now,   . . .
e. I'm sorry   . . .
f. to leave a message   . . .
g. to you as soon   . . .
h. after the tone,   . . .
i. we can't come   . . .

Do you like answerphones? Do you leave a message or do you hang up straightaway?

6 Business calls

Complete the following dialogues with the words and phrases below:

put you through	line	hold
left a message	hold the line	speaking
bear with me	available	extension

1. Hello. Could I speak to Paul Morgan, please?
   > . . . .
   Sorry, Paul. I didn't realise it was you.

2. Good morning. Glaxo and Son Ltd.
   > Judith Smart, please.
   . . . . , please. I'll . . . .

3. Good morning, I'd like to speak to the
   manager, please.
   > I'm afraid he isn't . . . . at the
   moment. Can anyone else help?

4. Good morning, Briggs and Powers.
   > . . . . 397, please.
   Sorry, there's no answer. Who did you
   want to speak to?
   > Andrew Brown. He . . . .
   for me earlier.
   Just . . . . for a moment. I'll see if
   I can find him for you.

5. Good morning. Import Export Trading.
   > Sylvia Parsons, please.
   I'm sorry, she's on another . . . . at the
   moment. Do you want to . . . . . . ?
   > No thanks. It's OK, I'll call back later.

*When you ring a company, the call is usually
answered by someone on the switchboard who
will put you through to the extension you need.*

55   Computers

1   Hardware

Match these words with the pictures:

palmtop	keyboard	printer
mouse	VDU (or monitor)	scanner
laptop	mouse pad	computer

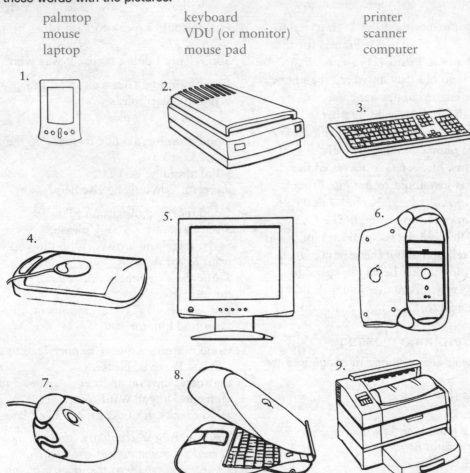

2   Basic computer operations

Here are the instructions that appear on the menu on most computers. Make sure you can translate all the instructions into your own language.

1. open   . . . . . .

2. close   . . . . . .

3. save   . . . . . .

4. save as   . . . . . .

5. select   . . . . . .

6. cut   . . . . . .

7. copy   . . . . . .

8. paste   . . . . . .

9. print   . . . . . .

10. delete   . . . . . .

11. insert   . . . . . .

12. merge   . . . . . .

3   Basics

Use these words in the text below:

helpline	pre-installed	software
hard disk	installation	CD-ROMs

People sometimes ask if you've got a PC or a Mac. Both systems have their strong points. Each system is a platform on which you run (1) . . . . programs. Software usually comes (2) . . . . or on (3) . . . . , which you then have to install yourself onto your computer's (4) . . . . If you have any (5) . . . . problems, you can always ring the (6) . . . .

4 Using a computer

Complete the sentences below with these words:

toolbar	template	spreadsheets
terminals	document	word processor
database	memory	modem

1. Most computers have enough . . . . to store a vast amount of information.

2. The central computer in this office serves thirty-two . . . .

3. You can't get onto the internet unless your computer has a . . . .

4. If you write a lot of similar letters, you can save a lot of time by using a . . . .

5. It's usually quicker to use the icons on the . . . . than to keep using the menu.

6. Many people only use their computer as a . . . . All they do is write letters and reports on it.

7. The three most important kinds of . . . . that your PC can create are word processor, database and spreadsheet.

8. We have a huge . . . . with detailed information about all our customers.

9. The . . . . save me a lot of time when I'm doing the accounts.

5 Computing verbs

Match the verbs on the left with the phrases on the right:

1. insert	a. a back-up copy
2. make	b. an e-mail
3. run	c. an icon
4. surf	d. a floppy disk
5. send	e. the internet
6. click on	f. part of the text
7. highlight	g. a program

6 Problems with computers

Complete the text with these words:

lost	viruses	hackers	crashed	bug

Everybody seems to be having problems with computers these days. Governments and big companies are worried about (1) . . . . who find their way into their systems and read confidential information. They are even more worried about (2) . . . . which can destroy all their programs.

It's not much better for ordinary people either – I bought a program myself last month and I suppose it must have had a (3) . . . . of some kind. My computer suddenly (4). . . . . . . and I (5) . . . . two hours' work.

7 Using the internet

Complete this extract from a guide to using the internet with the following:

on-line	web page	sites
chat room	download	newsgroup

The World Wide Web is made up of millions of (1) . . . . created by anybody from multi-media corporations to ordinary people like you and me. On the web you can read (2) . . . . newspapers or magazines; you can watch videos, (3) . . . . music or buy anything from a CD to a holiday. You can go into a (4) . . . . and talk to other people all over the world or join a (5) . . . . for more serious debate. If you are really ambitious you might even like to try creating your own (6) . . . . Then you can show your holiday pictures to the whole world!

Are you computer-literate? Have you got a PC? Are you on the net? How much time do you spend online?

Add your own words and expressions

56   Machines and equipment

1 Domestic equipment

Match the words with the pictures:

Musical and TV equipment

turntable   CD player   cassette deck   speaker   headphones   video/DVD player

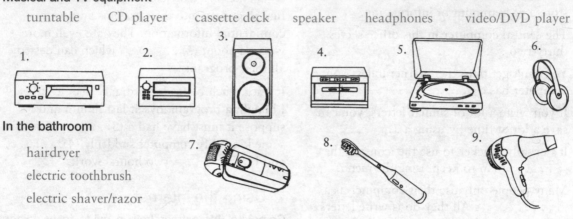

1.   2.   3.   4.   5.   6.

In the bathroom

hairdryer

electric toothbrush

electric shaver/razor

7.   8.   9.

Other equipment

sewing machine

iron

vacuum cleaner

video camera

fan

10.   11.   12.   13.   14.

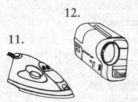
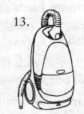

Plugs and things

plug   extension lead   switch   knob   socket   battery

15.   16.   17.   18.   19.   20.

2 Making things work

Use the correct form of these verbs below:

press   work   go   run   unplug

1. Do you know how this machine . . . . . . ?
   > All you do is just . . . . . . this button and it
   starts automatically.
2. Where's the lead for this CD player?
   > It . . . . . . on batteries. There's no lead.
3. Why isn't the video working?
   > I . . . . . . it earlier and didn't plug it in again.
4. What's wrong with the lamp?
   > Oh, the bulb . . . . . . when I switched it on.

3 Phrasal verbs

Add the correct preposition to the verbs below:

on   out/off   in   up   down

1. Remember to put the lights . . . when you go.
2. Could you turn the volume . . . a bit? I can't
   hear anything.
3. Did you remember to switch . . . the answerphone before we left the house?
4. Can you turn the volume . . . a bit, please?
   I'm trying to talk to somebody on the phone.
5. It's not surprising the toaster isn't working.
   You haven't plugged it . . . !

4 Appliances, machines etc

Appliances are all the electrical equipment you use to help you do jobs around the house. Most household appliances are powered by a motor.
Machine is a general word for electrical equipment. It can be used for household appliances – for example, a washing machine.
Machinery is a general term, used to refer to large industrial machines.
A device is a small, useful machine.
A gadget is an informal word for a small, modern device.

Complete the sentences below using these words:

gadgets	motor
machinery	device
appliances	machine

1. The vacuum cleaner's not working. I think there's something wrong with the . . . . It keeps making a funny noise.

2. Most cars nowadays are fitted with a security . . . . of some kind.

3. We're opening another factory next year, so most of this year's profit will be spent on new . . . .

4. He's got a really flashy new car with all the latest . . . .

5. It's surprising how much it costs to equip a modern kitchen. The electrical . . . . alone will cost at least two thousand pounds.

6. Sorry, madam, I think this . . . . is beyond repair. Perhaps you should think of replacing it with a newer model.

Are you good with machines? Have you got a mechanical mind or are you a technophobe (somebody who is afraid of technology)?

5 When machines don't work

Choose the correct ending for the following:

1. We can't use the video recorder today. It isn't
2. Could you have a look at the video? I think there's something
3. I'm worried about this washing machine. It's making
4. You can't use that phone. It's
5. I'm sick and tired of this old car. It keeps
6. I've fixed the washing machine. It's as

a. breaking down.
b. wrong with it.
c. out of order.
d. good as new.
e. working properly.
f. a funny noise.

If something doesn't work, you need to fix it, or get it fixed. Before you try to fix something electrical, make sure you unplug it. When you have fixed it, you can plug it back in again.

6 Revision

Without looking back at exercise 5, complete each sentence with one word:

1. There seems to be something . . . . . . with it.
2. It keeps . . . . . . down.
3. It's making a . . . . . . noise.
4. The phone's out of . . . .
5. It's as good as . . . .
6. It isn't working . . . .

Add your own words and expressions

119

57   Money

1   Basic vocabulary

Use the following words in the text below:

notes   coins   credit card   currency   cash   cheque   money belt

The less money you carry around with you, the better. I usually have about £40 in (1) . . . . . . in my wallet and a couple of pounds in (2) . . . . in my pocket. I pay (3) . . . . for things which cost under £10, but for anything over that I use my (4) . . . . I only use my (5) . . . . book to pay bills. When I go on holiday, I carry all my foreign (6) . . . . . . in a (7) . . . . round my waist under my trousers!

In the United States notes *are called* bills. *The American spelling of* cheque *is* check.

2   Situations

Complete the following dialogues with the words below:

credit card   cash   change   cheque

1. Um, I think £25 is a bit expensive.
   > Well, there's 10% off if you pay . . . .

2. We still haven't paid the telephone bill.
   > Don't worry, I put a . . . . . . in the post last night.

3. Can I pay by . . . . ?
   > Yes, we take Visa and Mastercard.

4. Have you got any . . . . . . ? I've only got a twenty-pound note.
   > Yes, I think I've got some pound coins.

We say pay cash *but* pay by cheque *or* pay by credit card.

3   Income

Most of us earn money from our regular jobs, but there are other ways of getting money too. Complete the definitions with these words:

a. pension   f. maintenance
b. grant   g. interest
c. fee   h. pocket money
d. salary   i. wage
e. income   j. bonus

1. A . . . . . . is what you earn weekly.

2. A . . . . . . is what you earn monthly or annually.

3. Your annual salary plus any other money you earn in a year is your . . . .

4. A . . . . . . is paid to a professional for some work – a lawyer, for example.

5. . . . . is given by parents to children.

6. People who have retired receive a . . . .

7. . . . . is paid by a man to his ex-wife.

8. . . . . . . is extra money you receive monthly or annually if you keep money in the bank.

9. Some people receive a . . . . . once a year if they have done a good job or if the company has had a good year.

10. A . . . . . . is money given to you to help you with your studies or to travel.

What social security benefits *are available in your country if you are ill or unemployed?*

4 Talking about your income

Complete the following dialogues with the correct form of the verb phrases below:

get £400 a week   earn pretty good money
make a lot more   get a rise

1. I've only just got enough to get by at the moment, but fortunately I . . . . next month.

2. She wears some lovely clothes, doesn't she?
   > Yes, and she bought a Porsche recently, so I guess she . . . .

3. How's the new job? Does it pay well?
   > Not too bad. I . . . . after tax.

4. My basic wage is only £200 a week, but I . . . . because I do so much overtime.

*In Britain it is not considered polite to ask somebody, "*How much do you earn?*" Can you ask this question in your country?*

5 Collocations with *pay*

Use these verbs with the correct pattern below:

pay   pay for   pay off

A	a meal, the drinks, my ticket
B	£10 for (the ticket), a lot of money for it, somebody to (fix your car), income tax, the bill, bills, a fine, the rent
C	a loan, your debts, the mortgage

Use the correct form of some of the phrases from patterns B and C to fill the gaps in the following:

1. Gas, electricity, telephone – all I ever seem to do is . . . .
2. I've got a loan of £10,000 to buy a car but it's going to take 5 years to . . . . it . . . . .
3. I've got a job at last! Now I can . . . . all my . . . . !
4. The landlord came round last night to see why we haven't . . . . yet.
5. It's great to own my own flat at last, but it's going to take a long time to . . . .
6. The more money you earn, the more . . . . you have to . . . .

6 Verb collocations

Match the verbs on the left with the phrases:

1. spend		a. to a beggar
2. lose		b. on food
3. give	money	c. in a will
4. save		d. at the casino
5. leave		e. by walking to work
6. lend		f. in a new business
7. invest		g. into the bank
8. waste	money	h. to a friend
9. pay		i. for your holiday
10. change		j. on silly things

7 Expressions with *money*

Complete the dialogues with these sentences:

What a waste of money!
It's very good value for money.
It'll save a bit of money.
He's got more money than sense!

1. That new French restaurant does a fixed price menu for only £18. . . . .
2. She's got more money than sense. That dress she's wearing cost £500!
   > You're joking. . . . . !
3. Let's take the ferry instead of the plane.
   > Good idea! . . . .
4. Have you seen Martin's latest car? It's an open-topped Mercedes.
   > . . . . !

8 Verb expressions with *money*

Here are some ways of earning money with little effort. Match these beginnings and endings:

1. I've never won any money
2. I inherited some money
3. They've organised an event to raise money
4. I'm hoping to borrow some money
5. Her father made a lot of money

a. from the bank.
b. when my grandfather died.
c. when he sold his house.
d. for charity.
e. on the lottery.

Add your own words and expressions

58   Rich and poor

1 Basic vocabulary

Read these sentences and put the words and phrases in green into the correct column below:

1. The wedding's at one of the best hotels in London. Her father's a very wealthy man.

2. They must be pretty well-off. They've just bought a six-bedroomed house.

3. I won't be able to have a holiday this year. I'm a bit short of money.

4. My father's got a very good pension so my parents have been quite comfortable since he retired.

5. I can't come out tonight. I'm broke.

6. I lent my brother some money last week. He's a bit hard up at the moment.

7. When the children were young, we couldn't afford to go on holiday.

8. They have three holidays a year so they must be loaded.

Lots of money	Little money
. . . .	. . . .
. . . .	. . . .
. . . .	. . . .
. . . .	. . . .

Now mark each of the following sentences (+) if they are about having a lot of money or (-) if they are about having very little or no money:

9. He won the lottery last year. They say he's a millionaire.

10. This latest tax will make life even more difficult for families on low incomes.

11. I can just about get by on what I earn.

12. Millions of people in developing countries live in poverty.

13. He's lived a life of luxury since he sold his business.

14. He's lost his house, his car – everything. He's been made bankrupt.

2 Rich and poor idioms

Mark each of the following sentences (+) if they are about someone who is rich, and (-) if they are about someone who is poor:

1. She's got money to burn.   . . .
2. He's on the breadline.   . . .
3. Money's a bit tight at the moment.   . . .
4. We need to tighten our belts.   . . .
5. They live in the lap of luxury.   . . .
6. We're struggling to make ends meet.   . . .
7. She hasn't got a penny to her name.   . . .
8. They just live from hand to mouth.   . . .
9. She's worth a fortune.   . . .

3 Borrow and lend

In one of Shakespeare's most famous plays – Hamlet – one of the characters gives this piece of advice:

Neither a borrower nor a lender be.

Complete this dialogue with these words:

pay you back   lending   owe
borrow   lent

Peter: Mark, can I . . . . £5 for a couple of days?
Mark: I'm always . . . . you money. You still . . . . me the £10 I . . . . you last week.
Peter: Don't worry. I'll . . . .
Mark: Sure, when? At Christmas?
Peter: No, on Friday. I promise.

Complete another version of the same dialogue with these words:

get it back   borrowing   lent
paid back   lend

Peter: Mark, could you . . . . me £5?
Mark: You're always . . . . money from me. You still haven't . . . . the £10 I . . . . you last week.
Peter: I know, I know. Don't worry. You'll . . . . on Friday.
Mark: I'll believe that when it happens!

Notice the patterns: *Could you lend me ...?*
                           Can I borrow ...?

4 World poverty

Complete the following article using these words:

debt   share   wealth
poverty   progress   poor

Although huge (1) . . . . has already been made in tackling global (2) . . . . , there is still a widening gap between the rich and the poor.

The unfair distribution of (3) . . . . means that while the world as a whole is getting richer, many poor people are excluded from their (4) . . . . . . of this wealth.

One sign of hope is that rich nations are starting to consider cutting Third World (5) . . . . Governments now recognise that without debt relief, there is little chance of poor countries like Rwanda and Tanzania achieving the growth necessary to lift their population out of absolute poverty.

Charities now have the ambitious target of cutting the world's (6) . . . . by half in the next fifteen years. They believe that this target will only be reached when governments and development agencies work together to achieve it.

5 Well-paid or badly-paid?

Put these phrases into the correct list:

hardly anything
far too much
a fortune
next to nothing
peanuts

1. Professional footballers are paid . . . .
. . . .

2. Children in developing countries who make footballs are paid . . . .
. . . .
. . . .

6 Revision

Complete each of the following expressions from this unit with one word:

1. I couldn't . . . . . . it.
2. We need to tighten our . . . .
3. I'm a bit . . . . . . of money.
4. They're a bit . . . . . . up.
5. She hasn't got a . . . . . . to her name.
6. They're paid . . . . . . to nothing.
7. He lives a life of . . . .
8. I can just about . . . . . . by.
9. Could you . . . . . . me £10?
10. Can I . . . . . . £10 for a couple of days?

Add your own words and expressions

123

59   At the bank

1   Basic vocabulary

Complete the sentences below with these words:

borrow	interest
cash	loan
overdrawn	overdraft
debts	account
cheque	cashpoint

1. I haven't got any . . . . . . with me. I'll need to go to the bank.
2. My salary is paid straight into my . . . . . . at the end of every month.
3. If you want to buy a new car, why not get a . . . . . . from the bank?
4. Interest rates are very low. Why don't you . . . . . . the money from the bank?
5. I'm going to the bank to pay in this . . . .
6. I'll have to stop spending so much money. I'm already . . . . by over £100.
7. If you are prepared to take more risk, you'll get higher . . . . . . on your investment.
8. Tom's got quite a few . . . . He's borrowed money from the bank and several of his friends.
9. I need some cash. Is there a . . . . near here?
10. I'm spending too much money. I've already got an enormous . . . .

A cashpoint is called an ATM in American English. In informal British English it is often called a hole in the wall.

2   Foreign currency

If you go abroad you will probably go to a bank to change money. **The** currency **in Britain is sterling (pounds and pence) and in the United States it is dollars and cents. The** current exchange rate **is $1.50 = £1. In which countries are the following currencies used?**

1. the rouble	4. the real
2. the yen	5. the euro
3. the rupee	6. the peso

3   Bank accounts and bank cards

Put these words in the correct list below:

current	credit	deposit
savings	cash	joint

. . . .
. . . .   account   . . . .   card
. . . .
. . . .

Now match the phrases with these definitions:

1. An account shared by two or more people.
2. An account that allows you to pay money in or take money out whenever you like.
3. A card used to buy things on credit. You have to pay money back each month.
4. A card used to take money out of a cashpoint.
5. These accounts earn higher interest.

In Britain different banks use different names for their accounts. Most people have a current account. If you want to leave money in the bank for longer periods, you will use a deposit, savings, or high-interest account.
In the United States a cash card is called an ATM card. A current account is called a checking account.

4   Using an account

Complete the sentences with these words:

electronic	write	direct debit
a withdrawal	a pay-in	standing order

1. If you pay money into your account you make . . . .
2. If you take money out of your account you make . . . .
3. If you need to pay a bill, you can . . . . a cheque.
4. If you have to pay money to the same person or company on a regular basis, you can pay by . . . . or by . . . .
5. Some people never need to visit their bank. They use an . . . . banking service. They can check their account and make payments using the internet.

5 Borrowing money from the bank

Complete the following dialogues with the words below:

debt	interest	loan
mortgage	overdraft	overdrawn

1. I'm glad it's nearly the end of the month. I've got absolutely no money left.
   > I know what you mean. I don't get paid for another week and I'm already . . . .

2. You're working long hours at the moment. Are you saving up for something?
   > No – nothing so exciting! I'm trying to pay off the . . . . on my Barclays account.

3. I'm sure the bank would lend you the money if you really need it.
   > No, I don't want to do that. I already owe my father £300. I really don't want to get further into . . . .

4. I hear you're thinking of starting up your own business. How are you going to get the money?
   > No problem. I've already applied to the bank for a . . . .

5. If you really want a new car, why don't you borrow some money from the bank?
   > I don't really want to do that. You have to pay so much in . . . .

6. So, I hear you're getting a flat of your own, are you?
   > Yes, I've found a really nice place, saved up enough for a deposit, and arranged a . . . .

A mortgage is a loan, but it is only used to buy a flat or house.

If your account is in the black, do you have a healthy account or do you owe money? What about if you're in the red?

6 At the cashpoint

Put the following into the most logical order:

a. Key in your PIN number.

b. Take your card.

c. Choose the amount of money you want.

d. Take your cash.

e. Insert your card.

f. Press the 'withdraw cash' button.

1. . . . 2. . . . 3. . . . 4. . . . 5. . . . 6. . . .

You can also use the cashpoint for other services. Complete the text below with these words:

statement	balance	transactions

If you just want to know how much money you have in your account, you can check your (7) . . . . You can also order a (8) . . . ., which your bank will send out to you within a few days and which shows all the (9) . . . . you have made.

7 At the bank – verbs

Make complete sentences:

1. I'd like to open
2. I'd like to pay
3. I'd like to transfer
4. I'd like to withdraw
5. I'd like to cash

a. these travellers' cheques.
b. a new account.
c. £200 from my current to my savings account.
d. this cheque into my account.
e. £300, please.

Add your own words and expressions

---

60   Shops and shopping

1   Different kinds of shop

Match these shops with what you buy in them:

greengrocer's   baker's   butcher's   chemist's
ironmonger's   florist's   off-licence   newsagent's

1. Meat . . . .
2. Flowers . . . .
3. Bread and cakes . . . .
4. Magazines and newspapers . . . .
5. Fruit and vegetables . . . .
6. Wine and spirits . . . .
7. Medicine . . . .
8. Tools, nails, candles etc . . . .

Which one of these is not the correct name for a shop?

bookshop   shoe shop   sweet shop
meat shop   pet shop   gift shop

Match these American English phrases with their British English equivalents above:

candy store   drugstore   liquor store

In British English stores *are large shops that sell lots of different things –* a department store, *for example,* which has a shoe department, a cosmetics department *and so on.* A chain store *has* branches *all over the country. A* shopping centre *or* shopping mall *is a place with lots of different shops under cover in one place.*

2   Supermarkets

Complete the following using these words:

aisle   checkout   baskets
plastic bag   organic   trolley

1. I hate carrying those wire . . . . I use
   a . . . . at the supermarket.
2. I think working on a . . . . must be a
   really boring job.
3. If everyone uses one . . . . every
   time they go shopping, that's an awful lot of
   pollution.
4. Could you tell me where the coffee is, please?
   > Third . . . . on the right.
5. Excuse me, are these potatoes . . . . ?
   > No, the . . . . section is over there, sir.

3   Shopping expressions

Who would say each of these – the customer **(C) or the** shop assistant **(S)?**

1. Can I help you? . . .
2. No, thank you. I'm just looking. . . .
3. Are you being served? . . .
4. Your receipt's in the bag. . . .
5. Okay, thank you. I'll take it. . . .
6. Thank you. I think I'll leave it for now. . . .

4   Talking about shopping

Complete the dialogues using the following verb phrases:

keep the receipt   make a list
got this   get a refund
try this on   pick up a bargain

1. I've got to go to the supermarket later. Is
   there anything you want?
   > Yes, lots of things. Why don't you . . . . . .
   . . . . so you don't forget anything?
2. I really need a new coat.
   > Well, wait till after Christmas. You might
   . . . . in the sales.
3. Can I . . . . , please?
   > Certainly, the changing rooms are over
   there.
4. I don't believe it! I've only had this alarm
   clock for three weeks and it's broken.
   > Well, why don't you take it back and see
   if you can . . . .
   > I'm not sure if I can do that. I didn't
   . . . .
5. Have you . . . . in dark blue?
   > I'm afraid not.
   Never mind. I'll take the black, then.

Notice the use of then *in the last example. It means 'in those circumstances' and comes at the end of what you say.*

If you're shopping for pleasure, you go shopping. *If you have to buy food and things for the house, you say "I've got to* do the shopping."

What are you doing if you're window-shopping?

5 Cost and price

It's a good idea to learn the words that collocate with the nouns cost and price. Complete the phrases below with either cost or price. Only one is possible in each case.

1. half . . . . . .
2. total . . . . . .
3. . . . . . . tag
4. . . . . . . of living
5. two for the . . . . . . of one
6. . . . . . . list
7. fair . . . . . .
8. included at no extra . . . . . .

Now use some of the phrases in the following:

9. Do you miss living in London?
   No, not really, because . . . .
   was so high, I never had any money.
10. That's a nice jacket. Is it new?
    > Yes, I bought it . . . . in the sales.
11. Why did you get two packets of coffee?
    It was a special offer – . . . .
12. I enclose a copy of our brochure and
    current . . . .
13. Can you tell me how much this jacket is?
    I can't see a . . . . on it.
14. The price of the air ticket alone was £120,
    but the . . . . was much more than
    that.

The nouns cost and price are very similar in meaning. The price is usually written on something (for example, price tag); the cost is the amount you have to pay (for example, the total cost).

These two questions mean about the same:

How much does it cost?
What's the price?

Notice price is usually a noun and cost is usually a verb, but cost can also be used as a noun. Have you heard the famous quotation: He knows the price of everything and the value of nothing.

6 Idiomatic expressions

Mark each of the following sentences to say something was free (F), cheap (C) or expensive (E):

1. Do you like my jacket? It's made of pure silk.
   > Really? It must have cost you a packet.
2. I thought the hotel was quite reasonable –
   considering how nice it was.
3. Wow! Two weeks in Barbados! It must have
   cost a fortune.
4. I'm not going to New York until February.
   The flights are a bit pricey at this time of the
   year.
5. I got this Beatles CD in the second-hand shop
   for a pound. It was a real bargain!
6. I like the new car. Was it expensive?
   > It didn't cost me a penny. My brother gave
   it to me.
7. New York was fantastic but the trip cost me
   an arm and a leg.
8. We had to get tickets at the last minute so we
   had to pay through the nose for them. It
   was a real rip-off.

7 A box of chocolates

Here are some things you might want to buy. Match the beginnings and endings of the phrases:

1. a box of   a. wine
2. a packet of   b. grapes
3. a can of   c. toothpaste
4. a tube of   d. cake
5. a bunch of   e. marmalade
6. a jar of   f. chocolates
7. a bottle of   g. crisps
8. a piece of   h. beer

Do you like shopping? Have you picked up any bargains recently?

Add your own words and expressions

61 Holidays

1 Basic vocabulary

Match the words with the definitions below. Guide has two different meanings.

1. package holiday
2. trip
3. tour
4. resort
5. guide (x 2)

a. A place where a lot of people go on holiday, usually by the sea.
b. A journey to visit different places.
c. A person who shows tourists around.
d. A holiday where your travel and hotel are arranged for you.
e. A short journey to a particular place.
f. A book that gives tourist information about a place.

In British English you go on holiday; in American English you take a vacation.

2 Collocations

Which word goes with which list below?

tour   holiday   resort   trip

1. summer, package, beach, adventure . . . . .
2. holiday, tourist, seaside, popular . . . . .
3. coach, sightseeing, package, guided . . . . .
4. coach, boat, day, business . . . . .

Notice when you travel as part of your job, you go on a business trip.

3 What people do on holiday

Match the verbs on the left with a word or phrase on the right:

1. stay   a. excursions and trips
2. send   b. a car
3. look round   c. sightseeing
4. hire   d. the museums and art galleries
5. go   e. some postcards
6. go on   f. some souvenirs
7. take   g. in a hotel or a guest house
8. buy   h. some photos

Now tick the activities that you enjoy when you go on holiday.

4 Different kinds of holiday

Complete the advertisements with these words:

beach   skiing
camping   cruise
adventure   sightseeing
safari

1. HOLIDAY OF A LIFETIME
   Enjoy a . . . . around the some of the most beautiful islands of the Caribbean.

2. PURE GREECE
   Clear blue sea and mile after mile of golden sand. Come to the Greek islands for a . . . . holiday you'll never forget.

3. EXPLORE AFRICA
   For fantastic scenery and wildlife, try a . . . . holiday in Kenya, Tanzania or Botswana.

4. NATURAL BREAK
   The best . . . . in France. Tents and mobile homes. Site near beach, pool, shops and bar.

5. SAVE £££'S ON YOUR . . . . holiday. We guarantee you the best snow, the best prices and the best equipment.

6. EXPLORE THE PLANET
   • jungle treks   • remote places
   • river journeys   • ancient cities
   • mountain walks   • white water rafting
   Get off the beaten track on any one of over 100 . . . . holidays in 85 countries. Call now for our new brochure.

7. ONE GREAT CITY!
   Probably the best . . . . in the world – visit the redwood forests, Alcatraz, the Golden Gate, the Waterfront. Ride the cablecar. Fantastic shopping.

Which city does the last advert refer to?
Which of these holidays appeal to you?

Some people take six months or a year off from their studies or job to go travelling. They often go backpacking to remote countries and stay in cheap hostels.

5 Deciding where to go

Complete the following dialogues with the words and phrases below:

long weekend   tourists
brochures   break
high season   abroad
travel agent's

1. Have you decided where you're going on holiday this year?
   > No, not yet. I might call in at the . . . . on the way home and pick up a few . . . .
2. I'm really fed up with work at the moment. I need a . . . .
   > Why don't you take next Friday off and have a . . . . in Paris or Amsterdam?
3. Are you going to Wales again this year?
   > Not likely! I'm going somewhere . . . . where I can be sure of some sun.
4. I fancy a few days in Venice this summer.
   > In August? Right in the middle of the . . . . ! You must be crazy. The place'll be absolutely full of . . . .

6 Asking about someone's holiday

Match these questions with the answers below:

1. What was the weather like?
2. What was the food like?
3. What was the hotel like?
4. What were the people like?
5. What was the beach like?

a. The room was very comfortable and they did great food.
b. Glorious! Warm and sunny every day.
c. Very warm and friendly.
d. A bit crowded, actually – and not as clean as I expected.
e. Absolutely delicious.

Can you answer those questions about your last holiday?

7 Travel advice

Match each extract from a travel guide with one of the words below. The words and phrases in green will help you to decide.

accommodation   money   food
transport   shopping   health

1. You can cash travellers' cheques in banks, exchange kiosks and large hotels.
2. If you're going to the Tropics, most doctors will advise jabs to protect against malaria and also vaccinations against typhoid.
3. Almost all the islands are connected by regular ferries. You can usually buy your ticket on the boat. For the most popular routes it is advisable to book your ticket in advance.
4. The regional cuisine is excellent, with many places serving local specialities.
5. The local market is the place for souvenirs. Prices are low and the quality of local handicrafts is excellent.
6. There are also family-run guest houses in all the major towns. The cheaper options are youth hostels and, away from the towns, there are plenty of well-equipped campsites.

The different arrangements for staying in a hotel are: room only; bed and breakfast; half-board (bed, breakfast and one other meal) or full-board (all meals). A holiday when you cook for yourself is called a self-catering holiday.

Add your own words and expressions

62   Beach holidays

1   At the beach

Match the words with the pictures:

the horizon   beach   rocks   cliffs   jet ski   pier   sunlounger   windsurfer   waves

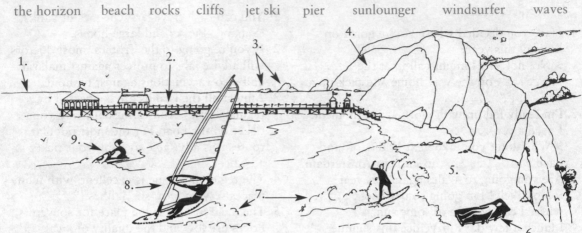

2   Things to take to the beach

Match the words with the pictures:

bikini   swimming costume   swimming trunks   beach towel
snorkel and mask   inflatable dinghy   flippers   lilo

Three people in the picture are wearing wetsuits.
If a woman only wears the bottom half of her bikini, she goes topless.

3   Describing beaches

Complete the sentences below with these words:

deserted   naturist   rocky   crystal-clear   unspoilt   crowded   golden

1. The beach is always . . . . at this time of the year. There's no room to put your towel down!
2. The beaches were absolutely . . . . Sometimes we were the only two people there.
3. Sri Lanka has some fantastic beaches – mile after mile of . . . . sand and . . . . water.
4. Ten years ago the place was completely . . . . , but now the whole seafront is full of bars and cafés. They've spoilt the place completely.
5. The coastline is very . . . . and most of the beach is pebbles. There's hardly any sand at all.
6. The . . . . beach is quite difficult to find, as it's about 2 kilometres outside town.

Pebbles are the small, smooth stones you find on many beaches.

4 A postcard

Complete the postcard with these words:

shining   glorious   deserted   soaking up   tide   luxurious   playing

> Dear Jane,
>
> Here we are in Portugal. The weather's absolutely
> . . . . – the sun's been . . . . ever since we
> arrived. The hotel is really . . . . and we're only
> five minutes from the beach, which is . . . . most
> of the time. That's where we are now. Peter's lying
> here next to me . . . . the sun and the kids are
> . . . . in the sea. The . . . . is coming in and
> we've got to move up the beach before we all get
> soaked! Wish you were here.
> Love
> Emma

Ms Jane Thomson

35 Beech Avenue

Coventry

CV2 3PQ

England

The tide comes in and goes out. We say that it's high tide when it's in, and low tide when it's out.

5 What people do at the beach

Complete the following expressions with the verbs below. Use two of the verbs twice.

keep   go   get   cool down

a. . . . . a lovely suntan   d. . . . . sunburnt
b. . . . . out of the sun   e. . . . . for a paddle
c. . . . . for a swim   f. . . . . in the sea

Now use the correct form of the expressions to complete the following dialogues:

1. This time next week I'll be lying on the beach in Spain.
   > You lucky thing! I'm sure you'll . . . . and make us all jealous when you get back.
2. Why don't you take your T-shirt off?
   > Because I don't want to . . . . The sun's really hot today.
3. My back feels sore. Is it looking a bit red?
   > Yes, it is. Perhaps you should . . . . for the rest of the day.
4. I'm not hot. I'm absolutely roasting!
   > Let's go and . . . .

5. Do you want to go for a swim?
   > No, it's too cold for me. But I will . . . . I'll just take my shoes and socks off.
6. The sea is beautiful. It's so warm.
   > Yes, I think I'll . . . . myself in a minute.

6 When it's really hot

Complete the following text with these words:

shade   sunbathe   exposure
factor   cancer   sunblock

If you're going to (1) . . . . in very hot weather, it's important to use suncream – at least (2) . . . . 10. And for children a (3) . . . . is essential. Even then, it's best to use a beach umbrella and to sit in the (4) . . . . rather than directly in the sun, as experts believe that (5) . . . . to direct sun, can be dangerous and may cause skin (6) . . . . It's better to be safe than sorry!

Add your own words and expressions

63   Forms of transport

1   On land

Match the words with the pictures:

car	train	bus	coach	minibus	lorry
van	motorbike	moped	scooter	bicycle	tram

People who ride motorbikes or bicycles usually just call them bikes.
A vehicle is anything that transports people on land. Lorries are sometimes called trucks in British English and always in American English.

2   On water

Match the words with the pictures:

cruise ship	car ferry	fishing boat	yacht	rowing boat
speedboat	barge	submarine	canoe	lifeboat

Ship is only used to talk about large boats.
If you go on a ferry, you hope the crossing will be calm because if it is rough, you might be seasick.

3   Air transport

Match the words with the pictures:

jet	light aircraft	helicopter	airship	balloon

4 Bikes

Label the parts of this bike using these words:

pedal

handlebars

crossbar

gears

saddle

tyre

chain

mudguard

brakes

spokes

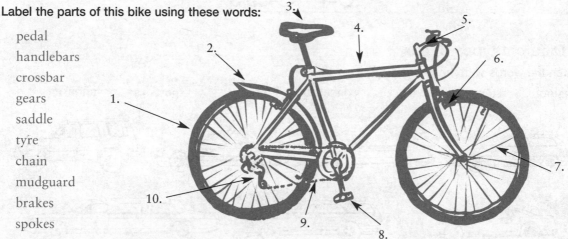

If you want to keep fit, it's a good idea to cycle to work.

5 Talking about transport

Put the highlighted words into the correct column:

1. I always get nervous just before take-off and landing.
2. Our cabin was fantastic and we could walk straight out onto the deck beside the pool.
3. Passengers for Hastings must use the first three carriages only.
4. I got a puncture on the way home and I didn't have a pump with me so I had to walk.
5. All the seats were taken and I didn't want to stand so I went and sat in a first-class compartment.
6. I had a seat right over one of the wings so I couldn't see much out of the window.
7. It isn't easy pedalling up that hill on the way into work, I can tell you.
8. Can you tell me which platform it leaves from, please?

ship	bike	plane	train
. . . .	. . . .	. . . .	. . . .
. . . .	. . . .	. . . .	. . . .
. . . .	. . . .	. . . .	. . . .

6 Collocations

Match each of these words with all of the words in one of the lists below:

car   bike   train   bus   boat

1. motor, speed, rowing, fishing   . . . . .
2. saloon, estate, family, sports   . . . . .
3. slow, express, commuter, freight   . . . . .
4. road, mountain, racing, exercise   . . . . .
5. school, airport, shuttle, double-decker . . . . .

Match the verbs on the left with a form of transport on the right:

6. ride   a. boat
7. drive   b. plane
8. fly   c. bike
9. sail   d. car

Remember you get on or get off the bus / train / plane / your bike, but you get into or get out of a car.

Add your own words and expressions

64 Cars

1 Different types of car

Match the words with the pictures:

saloon   estate   hatchback   convertible   off-road   sports car   limousine

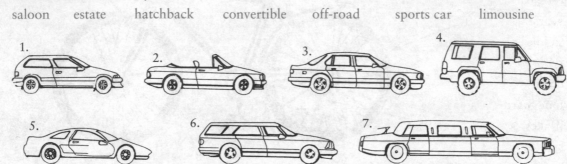

Cars are either automatic or manual. Off-road cars are also called four-by-fours.

2 Parts of a car

Match these words with the pictures:

windscreen wipers
number plate
bonnet
boot
tyre
bumper
wing mirror
headlights
windscreen
sunroof

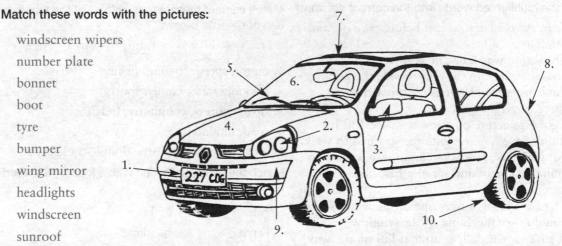

Now match these words with the pictures:

steering wheel
accelerator
dashboard
clutch
gear stick
brake
indicator
handbrake
heating controls
speedometer

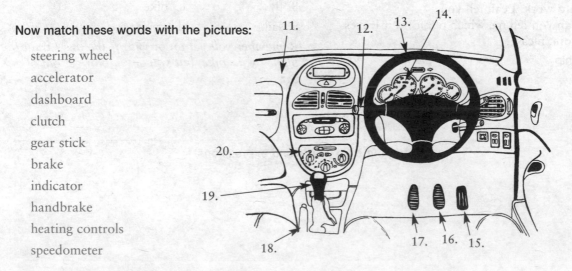

3 Features

Match up these common expressions:

1. central	a. features
2. safety	b. paint
3. power	c. locking
4. alloy	d. conditioning
5. air	e. wheels
6. metallic	f. steering

4 Driving a car

Match the verbs with the words and phrases:

1. fasten	a. the handbrake off
2. change	b. gear
3. start	c. the headlights on
4. take	d. your seatbelt
5. put	e. the engine

Now use one of the phrases to answer these:

6. What do you do when it starts to get dark?

7. What do you do to protect yourself in case you have an accident?

8. What don't you do if your car is automatic?

5 Running a car

Complete the following text with these words:

insurance   repairs   tax
comprehensive   servicing

It costs more than you think to run a car. First, there's the road (1) . . . . , which seems to get more expensive every year. Then there's (2) . . . . , which is very expensive if you are young. If you run an old car, you don't need (3) . . . . insurance – 'third party, fire, and theft' will do. If you're lucky your car will pass its annual MOT test. All cars need regular (4) . . . . If it breaks down, you've got the extra cost of (5) . . . .

The MOT is the annual car test by the Ministry of Transport. What is it called in your language?

6 Driving verbs

Use the correct form of these verbs below:

indicate   start   brake   park
overtake   push   reverse

1. You'll be lucky if you find anywhere to . . . . . . round here on a Saturday afternoon.

2. Wouldn't it be much easier if you . . . . into that parking space?

3. The driver behind didn't know what you were doing then. You really should . . . . . . before you turn.

4. Be careful – you can't see far enough ahead to . . . . . . safely on this stretch of road.

5. A dog ran out into the road and I had to . . . . . . really hard.

6. My neighbour couldn't . . . . . . his car this morning, so I helped him . . . . . . it.

Notice these three sentences: I came by car / I brought the car / I drove. If you go for a drive, you make a trip for pleasure.

7 Can I give you a lift?

Complete the dialogues below with these phrases:

pick you up   drop you off   give you a lift

1. I've got a meeting this morning. I need to get the seven o'clock train.
   > That's a bit early. I'll . . . . to the station if you like.

2. I'm not sure what time I'll be back this evening. I said I'd see Tony after work.
   > Well, give me a call when you get to the station. I'll come and . . . .

3. I'm a bit late this morning. I think I'd better call a taxi.
   > No, you don't need to do that. I'll . . . . at the station on my way to work.

What kind of car have you got? Is it reliable? What kind would you like?

Add your own words and expressions

65 Driving

1 Common collocations

Match the two halves of the following common collocations:

1. traffic	a. ticket
2. petrol	b. lines
3. unleaded	c. station
4. double yellow	d. jam
5. parking	e. petrol

Now use the expressions in these sentences:

6. Diesel, ..., and LRP (lead replacement petrol) are the three basic kinds of fuel you can buy at a . . . .

7. If you park on . . . ., you'll get a . . . ., or you might be towed away!

8. Avoid the rush hour and you won't get stuck in a . . . .

In British English a petrol station *is also called a* garage; *in American English it is called a* gas station.

2 Road signs 1

Match the words with the pictures:

roundabout　　junction　　wild animals
traffic lights　　steep hill　　danger
　　level crossing　　pedestrian crossing
　　　maximum speed limit

 1.　 4.　 7.

 2.　 5.

3.　6.　 8.

3 Road signs 2

Match the road signs with what they mean:

No entry　　One-way street　　No overtaking　　No right turn
Give way　　Bend ahead　　Two way traffic　　End of motorway

1.　2.　3.　4.　5.　6.　7.　8.

4 Motorways

Use these words in the sentences below:

hard shoulder　　inside lane
middle lane　　outside lane
emergency phone　　slip road

1. The . . . . is normally used by lorries and other slow-moving traffic.

2. The . . . . is used for overtaking.

3. The . . . . is sometimes called the fast lane and is used for overtaking when the other two lanes are full.

4. Never stop on the . . . . unless you have to use an . . . .

5. You use a . . . . to enter and leave the motorway.

In the UK motorways do not have tolls. You usually only pay a toll at certain bridges and tunnels.

5 Driving dangerously

Match these words to make common expressions:

1. speed   a. collision
2. reasonable   b. driving
3. dangerous   c. limit
4. head-on   d. speed

Now use the expressions to complete the following:

5. Slow down a bit. There's a 50 mph . . . .
   . . . . on this road.
6. Two drivers were killed this morning in a
   . . . . on a busy road just outside
   Derby.
7. David Petty, who caused the death of a cyclist
   after ignoring a red light, has been charged
   with . . . .
8. If he'd been driving at a . . . . ,
   he'd have had time to stop.

*If you exceed the speed limit, you may be
stopped by the police for speeding.*

6 A car crash

**If you have a road accident you have to give a
statement to the police. Complete the statement
below with the correct form of these verbs:**

crash	skid	damage
lose	knock	swerve

I was driving at a reasonable speed along
Brackley Road when a cyclist suddenly pulled
out into the road in front of me. He took me
completely by surprise and I very nearly
(1) . . . . him down. Fortunately, I
managed to (2) . . . . and avoid him, but
the surface was icy and the car (3) . . . .
across the road. I tried to steer back towards the
middle of the road, but I (4) . . . . control
of the car and (5) . . . . into a brick wall
on the opposite side of the road. I cut my head
and injured my shoulder in the accident. The
car was badly (6) . . . . , but fortunately
nobody was seriously injured.

7 Driving verbs

**Match the beginnings of the sentences with the
endings below:**

1. I wish you'd keep to
2. You've just gone through
3. You're driving
4. I wish you'd stop overtaking
5. You're going to cause

a. an accident.
b. a red light.
c. too close to the car in front.
d. the speed limit.
e. on these bends.

8 Driving fast or slowly

**Does the speaker want the driver to go faster (F) or
more slowly (S)?**

1. Slow down a bit. There's a police car!
2. Can't you speed up a bit?
3. You're supposed to reduce your speed when
   you approach a pedestrian crossing.
4. Take it easy! We've got all day to get there.
5. Come on! Put your foot down!
6. I think you'd better get a move on if we're
   going to get home before dark.

Add your own words and expressions

66   Public transport

1   Basic vocabulary

You catch the bus at a bus stop but you get the train at a station.

A single ticket takes you one way only, a return takes you there and back. If you make the same journey every day, you need a weekly, monthly or annual season ticket.

Sometimes you can buy a 10-journey ticket. These are sometimes called carnets.

2   Public transport verbs

Use the correct form of these verbs to complete the sentences:

miss	cancel	leave
catch	delay	run

1. Can you tell me where I can . . . . . . the number 8 bus, please?
   > Yes, the stop's round the corner in front of the Town Hall.
2. Which platform does the train go from?
   > 18. Hurry up or we'll . . . . . . it. We've got two minutes.
3. Come on, let's go. Our train . . . . . . in five minutes.
4. Sorry. I'll be a bit late for the meeting. My train's been . . . . . . by half an hour.
5. The buses are . . . . . . late again. I've been waiting for nearly twenty minutes now.
6. We regret to announce that the 18.04 train to Bristol has been . . . .

3   On the underground

Use these words to complete the directions:

stops	exit	line	tube	change

The quickest way from the airport to our office is by (1) . . . . Take the Piccadilly (2) . . . . . to Holborn and then (3) . . . . . . to the Central Line. From there it's three (4) . . . . . . to Bank and our office is immediately opposite the (5) . . . . . . to Bank station.

In the United States and Scotland the underground is called the subway. Some countries use the French word metro.

4   Talking about trains

Use these words to complete the sentences:

passengers	hold-up	fares	commuters
timetable	queue	rush-hour	unreliable

1. I see they've put train . . . . up again. That's the second increase this year.
2. I hate travelling during the . . . . I had to stand all the way home again last night.
3. The service is even worse since they changed the . . . . Now there are only two trains an hour instead of three.
4. Up and down to London every day – I don't know how these . . . . do it. It would drive me crazy.
5. I'd come by car if I were you. The trains are so . . . . these days.
6. Sorry I'm late again. There was another . . . . just outside the station – a problem with signals or something.
7. There was such a long . . . . at the ticket office that I nearly missed my train.
8. I sometimes think the only people the train companies don't listen to are their . . . .

In your country, do people often complain about the trains? Do they usually run on time or are there often delays?

5   Station announcements

Use these words to complete the texts:

calling	delay	change
running	arrival	standing

1. We apologise for the late . . . . of the 8.10 from Cambridge. This train will now arrive at platform 2 in approximately 15 minutes' time.
2. The 4.45 to Portsmouth is . . . . approximately 20 minutes late. We apologise to passengers for the . . . . and any inconvenience this may cause.
3. The train now . . . . at platform 4 is the 7.45 for London Victoria, ... at Gatwick Airport and East Croydon. Passengers for London Bridge should . . . . at East Croydon.

6 Travelling by plane

Translate these words into your own language:

1. flight	. . . .	5. cabin crew	. . . . .
2. terminal	. . . .	6. take-off (n)	. . . . .
3. passengers	. . . .	7. landing	. . . .
4. pilot	. . . .	8. trolley	. . . .

And these three common signs:

9. Customs   . . . .
10. Arrivals   . . . .
11. Departures   . . . .

At the beginning of your flight the plane taxis *along the runway before it* takes off. *At the end of the flight, it* lands. *An individual member of the* cabin crew *is called a* flight attendant.

7 Flying expressions

Match the words on the left with the words on the right to make common expressions:

1. departure   a. control
2. boarding   b. desk
3. hand   c. card
4. passport   d. luggage
5. check-in   e. lounge

Do the same with these:

6. baggage   f. desk
7. transit   g. card
8. landing   h. hall
9. information   i. baggage
10. excess   j. reclaim

You can buy a direct flight, *which takes you directly to your* final destination, *or a flight with a* stopover, *which gives you the chance to stop and visit another city on the way to your final destination.*

How do you make a flight attendant mad?
> Complain that it's too hot and ask her to help you to open the window.

8 At the check-in desk

Use these words to complete the sentences:

    window   aisle   pack   left

1. Did you . . . . your bag yourself?
2. Has it been . . . . unattended at any time?
3. Would you like a . . . . seat?
   > No, I'd prefer a seat on the . . . . , please.

Which sentence is said by the passenger?

Remember aisle *is pronounced like* I'll *in "I'll see you tomorrow."*

9 In-flight announcements

Match these words:

1. overhead   a. exits
2. life   b. position
3. upright   c. jackets
4. emergency   d. items
5. duty-free   e. lockers

Now use the expressions to complete these announcements:

6. Please store all hand luggage in the . . . .
7. The cabin crew will now point out the location of the . . . . and demonstrate the use of the . . . .
8. Please ensure that your seats are in the . . . . and your tray table stowed.
9. The cabin crew will shortly be coming round with our selection of . . . .

You need to keep *your seat-belt* fastened *during* take-off *and* landing *and if there is* turbulence *during the flight.*

Do you fly much? What's the longest flight you've ever made?

Add your own words and expressions

67 School

1 Subjects

Match the following school subjects with their definitions:

a. history   f. chemistry
b. music   g. biology
c. maths   h. IT (information technology)
d. economics   i. geography
e. physics   j. art

1. The study of plant, animal and human life.
2. The study of the world's physical features, climate, populations etc.
3. The study of the past.
4. The study of painting and drawing.
5. How to use computers.
6. The study of heat, sound, electricity etc.
7. Arithmetic, algebra, geometry, calculus etc.
8. The study of elements and how they combine and react.
9. The study of financial systems.
10. Playing instruments and singing.

Now mark each subject either 'S' (science subject) or 'A' (arts subject).

In Britain everyone has to do PE (physical education) and RE (religious education). Many people study languages, usually French, Spanish or German. Classics is the study of Latin, Greek, and perhaps ancient history.

2 Exams

Cross out the verb which does not collocate:

do / make / take / sit / pass / fail   an exam

Complete the dialogue with the correct form of these verbs:

re-sit   pass   fail   revise

A: Hi Tara, I'm so happy. I (1) . . . . . . all my exams. I even got a grade A in English!
B: I didn't do too badly, but I (2) . . . . . . biology. That means I'll have to (3) . . . . . . it next term.
A: Oh no, I'm so sorry. You spent ages on biology, didn't you? What happened?
B : Well, I guess I just didn't (4) . . . . . hard enough. Perhaps I'll get it next time.

3 Your school career

Use these verbs:

passed   graduated
sat   got
doing   applied

and these other words to complete the text:

primary   nursery
secondary   college
university   degree

When I was very young I went to a playgroup and then a (1) . . . . school. When I was five, I started at the local (2) . . . . school. School is compulsory in Britain for everybody between five and sixteen years old, but in lots of other countries children don't start until they are seven.

My primary school was mixed, but when I was eleven, I went to an all-boys (3) . . . . school. My favourite subjects were maths and English. After five years at secondary school, I decided to go to sixth form (4) . . . .

In my last year in the sixth form I (5) . . . . exams in four subjects – maths, physics, chemistry, and geography. I (6) . . . . them all and (7) . . . . A grades in maths and physics.

I (8) . . . . for a place at (9) . . . . to study astronomy. It was a three-year (10) . . . . course. I (11) . . . . with first class honours. I thought about (12) . . . . a postgraduate degree, but decided it was time to get a job and earn some money.

Most people go to state schools but some parents pay to send their children to private schools. In England the best known private schools are called public schools. Sometimes students live for the whole term at their boarding school. The most traditional are still single-sex schools but most are now co-educational (co-ed).

Americans go to high school and then college.

Pupils is used until children leave primary school; after that we usually call them students.

4 The school buildings

Match the different places with their definitions:

1. classroom   5. playing fields
2. hall   6. staff room
3. playground   7. chemistry / physics lab
4. gym   8. library

a. where you play football and other sports
b. the teachers' room
c. where students go during breaks
d. a quiet place to read or look things up
e. where you have most of your lessons
f. a special room where you can do experiments
g. a big room where the whole school can meet
   for assembly
h. where you do PE

5 Remembering your schooldays

Complete the text below with these words:

grade	rules
strict	discipline
hour	uniform
period	test

School was very different when I was young.
We all had to wear a school (1) . . . .
There were lots of (2) . . . . and the
teachers were very (3) . . . . We had to
stand up whenever a teacher came into the
room. Once a week we had a (4) . . . . and
anybody who got a (5) . . . . D or E had to
do extra work during the lunch (6) . . . .
My favourite subject was art, but we only had
that for one (7) . . . . a week. Schools are
more relaxed nowadays, but when you look at
the problems in society, I think perhaps we
should bring back some of the (8) . . . .
Is discipline strict in the schools in your country?
Do you (or did you) like school?

6 Being good or bad at school

Put the phrases below into the correct list:

a. work hard.
b. always do your homework.
c. get into trouble a lot.
d. play around in class.
e. pay attention all the time.
f. pick things up really quickly.
g. skip lessons.

1. If you are good at school, you:

. . . .
. . . .
. . . .
. . . .

2. If you aren't a good student, you:

. . . .
. . . .
. . . .

7 School staff

Match the following school staff with their job descriptions:

head teacher	caretaker
head of department	librarian
PE teacher	deputy head
learning support assistant	lab technician

1. I teach football and hockey and other sports.
2. I run the English department.
3. I provide extra help in the classroom.
4. I make sure the doors are locked at night.
5. I'm the boss!
6. I'm in charge of the library.
7. I'm number 2!
8. I help the science teachers prepare their
   experiments.

*The person who helps older students decide what
to do when they leave school is the careers
adviser.*

Add your own words and expressions

68 Further education

1 After school

Use these verbs to complete the text below:

stayed on   applied   got in   do   left

When I got to 16, some of my friends (1) . . . . .
school to get jobs, but most (2) . . . .
I wanted to (3) . . . . sociology, but it
wasn't possible at my school, so I (4) . . . .
to the local technical college. There were over
fifty applicants for only twenty places, so I was
really pleased when I (5) . . . . I really
enjoyed the course.

Now do the same with this text:

results   college   entry   course
degree   prospectus   diploma   high

I had wanted to be a doctor but the (6) . . . . . .
requirements to study medicine at university are
very (7) . . . . . . and my exam (8) . . . .
weren't good enough, so I got the (9) . . . .
from my local (10) . . . . to see what
alternatives there were. In the end, I got onto a
(11) . . . . in business administration. I
got a (12) . . . . , but I still sometimes wish
I'd been able to go to university and get a
(13) . . . .

Further education (FE) **usually means going to a**
college to do a *vocational* **course or degree.**
Higher education (HE) **usually means doing a**
degree at a university.

2 Expenses

Complete this text about paying for higher
education with these words:

part-time   fees   loan
expenses   grant   accommodation

Going to university is expensive. First, there's
the tuition . . . . Then there are all the
books you need. Then, if you live away from
home, you have to pay for your . . . .
The university halls of residence are not cheap.
Then you have all your other living . . . .
A few students get a . . . . , but most have
to take out a student . . . . from the bank,
which can take years to pay off! Most students
have to do a . . . . job in order to survive.

3 A student's week

Use these words to complete the text:

reading	lectures
presentation	term
seminar	notes
tutor	handout
lists	options

1. I've got two . . . . this morning and
   then I need to go to the library to do some
   background . . . . before tomorrow.
2. On Wednesday I've got to give a short
   . . . . at my English . . . .
3. I can't go to my history lecture on Thursday
   morning. I'll ask Jeff to pick up an extra
   copy of the . . . . and I can borrow his
   lecture . . . .
4. Professor Barnes is the only lecturer who
   gives handouts and his reading . . . .
   really save me a lot of time.
5. Later in the week, I've got to see my
   . . . . to decide what . . . . I'm
   going to do next . . . .

University teachers are called lecturers. *In the*
UK the heads of university departments and
some very important academics are Professors.
Professor is not used for any other kind of
teacher. In America professor *is a much more*
widely used term.

4 Subjects and specialists

What do you call a person who is a specialist in
these subjects? Complete the list, using your
dictionary if necessary. Then mark the stress.

1. physics   . . . .
2. philosophy   . . . .
3. psychology   . . . .
4. sociology   . . . .
5. architecture   . . . .
6. history   . . . .
7. mathematics   . . . .
8. chemistry   . . . .
9. astronomy   . . . .
10. engineering   . . . .

We say "He's studying engineering." "He's got a
degree in engineering."

5 Talking about your course

Use these words to complete the sentences:

placement	academic	drop out
qualifications	assignment	tutorial
specialise	vocational	qualify

1. The . . . . year begins in September and runs to the end of June.

2. So, what are you doing this weekend?
   > I'll probably be at home finishing the . . . . I have to hand in on Monday.

3. Hi Mark, where have you been? I haven't seen you for ages.
   > No, I've been away doing a work . . . . in an insurance company for the last four months.

4. The more . . . . you have, the more chance you have of finding a better job.

5. I wish I had done something more useful than philosophy – something more . . . . like nursing or hotel management.

6. Next year I have to decide which area of medicine I want to . . . . in.

7. Dr Hurst seems very remote in her lectures but when you have a . . . . with her, she's really friendly and helpful.

8. Mandy doesn't seem very happy at the moment. Is she finding the course difficult?
   > Yes, I think she's going to . . . . and get a job.

9. What will this course . . . . you to do?

6 Graduating

Use these words in the situations below:

finals	revising
paper	graduation
deadline	graduate
dissertation	coursework
results	term

1. It's your last . . . . at university, isn't it?
   > Yes, I've already done my oral, so now I've got to submit four pieces of . . . . The . . . . is next Friday. Then I've got to do a 10,000-word . . . . and hand it in by the end of May. Then I can relax.

2. Hi Susie, I haven't seen you around much recently.
   > No, I've been at home . . . . most nights. I've got my . . . . next month. I can't wait till it's all over. Can you believe it, we don't get our . . . . until the end of July?

3. Overall, the exams weren't too bad but the American history . . . . was really difficult.

4. It's my . . . . ceremony next week. I think my parents are looking forward to it more than I am. I don't think they realise being a . . . . doesn't guarantee you a job like it used to.

In American English semester *is used instead of* term.

In Britain your first *(undergraduate)* degree *is a* BA *(arts or humanities) or a* BSc *(science). If you do post-graduate study, you may get an* MA *or an* MSc. *After several years'* original research *and* publishing a thesis, *you can get a* PhD *(Doctor of Philosophy). Undergraduates usually write* essays; *a long essay is called a* dissertation. *A* thesis *is longer still and contains original research.*

Remember the different pronunciations of the noun graduate *and the verb* to graduate.

Add your own words and expressions

69 Learning a language

1 Basic vocabulary

Complete the dialogues with these words and expressions:

second language   bilingual   strong accent
mother-tongue   native speaker

1. So, Sandy, what language do you speak in Hong Kong?
   > Well, of course, Chinese is my . . . . ,
   but for almost everyone, English is spoken as
   a . . . .

2. So, Sven, you've been learning English for ten years. That's a long time.
   > I suppose it is, but I want to keep learning until I can hold a conversation like a
   . . . .

3. Where did you learn to speak such good Spanish, Mary?
   > Well my dad's Spanish and I went to school in Madrid until I was nine so I'm basically
   . . . .

4. I find it very difficult to understand Maggie when she speaks quickly.
   > Well, she comes from Liverpool and she's got quite a . . . . I'm sure you'll get used to it.

2 Typical classroom questions

Use these words to complete the questions below:

pronounce   say   difference
mean   spell   plural

1. How do you . . . . . . 'coche' in English?
2. What does 'rush' . . . . . . ?
3. What's the . . . . . . between 'for' and 'since'?
4. How do you . . . . . . this word?
5. How do you . . . . . . 'headache'?
6. What's the . . . . of 'calf'?

Now match the questions to the answers below:

a. It's h-e-a-d-a-c-h-e.
b. 'For' answers the question 'How long' and since answers the question 'When?'.
c. It means *go very quickly.*
d. Calves.
e. Car.
f. You pronounce it /bau/ like 'now'.

3 Learning and practising

Use the correct form of these verbs to complete the text below:

practise   study
say   improve
pick up   make
hold   do

When I first started learning English ten years ago, I could hardly (1) . . . . a word –
'hello,' 'goodbye', 'thank you' was just about it!
I went to classes two evenings a week and I was surprised at how quickly I (2) . . . .
progress. During the course we learned lots of vocabulary and (3) . . . . grammar rules.
The thing I enjoyed most was being able to
(4) . . . . speaking with the other students in my class.

After two years I went to England to a language school. It was in Cambridge. I (5) . . . . a three-week course at a very good school and I stayed with a local family. It was a fantastic experience and I (6) . . . . a lot of new language from speaking with my host family and with other students from all over the world. I really (7) . . . . my pronunciation as well. When I got back to Spain, I was so much more confident. I could actually
(8) . . . . a conversation with my teacher in English.

Now complete these whole expressions from the text. The first one has been done for you.

 9. I could hardly say *a word.*
10. I made . . . .
11. We studied . . . .
12. I enjoyed being able to . . . . speaking with the other students.
13. I did . . . . at a language school.
14. I picked up . . . .
15. I really improved my . . . .
16. I could actually hold . . . .

You can study English with a teacher in a group or you can have private or one-to-one lessons.

4 Grammar words

Choose one of the words in green from this text as an example of each part of speech:

A commuter was extremely annoyed because his morning train was late again, so he decided to go and complain to the station manager. "I pay a lot of money for my ticket and this is the third time this week that my train has been late. What's the point of having a timetable if the trains are never on time?" he asked. The manager thought for a moment, then said: "Well, how would you know that the trains were late if there wasn't a timetable?"

1. main verb   . . . .
2. adverb   . . . .
3. modal verb   . . . .
4. auxiliary verb   . . . .
5. countable noun   . . . .
6. definite article   . . . .
7. uncountable noun   . . . .
8. indefinite article   . . . .
9. adjective   . . . .
10. preposition   . . . .
11. pronoun   . . . .
12. conjunction   . . . .

5 Language terms

Match the language terms below with the highlighted words and phrases in the sentences:

a proverb   a gerund
a phrasal verb   an idiom
a collocation   the 'to' infinitive

1. I decided to do a conversation class.
2. Let me look it up in my dictionary.
3. I really enjoy trying to speak English.
4. "Too many cooks spoil the broth."
5. I'm a bit out of my depth in the advanced class.
6. Please correct me if I make a mistake.

6 What teachers say

Use the correct form of these expressions to complete the sentences:

do the exercises   correct   practise
listen carefully   repeat   hand in

1. I'm only going to play the tape once so . . . .
2. OK everybody, ... after me: "I think I'll call back later."
3. Remember to . . . . some of what you've learned today outside the classroom.
4. I want you to . . . . on page 78 for homework and don't forget you need to . . . . your essays on Friday.
5. I'm not going to . . . . every mistake you make. That would not be helpful.

Now use the correct form of these expressions:

make mistakes   write it down   revise
rub it out   look it up

6. If you're not sure what something means, ... in your dictionary.
7. Whenever you hear a new word that you think is important, ... in your notebook.
8. Don't worry about . . . . The important thing is to try to communicate.
9. Write the answers in pencil. Then if you get one wrong, you can . . . . and do it again.
10. Remember there's a test tomorrow. So, spend a bit of time . . . . this evening.

Add your own words and expressions

70 Jobs

1 Asking about someone's job

Two common questions to ask about someone's job are:

What do you do?

or *What do you do for a living?*

You start your answer by explaining the general area in which you work. For example:

I work in the tourist industry.

Match the beginnings of the sentences with the groups of endings below:

1. I'm	a. an (oil) company. a firm of accountants. IBM.
2. I work for	b. advertising. the (financial) sector. the (fashion) industry.
3. I work in	c. a consultant with a (software company). in the (catering) industry. self-employed.

If you are talking about someone else and you don't know exactly what they do, you can say:

She's some kind of financial adviser.

She's something to do with newspapers.

Here are some more words you can use with company or industry:

I work for a(n)	publishing television insurance pharmaceutical computer engineering electronics	company.

I work in the	travel banking motor construction oil film tourist	industry.

2 Areas of work

Match the description with the area of work:

1. You work for a big department store.
2. You deal with insurance, pensions, loans, etc.
3. You work for an advertising agency.
4. You're responsible for a company's sales strategy.
5. You work with computers and tele-communications.
6. You deal with your company's clients.

a. I'm in IT.
b. I'm in marketing.
c. I'm in financial services.
d. I'm in customer services.
e. I'm in retail.
f. I'm in advertising.

3 Office jobs

Match the job description with the position:

1. The person who welcomes visitors and deals with their enquiries.
2. The person who deals with any problems with the staff.
3. The person who does general jobs in an office.
4. The person who assists the managing director.

a. admin assistant   c. receptionist
b. personnel manager d. PA (personal assistant)

4 Factory jobs

Match the job description with the position:

1. (S)he is responsible for selling the goods.
2. (S)he is responsible for making the goods.
3. (S)he is responsible for testing samples as the goods are produced.
4. (S)he is in charge of a team of workers.
5. The boss!

a. quality controller
b. managing director
c. supervisor
d. sales manager
e. production manager

5 Skilled manual jobs

Match the following definitions with the jobs:

1. They build the walls of houses.
2. They install and repair pipes.
3. They work with wood.
4. They repair cars.
5. They install wiring and sockets.

a. mechanics   d. plumbers
b. electricians
c. carpenters or joiners   e. bricklayers

6 The professions

Certain traditional jobs are professions: the medical profession, the legal profession, the nursing profession and the teaching profession.

Match these jobs with the definitions:

1. Teachers   a. treat sick animals.
2. Doctors   b. perform operations in hospital.
3. Dentists   c. help look after patients.
4. Barristers   d. deal with routine legal work.
5. Solicitors   e. look after your teeth.
6. Nurses   f. present criminal cases in court.
7. Vets   g. treat patients at their surgery.
8. Surgeons   h. give children an education.

Lawyer is a general word for both solicitors and barristers. In Britain only a barrister is allowed to address the court in the most important courts.

7 The emergency and armed services

Use these words in the sentences below:

firefighter   police officer   pilot
soldier   paramedic   sailor

1. John's a . . . . . . in the Royal Navy.
2. He's a . . . . . . in the fire brigade.
3. He's a . . . . . . in the ambulance service.
4. I'm joining the army to become a . . . .
5. My father was a . . . . . . in the air force.
6. He's a senior . . . .

8 Two-word jobs

Match a word on the left with a word on the right to make the name of a job:

1. lorry   a. cleaner
2. shop   b. instructor
3. window   c. assistant
4. bank   d. clerk
5. driving   e. driver

Do the same with these:

6. taxi   f. worker
7. traffic   g. guard
8. security   h. warden
9. social   i. agent
10. estate   j. driver

Use your dictionary if necessary, then translate each of the jobs into your own language.

9 Other jobs

Match the words with the pictures:

chef   postman   photographer
hairdresser   waiter   architect

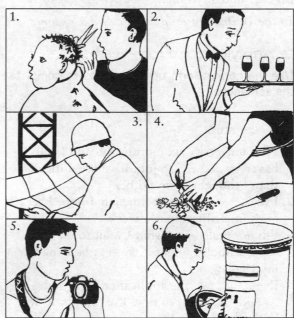

Add your own words and expressions

71 Employment

1 Looking for a job

Use the words below to complete the text:

qualifications	experience	section
application	interview	CV

I thought it would be quite easy to find a job when I left school, but it's been really difficult. I look through the job (1) . . . . in the local paper every week, but everybody seems to want people with lots of (2) . . . . and I didn't do very well at school. I've sent my (3) . . . . . . to dozens of companies in the local area but nobody has got back to me. I must have filled in at least thirty (4) . . . . forms and I've only had one reply. I went for an (5) . . . . last week but it didn't go very well – they said they wanted someone with more (6) . . . . , but I've never had a job! Sometimes I wonder if I'll ever find anything.

In the United States a CV *is called a* résumé.

2 Applying for a job – verbs

Use the correct form of these verbs to complete the sentences:

offer	send it off	find
go into	fill in	apply for

1. I left university six months ago and I still haven't . . . . a job. It's more difficult than I thought it would be.
2. I've . . . . a part-time job. I hope I get it – it's four afternoons a week.
3. I'm not really sure what I want to do when I leave school. I might . . . . banking like my Dad.
4. I've . . . . the application form and . . . . , so now I've just got to wait until I hear from them.
5. I can't believe it. They've . . . . me that job in New York. They want me to start next month.

When you apply for a job, the employer might ask for references *from people who know you, particularly a previous employer. The person who writes your reference is called a* referee.

3 Job advertisements

Use these words to complete the adverts:

salary	experience
temporary	rates
training	leave
applicant	apply
requires	position

Cleaner
Local hotel . . . . cleaner Monday – Friday, 9am – 1pm. Good . . . . of pay. Tel: 01345 876545

Accounts
Full-time . . . . in busy car hire company. To start immediately. Computer skills essential. . . . . according to age and experience. Phone Busby's on 01267 435 985.

Sales Assistant
The successful . . . . must be hard-working, responsible and honest. Previous . . . . an advantage but full . . . . will be given. . . . . to: Mr P Dale, Tel. 01274 768231.

Nurse
. . . . position for three months to replace nurse on maternity . . . .

Your annual salary *is the total amount you are paid over a year.* Salaries *are paid monthly; if you are paid daily or weekly you* get wages.

Sacked!

4 Personal qualities

Mark the sentences P (positive) or N (negative):

1. She's very ambitious. I'm sure she'll be very successful one day.
2. He isn't very reliable. He takes a day off sick every two weeks.
3. She's a bit lazy. She doesn't do anything if she doesn't have to.
4. He's extremely conscientious. He's often here long after everyone else has gone home.
5. She's very flexible. She can adapt to most situations.
6. He hasn't got much self-confidence. He worries about what people think of him.
7. He's very punctual. He's never late for meetings.
8. She's always on top of her work. Her desk is always tidy.

5 Verbal expressions

Match the first part of the sentences with the endings below:

1. I wish he was more independent. He tends to rely on
2. I have to keep telling him what to do. He doesn't really ever think
3. Whatever you ask him to do, he does it wrong. He doesn't seem to have
4. He's just so flexible. He'll adapt
5. You have to tell him what to do and when to do it. He never seems to use
6. You can always depend on him for an honest opinion. He's not afraid to speak

a. his initiative.
b. much common sense.
c. his mind.
d. for himself.
e. to any situation.
f. other people too much.

Notice the complete expressions in this exercise.

6 Unemployment

Use these expressions to complete the newspaper stories:

unemployed   was sacked   be made redundant

Office worker, Luke Bradshaw, lost his job yesterday. He (1) . . . . when he was discovered using the internet to book his holiday during work time. Mr. Bradshaw was amazed by his employer's decision. He said, "Everybody uses the internet at work – the company can't sack us all!"

Around 250 workers at the BMW car plant in Birmingham face unemployment after the company announced that it plans to close the factory next year. 100 men will (2) . . . . at the end of January and a further 150 in June. The closure will have a devastating effect in an area where 15% of the adult population is already (3) . . . .

Go back and use the following three expressions in the same gaps:

was fired   out of work   lose their jobs

You are dismissed, sacked or fired if you do something wrong at work or if you do not work to the required standard. You are made redundant when the company closes or does not have enough work.

Have you got a CV?
Have you applied for any jobs recently?

Add your own words and expressions

72   Working life

1   Working conditions

Read the sentences and then put the phrases in green into the correct list below:

1. I work very long hours.
2. It isn't very well-paid.
3. I get a company car.
4. I get six weeks' paid holiday.
5. They've got a good pension scheme.
6. I'm on a pretty good salary.
7. I'm hoping to get promoted next year.
8. I can do overtime if I like.
9. You can work your way up quite quickly.
10. They run a system of flexi-time.
11. I get a regular pay rise.
12. I get private health insurance.
13. They've said I can go part-time after I've had my baby.
14. I'm taking a few days off next week. The kids are off school.
15. I'm ambitious. I want to move up the career ladder.
16. They give us a bonus at Christmas.

Money	Hours
. . . .	. . . .
. . . .	. . . .
. . . .	. . . .
. . . .	. . . .

Benefits / Perks	Promotion
. . . .	. . . .
. . . .	. . . .
. . . .	. . . .

Holiday
. . . .
. . . .

Benefits are extras you get from your employer in addition to your salary. Perks is an informal word for benefits – "A company car is one of the perks of the job."

2   Talking about your job

These sentences describe what you like or dislike about your job. Match the beginnings and endings:

1. I hate having to attend
2. I love meeting
3. I wish I didn't have to do
4. I run my own business. I really enjoy being
5. I hate having to deal with
6. I get on really well with

a. so much boring paperwork.
b. my own boss.
c. new people.
d. difficult customers.
e. so many meetings.
f. all of my colleagues except one.

If you own your own business, you are self-employed. You can also say, "I'm my own boss."

3   Describing your job

Decide whether the words in green express a positive (P) or negative (N) idea:

1. My job's so boring. It's the same thing day after day.

2. It's so repetitive. I just sit there all day filling in forms.

3. It's very satisfying to know that you've helped somebody through their exams.

4. Knowing that I might have saved somebody's life is very rewarding.

5. I find it very challenging. It requires a lot of concentration and determination.

6. This job's so stressful. It's making me ill.

7. I wish I could do something glamorous like acting or modelling.

8. It's a very friendly place to work. All the staff were really helpful when I joined the firm a couple of months ago.

All of the people who work for a company are the staff; the people who work with you are your colleagues. You can refer to people in another department as "Our marketing / finance / security people".

4 Job satisfaction

Here are some things you might look for in a job. Match the beginnings and endings:

1. I need to be doing
2. I like to know that I'm helping
3. It's important to feel that I'm
4. I need to be given
5. I don't want to be stuck
6. I don't want to find myself doing

a. part of a team.
b. behind a desk all day.
c. the same thing day in day out.
d. something useful.
e. responsibility.
f. people.

If you work, tick (✔)the statements that are true for you in exercises 2, 3 and 4.

5 Problems at work

Use these words to complete the news item below:

strike	union	low pay	rejected
resigned	increase	demanded	crisis

NURSING IN CRISIS

The Government and nurses are no nearer reaching agreement over a new pay deal. Tina Jenkins, leader of the nurses'(1) . . . . , has warned the Government that the union may call a 24-hour (2) . . . . unless the Government improves the 2% pay (3) . . . . currently on offer. Earlier this week nurses (4) . . . . the offer and (5) . . . . an increase of at least 5%. Mrs Jenkins said this afternoon that long hours and (6) . . . . were forcing nurses out of the profession. Last year alone, thousands of nurses (7) . . . . from their jobs, leaving many hospitals in a state of (8) . . . .

Strike can be used as a verb or with 'go':
    Teachers have voted to strike.
    Miners have voted to go on strike.

6 Job or work?

Complete the sentences with work or job:

1. I'm a bit nervous. I'm starting a new . . . . . . next week.
2. I hear you're a lorry driver. I bet that's hard . . . . . . , isn't it?
3. I'm looking for part-time . . . . A full-time . . . . . . would be too much for me at the moment.
4. I didn't really want to go back to . . . . . . after I had the baby.
5. I'm sorry, I can't stop now. I've got a lot of . . . . . . to do.
6. Judging by the car he drives, I'd say he's got a pretty good . . . .
7. I'm hoping to find some casual . . . . . . while I'm at college – working in a bar or a shop.
8. I want to do something a bit different. I wouldn't like a regular nine-to-five . . . .

What is the easy grammatical way to do this exercise? Did you notice it?

7 Job or career?

Complete the sentences with job or career:

1. Jack started as the office junior. Now he's MD. He's had a very successful . . . .
2. I work in advertising. The pay's pretty good but there isn't much . . . . . . security.
3. I'd go mad if I had to do a dead-end . . . . . . like working on a supermarket checkout.
4. Ronaldo was the best footballer in the world until a bad knee injury ended his . . . .
5. Don't you think you should stop travelling and get yourself a steady . . . . . . ?
6. Janet's planning a . . . . . . in politics when she leaves university.
7. I'd go back to teaching if I could find someone to . . . . . .-share with.

What's more important to you – money or job satisfaction?

Add your own words and expressions

73   In the office

1   Around the office

Match the words with the numbers in the pictures:

wastepaper basket

fax machine

filing cabinet

desk

drawers

scales

photocopier

briefcase

computer

files

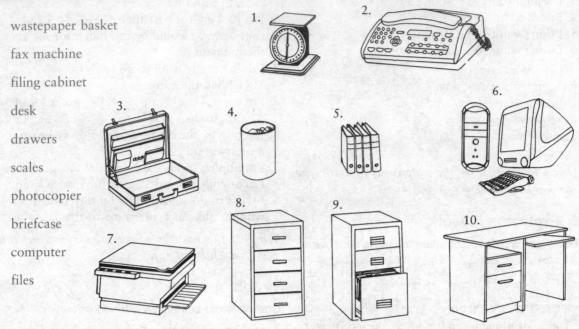

2   On your desk

Match the words with the pictures:

rubber   calculator   Sellotape   paper clip   drawing pins   pencil sharpener

stapler   in-tray   scissors   hole punch   envelope

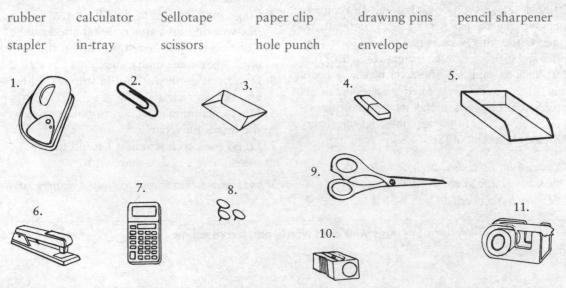

Often you have three trays on your desk – an in-tray, an out-tray and a pending tray.
*British English rubber = American English eraser. In English scotch is a drink, **not** a kind of tape.*

3 Jobs around the office

Match each verb with a group of nouns:

arrange   make   do   send   deal with

1. . . . . . . a problem, an enquiry, a customer
2. . . . . . . a letter, a fax, an e-mail, a copy
3. . . . . . . a meeting, a date, accommodation
4. . . . . . . paperwork, the accounts, the filing
5. . . . . . . a phone call, some photocopies, the
          arrangements, a complaint

4 More jobs around the office

Put each of these nouns with the correct group of verbs below:

a client   an order   a meeting   a problem

meet see (1) . . . . . . deal with	arrange attend be tied up in call off
deal with resolve (2) . . . . . . sort out look into	cancel chair go to (4) . . . . . . have hold
lose place confirm (3) . . . . . . cancel	open postpone report on set up

5 Requests around the office

Match the beginnings of these requests with the pairs of endings below:

1. Can / could you   3. Don't forget
2. Do you mind   4. Make sure

a. ringing back after four o'clock?
   if we rearrange the meeting for next week?
b. you put the date on all the documents.
   the map is enclosed with the documents.

c. to send those disks to Unipart.
   we've got a meeting this afternoon.
d. phone Mr. Baxter in Liverpool?
   fax this through to head office?

6 A busy day at the office

Make answers to the question by matching the beginnings and endings of the sentences below:

What sort of day have you had?

1. Terrible. It's been
2. Really boring. I spent
3. Busy. I had to work
4. Hectic. I haven't
5. Terrible. The phone hasn't

a. right through my lunch break.
b. had a break all day.
c. one thing after another.
d. stopped ringing all day.
e. the whole day putting addresses into the
   computer.

7 Revision

Without looking back answer these questions using words from this unit:

1. What do you put on the wall to remind you
   of the date?
2. Where do you write the date of an important
   meeting that you have to go to?
3. What would you use to cut paper?
4. What do you use to add up figures?
5. Where do you keep all the office files?
6. Where do you throw away pieces of paper
   that you don't need?
7. What do you use to make holes in a piece of
   paper?
8. What do you use to hold two pieces of paper
   together? (two answers)

Add your own words and expressions

74   Business

1   Starting a new business

Complete the text below with these words:

capital	competition	plan
market	facility	investment
flow	products	expenses
overheads	stock	sales

A few years ago I decided to start my own business. I live by the sea and I love surfing, so I knew that there would be a (1) . . . . for surfboards, wetsuits and all the other equipment surfers need. There were already other shops in the area selling similar (2) . . . . , so I knew there would be quite a lot of (3) . . . . , but I still thought I could make a success of it.

I had already built up a certain amount of (4) . . . . in my bank account but I knew I would need an overdraft (5) . . . . , so I asked the bank what I needed to do. They told me I needed to prepare a business (6) . . . . with a detailed cash (7) . . . . I was pleasantly surprised that they immediately agreed to provide the overdraft.

I deliberately opened my shop in May so I knew (8) . . . . would be good, but when you start a business, the (9) . . . . are very high as well. In addition to (10) . . . . – rent, regular bills and so on – you also have to make quite a big (11) . . . . in computers, equipment and of course, (12) . . . .
It's too early to say, but things seem to be going OK. I'm keeping my fingers crossed!

After you've started your business, you then run it, expand it, sell it and then retire!

2   Verbs to describe a business

Choose the correct ending for each sentence:

1. We produce
2. We import
3. We export
4. We've just opened
5. We've just launched
6. We're negotiating
7. We do

a. most of our products to the States.
b. a new range of skin-care products for men.
c. a new branch in Singapore.
d. all our parts from Germany.
e. luxury goods, which are sold all over the world.
f. the final details of the agreement tomorrow.
g. a lot of business in the Far East.

3   Different kinds of business

Match the different types of business with the definitions below:

a. subsidiary
b. limited company
c. multinational
d. parent company
e. franchise

1. A very large company with offices in many different countries.
2. A business that is owned by another larger company.
3. A company which controls a smaller company.
4. A company which sells its shares to the public.
5. A business which has a licence to use the name and sell the products or services of a larger company which provides support.

Now use these words to complete the sentences:

private enterprise	family	firm
shareholders	branches	directors

6. It's a small . . . . business. My brother and I started it three years ago.
7. It's a huge company. They have . . . . in every major city.
8. The . . . . are the people who oversee the running of a company.
9. She works for a . . . . of solicitors.
10. This Government believes in . . . . , so they do a lot to help people starting new businesses.
11. As a limited company we have a responsibility to our . . . .

4 Departments in a large company

Match the departments with their area of responsibility:

1. Accounts / Finance
2. Personnel
3. Sales and Marketing
4. Research and Development (R&D)
5. Customer Services
6. Public Relations (PR)

a. selling the company's products or services
b. developing new products
c. staff problems and recruitment
d. the company's image
e. invoices, salaries, expenses and budgets
f. dealing with customers' enquiries and complaints

5 How's business?

Decide whether the following mean that a business is going well (W) or badly (B):

1. We've just had our end-of-year figures. Profits are up on last year.
2. January and February were quiet but business has picked up in the last three weeks.
3. We're going through a bad patch but I'm sure things will start to pick up soon.
4. Business is pretty slack at the moment.
5. Business is booming. We sold more in the last three months than in the whole of last year.
6. If business continues like this, a lot of small companies will go to the wall.
7. We are now the market leader in our field.
8. We've just taken over one of our competitors. We're expanding all the time.
9. Apparently, they've just gone bankrupt.

If you go bankrupt, you are unable to pay your debts and your creditors can force you out of business. It is then very difficult to start another business.

6 Figures

Only one of the expressions in green in each example is correct. Delete the wrong one.

1. Companies shouldn't expect to make much profit / do much profit in their first year of business. In fact they are probably doing quite well if they get even / break even.
2. We made a huge loss / got a huge loss in the first year. We seriously considered giving up.
3. The company's annual turnover / annual turnaround is over £2,000,000.
4. The budget / expenditure for this project is £12,000. We really mustn't go over that.
5. This month's sales figures / sales numbers are a lot better but the year to date still doesn't look very good.
6. We have set ourselves more realistic sales targets / sales goals this year and we're on course to reach the target for the year by the end of November.
7. We've had a 7% increase / addition in sales so far this year.
8. Sales are up but costs are up too, so the bottom figure / bottom line is disappointing.

The bottom line (in a set of company accounts) is the final profit or loss. "What's the bottom line?" is an idiom meaning, "Tell me what the overall result will be without going into the details."

7 Trends

When numbers change, we usually talk about a rise or fall with an adjective to describe the change. For example, "We anticipate a slight rise in costs." Match the adjectives with the definitions:

1. a slight fall
2. a steady rise
3. a sharp drop
4. a dramatic fall
5. a marginal increase

a. very quick
b. large and sudden
c. changing slowly
d. small
e. extremely small

Add your own words and expressions

75   Crime and punishment

1   Basic vocabulary

Choose two of these expressions to complete each sentence below:

a. serious
b. illegal
c. crime
d. violent
e. criminal offence
f. commit a crime
g. against the law
h. break the law

1. Young men are more likely to __ / __ than any other group in society.
2. In most countries carrying a gun is __ / __ .
3. In most countries drink driving is a __ / __ .
4. Latest figures show that __ / __ crime, such as murder and rape, is on the increase.

2   Crime – nouns

Use these nouns to complete the text:

trial
court
crime
case
defence
judge

If you commit a (1) . . . . and are caught, you can expect to go to (2) . . . . If the crime is a serious one, you will be sent for (3) . . . . Your (4) . . . . will be heard before a (5) . . . . and jury. The prosecution will try to show why you are guilty, while the (6) . . . . will try to show that you are not.

sentence
evidence
fine
prison
jail
verdict

When all the (7) . . . . has been heard, the jury will be asked for their (8) . . . . – 'Guilty' or 'Not guilty'. If you are found guilty, the judge will pass (9) . . . . He might impose a two-year (10) . . . . sentence. If you are lucky, you might get away with a (11) . . . . of £500. The time you actually spend in (12) . . . . will depend on your behaviour while you are there.

In England minor offences are dealt with in a Magistrates' Court. More serious cases go to a Crown Court. If you are not happy with the verdict, you can go to the Appeal Court. To talk about your country's system, you can say, "It's the (Spanish) equivalent of a Crown Court."

3   Crime – verbs

Use these verbs to complete the story:

suspected
questioned
arrested
charged
heard
convicted

A few months ago Ron was (1) . . . . by the police, who (2) . . . . him of being involved in a robbery at a local post office. He had been (3) . . . . previously of petty crime, but never anything serious. The police (4) . . . . him for several hours and finally (5) . . . . him with robbery. A few weeks later he got a letter saying that he had to appear in court the following month when his case would be (6) . . . .

identified
committed
called
pleaded
sentenced
defend

Ron hired the best lawyer he could find to (7) . . . . him. He (8) . . . . not guilty. When he was (9) . . . . to give evidence, he said he had been somewhere else over 100 miles away when the crime was (10) . . . . Unfortunately for Ron, three witnesses (11) . . . . him as the man they had seen at the scene of the crime. He was found guilty and (12) . . . . to three years in prison.

Did you notice the expression petty crime for less serious offences?

Before you give evidence in court, you have to take the oath. You promise to tell the truth. In a British court the full oath is:

> *I swear by Almighty God, that the evidence I shall give is the truth, the whole truth, and nothing but the truth, so help me God.*

If you do not wish to take the oath, you can affirm: "I promise on my honour that the evidence..."

4 Punishments

Choose the correct ending for each sentence:

1. She was sent
2. He was sentenced
3. First offenders can be put
4. She was fined
5. He was banned

a. to life imprisonment / to death.
b. from driving for three years.
c. to prison for 3 months.
d. on probation.
e. £200.

If you are given a suspended sentence, you only have to go to prison if you commit another crime within a certain period of time.

If you are on probation, you stay at home, but you have to report regularly to and receive help from a probation officer. For a less serious offence, committed particularly by a young person, community service is often a more appropriate sentence.

Tagging is when a prisoner is allowed home, but is fitted with an electronic 'tag' so that the police know where he is.

5 Prison life

Use these words to complete the text:

society	inmates
rehabilitate	cells
integrate	released
criminals	recreational

The (1) . . . . of most prisons spend most of the day locked in their (2) . . . . In older prisons, there are few (3) . . . . facilities. Prison is supposed to (4) . . . . offenders, but in many cases the prisoners mix only with other more hardened (5) . . . . and get deeper into the world of crime. When they are (6) . . . . , many find it very hard to (7) . . . . back into (8) . . . .

6 Talking about criminals

Use these phrases to complete the dialogues:

lock them up
get away with it
be behind bars
make an example
bring back the death penalty

1. Did you read about those two men who killed that young policeman?
   > Yes, I couldn't believe it. They should . . . . for people like that.
2. It makes me so angry that so many criminals are let off with a fine these days.
   > I couldn't agree more. Most of them should . . . . Then the world would be a much safer place for the rest of us.
3. Did you see those football hooligans on the news again last night?
   > Yes, they should . . . . and throw away the key!
4. Did you see that story about that guy who was caught selling drugs right outside a school?
   > Yes, they should . . . . of him. Maybe if he gets a really stiff sentence, it'll stop other people doing the same thing.
5. It's absolutely terrible that there are still people who think drinking and driving is OK.
   > I agree. They shouldn't be allowed to . . . . They should be banned from driving for life, as far as I'm concerned.

The death penalty or capital punishment has been abolished in many countries. It has been brought back in some states in the United States, where people are executed usually by lethal injection.

Add your own words and expressions

157

76 Serious crime

1 Violent crimes

Match the following violent crimes with the extracts from newspaper articles:

terrorism   kidnapping   rape
mugging   hijacking   murder

1.
The body of a man was discovered at 10.30am by a man walking a dog in the park.

2.
Three people were killed and more than twenty injured in an explosion this morning. The bomb went off without warning in a busy shopping centre.

3.
The man, armed with a knife and a hand grenade, forced the pilot of the 737 to fly to Madrid, where six elderly passengers were allowed off.

4.
The twenty-year-old woman was dragged into bushes and attacked at knifepoint.

5.
The young boy was snatched on his way to school this morning. Three hours later his family received a ransom demand for £100,000.

6.
Two youths came up behind 73-year-old Arthur Potter, knocked him to the ground and ran off with his wallet and watch.

2 Criminals

Use your dictionary to complete this list of criminals. The first one has been done for you.

1. armed robbery   *armed robber*
2. arson   . . . .
3. blackmail   . . . .
4. hijacking   . . . .
5. kidnapping   . . . .
6. mugging   . . . .
7. murder   . . . .
8. rape   . . . .
9. smuggling   . . . .
10. terrorism   . . . .

3 Other serious crimes

Match these serious crimes to the descriptions:

smuggling   arson   armed robbery
drink-driving   fraud   blackmail

1. Police believe the fire which destroyed a factory last night was started deliberately.
2. Customs seized two kilos of heroin, hidden in a secret compartment in Miss Henley's suitcase.
3. Three men with shotguns held up a security van in East London this afternoon.
4. The woman threatened to send Mr Baxter's wife the photographs unless he paid her £2000.
5. Mr Grey was stopped by police on his way home from the pub and found to be three times over the legal limit.
6. Mr Baker admitted using both his father's and mother's credit cards and forging his father's signature on several cheques.

4 Police work

Match each verb with a noun on the right:

1. interview   a. a crime
2. search   b. an enquiry / investigation
3. launch   c. evidence
4. investigate   d. the area
5. take   e. witnesses
6. gather   f. statements

Put the following events into the order in which they usually happen. The first one is correct.

g. Detectives gather evidence at the scene of the crime, including fingerprints, DNA samples and other forensic evidence.
h. The suspect is kept in custody or released on bail.
i. A suspect is arrested.
j. The suspect appears in court.
k. The suspect is taken in a police car to the police station where he is questioned.
l. The suspect is charged.

If you are in custody, you are kept in prison. You could be released on £1000 bail. Bail is money you lose if you fail to appear in court.

5 Serious crime verbs

Use the correct form of these verbs to complete the sentences:

murder	rob	rape
set fire to	kidnap	smuggle

1. Firefighters were called to a pub in Croydon this morning. Police believe a man . . . . the building after an argument with the owner last week.

2. Police believe that Jenkins . . . . his victim at his home and then drove the body out to the forest, where it was found this morning.

3. The boy was . . . . as he played outside his house this afternoon. A man was seen forcing him into a car. He has not yet made contact with the boy's family.

4. Miss Davies is accused of trying to . . . . . . £100,000 worth of heroin into the country.

5. Two men . . . . . . a post office in Brighton this afternoon. They got away with £20,000.

6. A young woman was . . . . on a train between London and Oxford last night. Police think her attacker may be the same man they believe to be responsible for three other similar sexual assaults in recent weeks.

Now choose the correct ending for each of these sentences:

	a. assaulted by a gang of youths as he left the nightclub.
7. The bomb was	
8. The plane was	b. planted in a litter bin in the shopping mall.
9. The man was	
	c. hijacked thirty minutes into the flight.

If someone attacks you, you are the victim of an assault. They might use an offensive weapon such as a knife.

6 Murder

Match the evidence the police found to what happened to the victim:

1. A gun
2. A knife
3. A baseball bat
4. Marks around his throat
5. Something in his drink
6. The body was in the swimming pool

The victim had been:

a. beaten to death.	d. stabbed.
b. poisoned.	e. shot.
c. drowned.	f. strangled.

Now complete the sentences with these words:

weapon	murder	killer

7. Police are still searching for the *murder*
8. Police now think they are looking for a *serial*
9. Police are treating the case as *attempted*

A serial killer / rapist is someone who commits the same sort of crime again and again.

Attempted murder is when someone tries to kill another person but fails.

Manslaughter is the charge of killing someone when you do not intend to. This could be in a road accident or in a fight.

Add your own words and expressions

77   Theft, drugs, and other crimes

1 Stealing, theft, burglary etc

Match each crime with one of the situations:

burglary   shoplifting   mugging
theft   robbery   embezzlement

1. I can't believe it. Somebody stole my bike from outside the library yesterday.
2. Did you hear that somebody broke into our house when we were away on holiday and took our TV and video?
3. Two armed men attacked security guards as they were delivering money to a bank.
4. A woman was caught leaving the store with four bottles of perfume in her bag.
5. The head of the accounts department had been transferring money to his own account systematically for several years.
6. I was walking down the street when a guy knocked me down, grabbed my handbag and ran off with it.

Use a dictionary to complete this list of criminals:

Crime	Criminal
theft	. . . .
burglary	. . . .
shoplifting	. . . .

Theft is the general word for stealing. The plural of thief is thieves.
Burglars break into people's homes.
Pickpockets steal from your pockets or bags.
In spoken English pinch is an informal word for steal: "Somebody's pinched my bike."

2 Steal or rob

Use the correct form of steal or rob to complete the sentences below:

1. Two men . . . . . . a bank in central London this morning.
2. Somebody . . . . . . my bike from outside the school yesterday.
3. Somebody's . . . . . . the money that I left in this drawer.
4. My car was . . . . . . last month. When I got back to the car park, it wasn't there.
5. We were . . . . . . last weekend while we were in Copenhagen.

3 Crime collocations

Match the words on the left with those on the right:

1. the black	a. £10 note
2. a forged	b. goods
3. stolen	c. market
4. tax	d. limit
5. the legal	e. evasion

Use each expression in one of these sentences:

6. Somebody gave me . . . . in my change yesterday.
7. My brother's lost his driving licence. He was three times over . . . . , so he was lucky to get away with only a two-year ban.
8. The police say that if everybody refused to buy . . . . , it would help to reduce the number of burglaries.
9. It's quite easy to buy tapes of new films on . . . .
10. The Government loses millions of pounds a year because of . . . .

Tax evasion is illegal. Tax avoidance is making arrangements which are legal so that you pay less tax.

4 Anti-social behaviour

Match the words with the newspaper extracts:

speeding   prostitution
vandalism   hooliganism

1. English and Dutch football fans fought a running battle in the centre of Paris today.
2. The local authority has plans to clean up the red-light district near the station.
3. The two teenagers were arrested after they smashed car windscreens and destroyed a public phone.
4. Police said he had been doing at least 65mph in an area with a 30mph speed limit.

Vandals damage property by, for example, spraying graffiti, breaking windows etc. Gangs of hooligans fight in public, for example, football hooligans. Newspapers often use the word thug for anyone who behaves in a violent way. A riot is large-scale public disorder.

5 Drugs

Use these words to complete the text:

| possession | soft | hard |
| decriminalise | barons | pushers |

In most western countries drugs are becoming a bigger and bigger social problem. Many young people see nothing wrong with (1) . . . . drugs such as cannabis. Experts worry that if they experiment with drugs at all, (2) . . . . soon move them on to (3) . . . . drugs. It is quite easy for the police to arrest pushers, but it is much more difficult to catch the powerful drug (4) . . . . who control the trade. Some people believe that it would be better to (5) . . . . the (6) . . . . of soft drugs and to concentrate police efforts on the highly organised gangs who control heroin and cocaine smuggling.

6 Crime verbs

Use the correct form of these verbs to complete the sentences:

| burgle | snatch | vandalise |
| mug | forge | embezzle |

1. Jill's very upset. A man just tried to . . . . her handbag as she came out of the bank.
2. The telephone box at the end of our street is always being . . . .
3. Three houses in our street have been . . . . in the last month.
4. My boyfriend was . . . . on his way home from work last night.
5. Over a period of five years Mr Martin . . . . more than £15,000 from the company he worked for.
6. One of my colleagues was caught . . . . the boss's signature on a company cheque.

7 Contact with the police

Certain verbs are used very often when talking about contact with the police. Choose the correct set of endings for these sentences:

1. He was accused
2. He admitted
3. He denied
4. He was let off
5. He was warned

a. not to drive so fast in future.
   to be more careful in future.

b. of stealing money from his employers.
   of shoplifting.

c. that he'd stolen the money.
   stealing the money.

d. that he was involved.
   being involved himself, but admitted he knew who'd done it.

e. with a fine.
   because it was his first offence.

When the police arrest someone, they don't always prosecute. Sometimes, particularly with young offenders, they let them off with a caution.

They say that crime doesn't pay. Do you agree?

Add your own words and expressions

78 War

1 Basic vocabulary

Use your dictionary to translate the words in green:

1. Do you have to do military service in your country?
2. The conflict in the Middle East is escalating.
3. The trouble began with a dispute over territory.
4. A bomb exploded in the city centre.
5. The United States has been supplying arms to Israel.
6. Russia has been supplying them with weapons.
7. The Government has called the bombing of civilians an act of terrorism.
8. Several soldiers were killed in the fighting.
9. More troops arrived in the capital today.

2 War and weapons

Which word goes with which list below?

bomb   war   weapons

a. nuclear, conventional, chemical, biological
b. nuclear, car, petrol, letter
c. civil, world, nuclear, guerrilla, global

Use words from above to complete these sentences.

1. There have been two . . . . wars in the past hundred years. Let's hope they were the last.
2. The worst kind of war is . . . . war when neighbours end up killing each other.
3. The . . . . war in the mountainous region of North India shows no sign of ending.
4. Thousands of people are suffering from diseases caused by the use of . . . . and . . . . weapons during the recent conflict.
5. Youths threw rocks and home-made . . . . bombs at soldiers during last night's fighting.
6. A Government official was seriously injured by a . . . . bomb, which arrived in his post yesterday.

3 The armed forces

Write the following nouns in the list where they usually belong:

cruiser	submarine	landmine
rifle	aircrew	machine gun
grenade	artillery	minesweeper
bomber	aircraft carrier	helicopter
soldier	tank	parachute
fighter pilot	landing craft	torpedo
warship	destroyer	sailor

the army	the navy	the air force

4 War verbs

Use the correct form of the verbs below:

supply   clear   blow up
bomb   shoot down   explode

1. The United States has been . . . . arms to anti-government troops for years.
2. Planes have been . . . . the city for three days now.
3. They . . . . the bridge in order to cut off the enemy's supply lines.
4. The bomb . . . . as soon as the General started his car.
5. It will take years before all the mines have been . . . . from the area.
6. They claim to have . . . . 5 of our planes.

5 The start of a war

Use these words to complete the sentences:

ethnic	attacks
deteriorates	disputes
process	escalates
involved	force

1. Most wars are caused by . . . . over territory by different . . . . groups.
2. Often there are months of small, separate . . . . before the situation . . . . and . . . . into all-out war.
3. The international community is usually unwilling to get . . . . , but in the end it usually has no choice.
4. Pressure increases and someone – usually the US – puts together some kind of international . . . . to try to restore peace.
5. It is ironic that as soon as a war starts, so also does the peace . . . .

6 War reporting

Choose the correct ending for each sentence in these reports of a recent conflict:

1. The Government has decided to send in
2. The invasion was launched
3. Rebel troops claim to have taken over
4. Several civilians were wounded
5. The rebels attacked
6. Fighting has spread
7. The rebels sought
8. The guerrillas have agreed to release

a. the Government television station.
b. ground troops.
c. to neighbouring villages.
d. help from their allies in neighbouring Chad.
e. in the early hours of this morning.
f. two of the hostages unharmed.
g. in the fighting in the city centre.
h. Government forces with grenades and missiles.

7 Restoring peace

Use these words to complete the text:

ceasefire	talks
peacekeeping	treaty
sides	deal

Three weeks after the United Nations sent a (1) . . . . force to the area, both sides in the conflict have agreed to a temporary (2) . . . . while peace (3) . . . . are held.

A UN spokesperson said that they hoped to negotiate a peace (4) . . . . in the next few days which would be acceptable to both (5) . . . . . . in the conflict. The official added that he was confident that a formal peace (6) . . . . could be signed before the Presidential elections take place in March.

Now without looking back, complete these common collocations:

a. send an international . . . . force
b. agree to a . . . . ceasefire
c. hold peace . . . .
d. negotiate a peace . . . .
e. sign a formal peace . . . .

A ceasefire can be temporary or permanent.

Add your own words and expressions

79 Politics

1 Political systems

Complete the list below with these words:

democracy   president   king / queen
Prime Minister dictator   dictatorship (2)

1. Britain is a parliamentary democracy with either a . . . . . . or a . . . . . as Head of State. The government is headed by the . . . .
. . . .

2. Under the . . . . , Mussolini, Italy was a . . . . It is now a republic with a . . . .

3. People living in a . . . . want to vote, but can't. People living in a . . . . can vote, but often don't exercise their right.

Every country has a different political system. To talk about the British system, for example, you need: MP (Member of Parliament), House of Commons / Lords. For the American system you need: Federal government, Senate, senator etc. For your own country you may say, for example, "The Duma is the Russian parliament."

2 The political process

Only one of the expressions in green is correct. Cross out the wrong one.

1. Politicians / Politics are all the same. They never do what they say they will.

2. I think there should be an election / a referendum on really important issues so the Government knows what the people think.

3. It's easy for the opposition / opponents to make promises but it's much harder to carry them out once they get into power / control.

4. No party had a clear majority. Two parties have formed a co-operative / coalition.

5. No American President can serve more than two four-year terms / periods in office.

6. Britain has to have a national / general election at least once every five years.

7. The Manager / Minister of Finance has said that taxes will be cut in the budget in May.

8. The most important members of the government are all in the cupboard / cabinet.

3 Elections

Complete the dialogue with these words:

voter   candidate
manifesto   power
campaign   polling station
vote   parties
constituency   policies

A: Have you voted yet?

B: No, but I'm going to the (1) . . . . . . on my way home.

A: Sometimes I don't know why we bother. The main (2) . . . . . . might have a few different (3) . . . ., but basically they're all the same – they make lots of promises during the election (4) . . . . and as soon as they're in (5) . . . ., they do something completely different.

B: I know. I saw the Conservative (6) . . . . in town yesterday, but he didn't say anything I haven't heard a thousand times before, and in my (7) . . . . . . the Social Democrat always wins anyway.

A: I voted for the Green Party last time, and Social Democrat the time before, but this time my (8) . . . . . . is going to somebody who promises to reduce income tax and that's in the Conservative (9) . . . . . . , but none of the others.

B: A different party every time! You're a politician's nightmare – the floating (10) . . . . . . !

Use the correct form of these verbs to complete the sentences:

get   call   hold   win

a. I've just heard on the news, the Government has . . . . . . an election. It's going to be . . . . . . on June 6th.

b. In the last election the Social Democrats . . . . . . with a huge majority.

c. I don't agree with anything the Socialists say. They'd never . . . . . . my vote.

Another way to say 'won with a huge majority' is won by a landslide.

4 Political promises

Political parties often make promises in their election manifestos. Match the verbs and the endings:

We are going to ...

1. build
2. create
3. protect
4. reduce, fight, tackle
5. reduce, cut
6. provide

a. crime, unemployment
b. more houses, schools, hospitals, roads
c. more jobs
d. the environment
e. better education, better health care
f. taxes

5 Political ideologies

Use a dictionary if necessary to complete the table:

System / belief	Person
1. capitalism	. . . .
2.	socialist
3. communism	. . . .
4.	fascist
5. nationalism	. . . .
6.	anarchist

Complete this comment using the following words:

socialists   middle   working-class
extreme   right-wing   independence

In Britain both the Conservative Party and the Labour Party like to think they occupy the (7) . . . . ground of British political life. Both parties, however, find it difficult to escape their roots: the Labour Party in traditional (8) . . . . and trade union politics; the Conservatives in the countryside and business communities.

In many parts of the world groups like the Scottish Nationalists would like (9) . . . .

It can be difficult to say exactly what many political words mean because they can mean different things to different people and different things in different countries. As a rule, (10) . . . . . . are more left-wing than social democrats, while conservatives are more (11) . . . . Fascists are people with (12) . . . . right-wing views.

6 Personal views

Use these words to complete the sentences:

liberal   left-wing   extreme
patriotic   right   politically aware

1. My Dad gets very upset if I say anything negative about Britain. He's very . . . .
2. She's got some very . . . . views. She thinks all immigration should be stopped.
3. My parents didn't mind when Dave and I said we were going to live together. They've got quite . . . . views on most things.
4. Students tend to be more . . . . than most other sections of the community. Like most young people, they're usually fairly . . . . As they get older, they move more to the . . . . !

People can have reactionary / conservative / progressive / liberal / radical views on political and social issues.

Mark each of the following ideas:

L (left-wing)   R (right-wing)

5. The rich should be taxed more to pay for education and health care for the poor.
6. People should take out private pensions.
7. Immigration laws should be stricter.
8. We should give more to help developing countries.
9. Nursery education should be free for everyone.

Add your own words and expressions

80   Religion

1   World religions

Complete the text with these words:

Jews   Islam   Hindus
Catholics   Christianity   Buddhism

The main religious tradition in the West is
(1) . . . . Among mainstream
Christian churches are: Anglicans, Baptists,
Methodists, Roman (2) . . . . and
Orthodox. Others are: Free, Evangelical,
Lutheran and Reformed.
In countries such as Thailand and Japan, the
main tradition is (3) . . . .
In the Arab countries of the Middle East, the
main tradition is (4) . . . . , whose
followers are called Muslims.
The (5) . . . . have spread all over the
world from Israel.
Sikhs and (6) . . . . come mostly from
India.
*Fundamentalists are people who take a strict
and traditional view of particular parts of their
religious doctrine.*

2   People and places

**Put the following words into the correct column.
Then mark each person or place C, I, B, J
according to which religion(s) they belong to.**

temple	bishop	the Pope	mosque
priest	church	nun	monk
chapel	minister	muezzin	synagogue
vicar	shrine	convent	monastery
imam	rabbi	minaret	cathedral

People		Places	
. . . .	. . .	. . . .	. . .
. . . .	. . .	. . . .	. . .
. . . .	. . .	. . . .	. . .
. . . .	. . .	. . . .	. . .
. . . .	. . .	. . . .	. . .
. . . .	. . .	. . . .	. . .
. . . .	. . .	. . . .	. . .
. . . .	. . .	. . . .	. . .
. . . .	. . .	. . . .	. . .

3   Verbal expressions

Match each verb with the correct endings:

	a. a sin, an immoral act
	b. God, Heaven and Hell, the devil, evil spirits, reincarnation, life after death
1. worship	
2. believe in	
3. pray	c. God, an idol, a superior being
4. go	
5. commit	d. a prayer, your prayers
6. read	e. the Bible, the Koran, St John's gospel
7. say	
	f. to Heaven or Hell, to church, on a pilgrimage
	g. for peace, that your son will get better

4   Beliefs and rituals

**Now use words or expressions from the box above
to complete these sentences:**

1. In some religions, people say a . . . .
   before starting a meal.
2. Some people believe in . . . .
   but others believe death is the end.
3. Muslims try to go on a . . . . to Mecca
   at least once during their life.
4. Nowadays, in times of conflict, religious
   leaders from different traditions often get
   together to pray . . . .
5. In most western European countries, fewer
   people go . . . . than twenty years ago.

*The person who leads Christian religious services
is a minister. Roman Catholics call their
ministers priests and address them as 'Father.'
Vicar is only used in the Anglican tradition. The
word which is used for all priests, ministers etc is
clergy. Monks live in monasteries and nuns live
in convents.*

*The main Catholic service is the Mass. This is
called either Communion or the Eucharist in
other Christian traditions.*

5 Christian festivals

Use the following words in these descriptions of the most common Christian Festivals:

Good Friday   Easter   Ascension   All Saints
Holy Week   Advent   Christmas   Lent

1. Giving presents is what makes . . . . so popular with Christians and non-Christians all over the world.
2. The week before Easter is known as . . . .
3. Christ's death is remembered on . . . .
4. The forty-day period before Easter is known as . . . .
5. The date of . . . . moves from year to year. The Orthodox churches usually celebrate it on a different date.
6. The four-week period before Christmas is known as . . . .
7. The day when Jesus went to Heaven is known as . . . . Day.
8. The day when Christians remember everyone who has died is known as . . . . Day.

6 In church

Use these words to complete the sentences:

hymn   aisle   altar
pulpit   service   pew
lectern   sermon   font

1. You walk down the . . . .
2. You sit in a . . . .
3. You sing a . . . .
4. The minister goes into the . . . . to preach the . . . .
5. You attend a morning or evening . . . .
6. The main focus of most Christian churches is the . . . .
7. In many churches there is an open Bible on the . . . .
8. The . . . . contains water which is used to baptise children.

7 Talking about belief

Complete the dialogue below with these words:

faith   atheist   devout
religious   agnostic

A: So, Paul, I hear you're getting married. Will it be a church wedding?
B: Well, we haven't decided yet. It's a bit of a problem. Liz and I aren't very . . . . I'm actually an . . . . – I don't believe in God and Liz is an . . . .
A: So, she can't make up her mind if he exists or not! I can see your problem!
B: So, we'd really like to just have a civil ceremony, but her mum and dad are . . . . . . Catholics. Their . . . . is very important to them. So, they'll be really upset if we don't have a church wedding.

8 Religious idioms

Religious words are often used in metaphorical ways. Use these words to complete the sentences:

paradise   idolise   faith   pray   Bible
worships   Mecca   angel   shrine

1. You've done the washing up. You're an absolute . . . .
2. Mark has fallen in love with a girl called Kirsty. He . . . . . . the ground she walks on!
3. We've just come back from a week in Barbados. It was absolute . . . . !
4. Brian was doing a great job at first but recently the team have lost . . . . . . in him.
5. Most young boys . . . . . . David Beckham.
6. The Michelin guide is my . . . . . when I go to France.
7. The barbecue is on Saturday. Let's just . . . . . it doesn't rain.
8. Elvis Presley's house in Memphis has been turned into a . . . . . . in his memory.
9. St Andrews is a . . . . for golfers from all over the world.

Add your own words and expressions

81 Social issues

1 Contemporary issues

Match these issues with the extracts from the newspaper reports:

sexual discrimination	drug abuse
teenage pregnancies	animal rights
gay rights	racism
homelessness	class

1.
The Government has expressed concern that the number of school-girls under the age of sixteen becoming pregnant has risen rapidly and Britain now heads the European league table.

2.
Statistics show that 20% of teenagers in the area are regularly using heroin. Police believe that at least half of the crime in the area is drug-related.

3.
The Government wants us to believe that we are living in a classless society but a recent report shows that 45% of people still believe they are working class while only 25% describe themselves as middle class.

4.
A number of people were arrested today during a protest outside a laboratory where they say scientists are testing cosmetics on monkeys.

5.
The Government is becoming worried about the number of teenagers sleeping rough on the streets in London. Many of them are in danger of becoming involved with drugs and prostitution.

6.
Mrs Fenton claims that she was denied promotion after she told colleagues she was planning to have a baby.

7.
Cardiff police are investigating after a young black student was attacked by a group of white youths last night. They believe the attack was racially motivated.

8.
Airline steward Alan Paul claims he is being discriminated against on grounds of his sexual orientation. He is demanding the same travel privileges for his gay partner as are available to the husbands and wives of his married colleagues.

Now complete the phrases in green with words from the extracts opposite:

a. Politicians say we are living in a . . . . society.
b. More and more young people are sleeping . . . . on the streets.
c. Homeless youngsters can easily become . . . . with drugs and prostitution.
d. Police believe the attack was . . . . motivated.
e. A lot of crime in the area is drug-. . . . .
f. Many people believe it is wrong to discriminate against people on the basis of their sexual . . . .

2 Collocations

Match each word on the left with a word on the right:

1. race	a.	families
2. the gay	b.	rights
3. inner-city	c.	minorities
4. ethnic	d.	relations
5. human	e.	community
6. single-parent	f.	areas

Now use the complete phrases in the following sentences:

7. In some countries people are denied basic . . . . like free speech.
8. Community leaders are working to improve . . . . after a number of recent incidents involving black and white youths.
9. Senior police officers, concerned that there are so few black and Asian officers, are hoping that a new campaign will encourage more people from . . . . to join the force.
10. A recent report confirms that schools in . . . . have the worst exam results.
11. Members of the . . . . have been warned to take extra care after a rise in the number of homophobic attacks in the area.
12. Many of our current problems are unfairly blamed on the growing number of . . . .

3 Problems with drugs

Match the verbs on the left with the phrases on the right to make four sentences. Use one of the endings twice.

Children	are	drugs.
	are taking	with drugs.
	are using	on drugs.
	are experimenting	

Now use these words to complete the text below:

addicts   overdose   soft drugs
hard drugs   dealers

A recent report says that in some parts of the city, more than a quarter of young people are regularly using drugs.

Most teenagers start by taking (1) . . . . like cannabis and marijuana, but many soon begin to experiment with cocaine and heroin. Once they have moved on to (2) . . . . , they are much more likely to become addicted.

People in the worst affected area say that it's impossible to leave the house without being stopped by (3) . . . . asking for money to buy drugs or by (4) . . . . trying to sell them. Last week a 14-year-old boy died from a heroin (5) . . . .

4 What you can do

Choose the correct ending for each sentence:

1. I'm protesting	a. the petition.
2. I went on	b. a demonstration / protest march.
3. I'm boycotting	c. against the new motorway / the arms trade / nuclear weapons.
4. I've already signed	d. them until they pay their workers properly / the meeting.

5 Taking action

Do these verbs fit in sentence A or B?

avoid   tackle   face   ignore   address

A. The Government needs to . . . . . the problem.
B. The Government can't . . . . the problem.

Now mark each of the expressions below, C or D, depending on which pattern it fits:

C. The Government needs to . . . .
D. The Government can't just . . . .

1. leave things as they are
2. do something about it
3. hope the problem will go away
4. take action
5. do nothing
6. act now

6 Other issues

Use the following words to complete these short descriptions of other social issues:

trap   bullying   housing   abuse   domestic

1. We hear a lot today about child . . . . , but it's not new. In the past people just didn't talk about it.
2. One issue which is still a taboo subject in a lot of families is . . . . violence.
3. We don't like to admit it, but there is still far too much sub-standard . . . . around.
4. A major cause of suicide among young people is . . . . at school.
5. Today thousands of people are caught in the poverty . . . .

Add your own words and expressions

169

82   The environment

1 Basic vocabulary

Use these words to complete the sentences:

waste	pollution
protect	factory
recycled	emissions
damage	environmentalists

1. During the last hundred years we have done great . . . . to the environment.
2. There's a large chemical . . . . in our town which has polluted the river twice in the last year.
3. The Government is very worried about the . . . . of our rivers and beaches.
4. A lot of household . . . . like bottles and newspapers can be . . . . and used again.
5. . . . . are furious with the American Government for delaying measures which will reduce greenhouse gas . . . .
6. There are lots of things we can all do to . . . . the environment.

2 What causes the damage

Use these words to complete the sentences:

exhaust fumes	toxic waste
emissions	deforestation
pesticides	crops

1. The Government is introducing strict new rules on the dumping of . . . . by industry.
2. Farmers contribute to environmental damage by spraying . . . . with . . . . which stay in the soil for years.
3. . . . . from factories in northern Germany affect the environment in large parts of Scandinavia.
4. Tropical rainforests have always helped to keep the environment in balance but recent . . . . means they no longer absorb as much carbon dioxide as they used to.
5. . . . . from cars and other vehicles cause a great deal of damage to the environment.

Which verbs cannot be used with *environment*?

damage, harm, injure, destroy, hurt, pollute

3 Consequences

Match a word on the left with a word on the right to make common expressions:

1. global		a. rain
2. greenhouse		b. warming
3. ozone		c. effect
4. acid		d. layer

Now use the phrases in the following sentences:

5. The gradual rise in the Earth's temperature is known as . . . .
6. When heat gets trapped in the Earth's atmosphere, it is known as the . . . .
7. Scientists have found holes in the . . . . , particularly over Antarctica.
8. Rain mixed with toxic chemicals from factories is known as . . . .

4 Global warming

Use these words to complete the text:

floods	radiation	sea level	climate
deserts	ice caps	oceans	gases

Scientists have shown that the temperature on Earth is increasing by 0.1° every ten years. That's one degree every century. The (1) . . . . . . that are produced by factories and cars are allowing more (2) . . . . from the sun to reach Earth. In the future this will have very serious consequences for humanity.

As the Earth gets hotter, the Arctic and Antarctic (3) . . . . will slowly melt and the level of the (4) . . . . will rise. A recent report says that the (5) . . . . will rise by 70 metres over the next hundred years, causing (6) . . . . in many low-lying parts of the world.

There will be (7) . . . . changes, too. Some areas will become wetter while others will become much drier. Some areas which today are green and fertile will eventually turn into (8) . . . . Tropical diseases like malaria will become common in areas where today they are unknown.

5 Environmental problems

Use these expressions to complete the text:

natural habitats	in danger of extinction
long-term	natural resources
way of life	indigenous people
destruction	future generations

The (1) . . . . of the rainforest is very worrying. Thousands of acres of forest are being cut down every year and the (2) . . . . of many animals are being destroyed. As a result, many species are (3) . . . .

This, in turn, threatens the traditional (4) . . . . of many of the (5) . . . . who live in some of the most remote areas of our planet. As with most environmental issues, we need to think more (6) . . . . and realise that everything we do has implications for (7) . . . . If we want to hand on our world to our children and grandchildren, we simply can't continue to misuse the world's (8) . . . . as we are at the moment.

Do the same with this text:

heavily polluted	cloud of pollution
uninhabitable	air quality

The (9) . . . . in many of the world's largest cities is so poor that we have seen an enormous increase in chest and lung illnesses such as asthma. These cities are (10) . . . . and some are permanently covered by a (11) . . . . Unless we begin to take the problems more seriously and start to do something about them, many of our biggest cities, particularly in the developing world, will become (12) . . . .

6 Protecting the environment

Match a word on the left with a word on the right to make common expressions:

1. unleaded   a. bank
2. public   b. friendly
3. recycling   c. energy
4. bottle   d. point
5. environmentally   e. transport
6. renewable   f. petrol

If you want to protect the environment, here are some things you should do. Use the expressions above.

7. Make sure your car runs on . . . . and your home uses sources of . . . .
8. Use . . . . instead of taking your car.
9. Take glass, paper and plastic to a . . . . and your empty bottles to a . . . .
10. Buy . . . . products whenever possible.

7 Green politics

Use a dictionary to fill the gaps below:

noun	adjective	person
environment	. . . .	. . . .
ecology	. . . .	. . . .

Conservationists *campaign* *to* *protect* *the* *environment.*

In most countries there are political parties which aim to protect the environment – the Green Party or the Ecology Party, for example. Greenpeace is an international group that protests against anything which is a threat to the environment, like dumping nuclear waste and, more recently, growing genetically modified crops.

Are you worried about the environment? What do you do to help protect it?

Add your own words and expressions

83   The natural world

1   Natural features

Match the words and pictures below:

river   lake   island   waterfall   valley   cliffs   mountains   rocks   cave   forest

A stream is smaller than a river. Hills are lower than mountains. The Andes, the Himalayas and the Alps are mountain ranges. Forests and woods are sometimes very similar, but use forest if it is very large. For example: the tropical rainforests; much of Sweden is covered by forest.

2   Collocations

Match these adjectives and nouns:

1. thick or dense   a. path
2. fertile or arid   b. hill
3. winding or mountain   c. land
4. steep or gentle   d. shore
5. sandy or rocky   e. forest

Put two of the following adjectives with opposite meanings in front of each of the nouns:

flat   deep   high   low   hilly   shallow

6. . . . . , ... countryside
7. . . . . , ... tide
8. . . . . , ... river

Now use some of the adjectives from 1-8 above to complete these sentences:

9. At . . . . tide you can walk across the sand to that island.

10. Cycling into work is OK, but cycling home isn't easy. There's a really . . . . hill!
11. We should be able to get across the river here – it's quite . . . .
12. Be careful if you go swimming here. The water's quite . . . .
13. The land in this part of the country is very . . . . We can grow anything here.
14. The Netherlands is incredibly . . . . There are hardly any hills at all.
15. Mushrooms grow best on the floor of . . . . , damp forests.
16. The countryside round here is very . . . . so not many people use a bike.

The shore is where the land meets the sea, or the side of a lake.

At high tide we say the tide's in. At low tide we say the tide's out.

3 Describing the natural world

In the following texts one of the words or phrases in green is wrong. Delete it.

1. My favourite part of England is Cornwall. There's some absolutely beautiful nature / countryside / scenery there. There's a pretty little fishing village by the sea / on the coast / on the beach called Clovelly. There's a path that follows / leads / goes out of the village to a beautiful 14th-century church.

2. Bath is one of my favourite places. The river runs / flows / leads right through the centre of the city. It's a very relaxing place and at the weekend people sit and picnic by the side / on the bank / on the shore of the river.

3. Costa Rica is one of the most beautiful places I have ever visited. Wherever you go, you can see the tops / peaks / ends of volcanoes, some of which are still active / alive. Almost as soon as you leave town, you find yourself deep in the wood / jungle / rainforest.

Landscape is a very difficult word to use correctly in English. It is usually better to use countryside or scenery.

4 Trees and flowers 1

Match the words with the pictures:

roots   trunk   branch   leaf   fruit   blossom

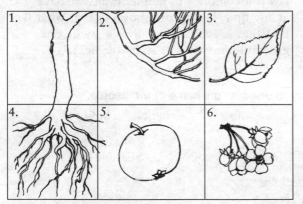

5 Trees and flowers 2

Use your dictionary to translate the following. Mark each of them (T) trees or (F) flowers:

1. oak   . . .   7. willow   . . .
2. rose   . . .   8. lily   . . .
3. tulip   . . .   9. daffodil   . . .
4. birch   . . .   10. chestnut   . . .
5. olive   . . .   11. carnation   . . .
6. fir   . . .   12. chrysanthemum . . .

Blossom is the flowers of a tree (cherry blossom, orange blossom). Buds are flowers before they open. Once they are open all the petals spread out. All trees and plants produce seeds which fall to the ground in autumn. You plant seeds in soil. The plural of leaf is leaves.

6 Famous places

Match the words on the left with a word on the right to make the name of a famous place:

1. The Pacific   a. Canyon
2. The Dead   b. Falls
3. The Sahara   c. Garda
4. The Great Barrier d. Rock
5. Grand   e. Ocean
6. Mount   f. Reef
7. Niagara   g. Ness
8. Ayers   h. Sea
9. Lake   i. Everest
10. Loch   j. Desert

7 Revision

Which is bigger?

1. a forest or a wood?
2. a stream or a river?
3. a lake or a sea?
4. a sea or an ocean?
5. a mountain or a hill?
6. a tree or a bush?

Add your own words and expressions

84 Science

1 Basic vocabulary

Translate these nouns into your own language:

1. scientist   . . . . . .
2. experiment . . . . . .
3. research   . . . . . .
4. test   . . . . . .
5. theory   . . . . . .
6. conclusion . . . . . .
7. discovery   . . . . . .
8. observation . . . . . .
9. results   . . . . . .
10. statistics   . . . . . .
11. sample   . . . . . .
12. evidence   . . . . . .

2 Collocations

Delete the verb which does not collocate well in the following groups:

1. do, carry out, take, perform   an experiment
2. do, make, carry out, conduct   research
3. do, carry out, conduct, put   some tests

Now delete one noun from each line which does not make a strong collocation with the verb:

4. analyse information, results, statistics, somebody's eyes, a blood sample
5. test nuclear weapons, a new engine, drugs on animals, somebody's eyes, the evidence
6. examine the results, drugs on animals, a blood sample, somebody's eyes, the research
7. develop an idea, a theory, a conclusion, a new engine, a new drug

3 The scientific method

Use these words to complete the text:

recorded	discarded
performed	controlled
accepted	formulated
replicated	modified
ignored	tested

Advances in scientific knowledge depend on all scientists following a strict procedure. Firstly, a theory is (1) . . . . in such a way that it can be empirically (2) . . . . Experiments are (3) . . . . under carefully (4) . . . . conditions which can be (5) . . . . by other scientists. The results must be precisely observed and accurately (6) . . . .
If the results contradict the theory in any way, the theory must be (7) . . . . or at least (8) . . . . to take account of the results.
In no circumstances can the results be (9) . . . . Experimental evidence may support a theory but many advances are made when observations disprove current theory. In science, something is a fact or a law if it conforms to all the results we have at any time, but history shows us that what is (10) . . . . as fact or as a law in one generation may not be so by the next.

4 Scientific fields

Complete the table below. You may need a dictionary to discover the name of the people.

botany   physics   astronomy   chemistry   zoology   genetics   biology

SUBJECT	THE SCIENTIFIC STUDY OF:	SCIENTIST
. . . .	fundamental forces, light, heat etc	. . . .
. . . .	how elements combine and react	. . . .
. . . .	space, stars, planets etc	. . . .
. . . .	living things	. . . .
. . . .	the habits and classification of animals	. . . .
. . . .	plants	. . . .
. . . .	inherited characteristics	. . . .

5 Causes and links

Use these words and phrases to complete the patterns below:

what causes   the cause   a cure
a link   why   a way

find   ...... for AIDS
find   ...... of death
discover   ...... of reducing heart disease
discover   ...... between smoking and
                   heart disease
find out   ...... malaria is spreading
discover   ...... the plane crashed
find out   ...... infertility
discover   ...... a plant species to die out

6 How people feel about science

Are the following statements for (F) or against (A) experiments in genetic engineering?

1. I think it's all wrong.
2. I can't see anything wrong with it.
3. I don't see why we shouldn't do it.
4. I can't see any harm in it.
5. We could upset the balance of nature.
6. It's totally unethical.
7. The advantages outweigh the dangers.
8. We shouldn't interfere with nature.

7 Science and society

Use these words to complete the texts:

microsurgery   lasers   robots
test-tube baby clone   breed

1. Scientists can grow crops that are not affected by disease and . . . . animals that produce more meat. They can . . . . plants and animals, by taking a cell and developing it artificially.
2. Since the first . . . . was born in 1978, modern science has helped thousands of couples who could not have children naturally to become parents.
3. Using the latest . . . . doctors can perform operations on parts of the body too small to see with the human eye. In the future patients will not have to worry about operations leaving scars as they will be performed with . . . .
4. Life in the twenty-first century will be much easier for most people. More and more dangerous jobs will be done by . . . .

Now match each of the following headings with one of the texts above:

genetic engineering   automation
medical science   fertility treatment

What happened?
I'm half man...
...half fly!

TRANSPORTER 1

Add your own words and expressions

85   Materials

1   What's it made of?

Use the following words in the sentences below:

metal	wood	glass	rubber
plastic	leather	wax	cardboard

1. The characters in Madame Tussaud's are made of . . . .
2. Most wine bottles are made of green, brown or clear . . . .
3. Car tyres are made of . . . .
4. A few cars are made of fibre glass, but most are made of . . . .
5. Shampoo bottles and washing-up liquid both come in . . . . bottles.
6. Today most yachts are made of fibre glass, but they used to be made of . . . .
7. Most people wear shoes with . . . . uppers, but plastic soles. The most expensive shoes also have . . . . soles.
8. Cornflakes and other breakfast cereals come in . . . . boxes.

Divide the 8 words above into two groups and add the following words to the groups:

oil	paper	fibre glass	nylon
cotton	chalk	wool	petrol

A: bio-degradable: . . . .

B: non-bio-degradable: . . . .

2   Metal, wood and precious stones

Put the following words into the correct list:

iron	gold	diamond	steel
oak	silver	emerald	tin
pine	copper	platinum	ruby
lead	walnut	mahogany	bamboo
brass	beech	aluminium	bronze

precious stones   **precious metals**

. . . .

. . . .

. . . .

other metals   **types of wood**

. . . .

. . . .

. . . .

. . . .

. . . .

. . . .

What are each of the following made of? Use words from the lists opposite:

1. The blade of a kitchen knife.
2. The medal if you win an Olympic event.
3. The medals if you come second or third.
4. A trumpet or trombone.
5. Railway tracks.
6. A coke can.

Now answer the following questions, using the words opposite:

7. Which precious stone is green?
8. Which type of wood is the most expensive?
9. Which metal has the symbol Pb?
10. Which metals are alloys?

Metals and other minerals are mined from the earth by miners working in diamond, gold, tin, or coal mines.

Many semi-precious stones, and pearls, which are found in oysters, are used to make jewellery.

British English aluminium = American English aluminum.

176

3 Fabrics

Are the following fabrics natural (N) or synthetic (S)?

1. cotton		4. polyester	
2. nylon		5. denim	
3. wool		6. silk	

Now match the groups of adjectives with the most likely noun:

7. cotton, woollen, woolly   a. handbag

8. leather, denim, sheepskin   b. stockings

9. leather, plastic, snakeskin   c. jumper

10. silk, nylon   d. jacket

Suede is very soft leather with a rough finish, used to make shoes, handbags, jackets and coats.

4 Word pairs

Match the materials with the objects:

1. a tin   a. ring

2. a diamond   b. jacket

3. a suede   c. can

4. a pearl   d. scarf

5. a silk   e. necklace

Do the same with these more unusual materials:

6. a pine   f. glass

7. a copper   g. spoon

8. a wooden   h. band

9. a rubber   i. table

10. a crystal   j. bracelet

Which one of the following collocations is wrong?

> pure gold
> pure leather
> pure silver
> pure silk
> pure wool

Do you know the correct way to say it?

5 Materials idioms

Types of material are often used in idiomatic expressions. Use these words to complete the dialogues:

wood	stone	silver	gold
golden	iron	lead	steel

1. I'm hoping to go and see the men's tennis final at Wimbledon this year.
   > You'll be lucky! Tickets are like . . . . . . dust.

2. I thought Jane would be nervous giving that lecture. There were more than two hundred people there.
   > No, not Jane. She's got nerves of . . . .

3. How long have you been driving now?
   > Ten years and I've never had an accident. Touch . . . . . . !

4. I hear you've lost your job.
   > Yes, it seemed like really bad news, but every cloud has a . . . . . . lining – I've got a new job at double the salary!

5. What's your boss like? I hear he's a bit of a dictator.
   > He rules with an . . . . . . fist. If anybody disagrees with him, they're out!

6. I've been offered a job in New York, but I'm not sure about going to live abroad.
   > You really should think about it. It sounds like a . . . . . . opportunity to me.

7. We need to go to the supermarket.
   > Yes, and I need some cash. Let's go to Asda – they've got a cash machine there. We can kill two birds with one . . . .

8. Did you have a good day at work?
   > Not exactly! When I told my boss I needed a couple of days off, it went down like a . . . . . . balloon. She was not a happy woman!

Now go back and underline the complete idioms. How many of them are the same in your language?

Add your own words and expressions

86   History

1 Basic vocabulary 1

Use these words to complete the sentences:

> ancestors   ancient   empire
> date   event   primitive

1. In the future, historians may well think that man landing on the moon was the most important . . . . of the 20th century.
2. Our . . . . invented writing nearly 10,000 years ago.
3. . . . . humans lived in caves and hunted animals for food.
4. Many . . . . civilisations, for example, the Mayan and Roman, were very advanced and in many ways surprisingly modern.
5. The Romans built a huge . . . . which stretched from Britain to parts of Asia.
6. The tools found on this site . . . . from around 250,000 BC.

Prehistoric refers to the time before anything was written down. Ancient is mostly used in the expressions: ancient Greece, Egypt, or Rome.

2 Basic vocabulary 2

Use the following words to complete these paragraphs:

> records   artefacts   origins   archaeologists

History is the study of the main events, people and periods of the past. Experts who wish to know about our very earliest (1) . . . . need to rely on evidence such as buildings and (2) . . . . uncovered by (3) . . . . as we have no written (4) . . . . from the earliest times.

> accounts   sources   documents   periods

Those who study later (5) . . . . often have access to written records, but to give a balanced and accurate account of a historical event, historians also look at literature, art and, if they are lucky, study eye-witness (6) . . . . of the events. These may be found in private letters or other (7) . . . . Good historical research depends on the use of a wide range of original (8) . . . .

3 Verbs to talk about historical events

If you write about history, you need lots of verbs which describe changes. Choose the correct ending for each of these sentences:

1. Television was	a. invaded by the Romans 2,000 years ago.
2. Many parts of Africa were	b. discovered by Michael Faraday.
3. Britain was	c. signed in June 1919.
4. Electricity was	d. abolished in the United States in 1865.
5. John Kennedy was	e. reunited after the collapse of Communism.
6. Slavery was	f. caused by potato famine in the 1840's.
7. Mussolini was	g. invented in 1926.
8. The Treaty of Versailles was	h. assassinated in 1963.
9. The European Union was first	i. deposed in 1943.
10. Irish emigration to the United States was	j. formed over forty years ago.
11. The Health Service in the UK was	k. colonised in the eighteenth century.
12. Germany was	l. introduced shortly after the Second World

Form nouns from some of the verbs above to complete these phrases:

13. The . . . . of Britain by the Romans
14. The . . . . of electricity
15. The . . . . of Africa
16. The . . . . of slavery
17. The . . . . of television
18. The . . . . of John Kennedy

4 Historical events

Match the periods and events with the dates:

1. The Second World War ended	a. approximately 75 million years ago.
2. The Egyptians built the pyramids	b. around 50,000 BC.
3. Cavemen made the first tools from stone	c. around 3,000 BC.
4. The Russian Revolution took place	d. from 1914 to 1918.
5. The Space Age started	e. in late 1917.
6. Dinosaurs lived on Earth	f. until the middle of the 19th century.
7. The First World War lasted	g. from 1945 to the end of the 1980's.
8. The Cold War lasted	h. in 1945.
9. The slave trade lasted	i. when the Russians launched the Sputnik.

A historical event is anything that happens in history, but a historic event is an important event. So you can say, for example, "Today is a historic day for our country as we vote for a new President." Notice that we refer to decades as the twenties, the sixties etc.

5 Periods in history

Put the following historical periods in the correct order. Number them 1 – 10, with 1 the earliest.

the Roman Empire	the Stone Age
the French Revolution	the Reformation
the end of the last century	the Ice Age
the early nineteenth century	the Middle Ages
the Great Depression	the Renaissance

6 Historical figures

Cover the right hand column and try to describe each of the historical figures in the list. Then match the names and descriptions:

1. Tutankhamun	a. a Roman emperor
2. Cleopatra	b. a Nazi dictator
3. Plato	c. a king of England
4. Julius Caesar	d. a Greek philosopher
5. King Henry VIII	e. an Egyptian queen
6. Genghis Khan	f. an Indian spiritual leader
7. Mahatma Gandhi	g. an Egyptian pharaoh
8. Adolf Hitler	h. a Russian revolutionary
9. Leon Trotsky	i. a Mongol warrior

7 Time phrases

Translate the phrases in green into your own language.

In ancient times people believed the Earth was the centre of the universe. More recently, Galileo showed that the Earth moved round the sun.

Early in the 20th century, Einstein proposed his theory of relativity. Until then, most scientists believed Newton's laws were a perfect description of our universe. Subsequently, quantum theory and, later still, chaos theory have changed our understanding again. In our own times, new discoveries are being made which will mean further changes to our understanding.

1. in ancient times   . . . .
2. more recently   . . . .
3. until then   . . . .
4. subsequently   . . . .
5. later still   . . . .
6. in our own times   . . . .

Add your own words and expressions

87   Countries and nationalities

1   Parts of the world

Match these parts of the world with the numbers 1 – 16 on the map:

. . . Africa	. . . the Mediterranean	. . . South America	. . . the Middle East
. . . the Arctic	. . . South East Asia	. . . Central America	. . . Scandinavia
. . . Antarctica	. . . the British Isles	. . . the Far East	. . . North America
. . . Asia	. . . North Africa	. . . the Caribbean	. . . Central Europe

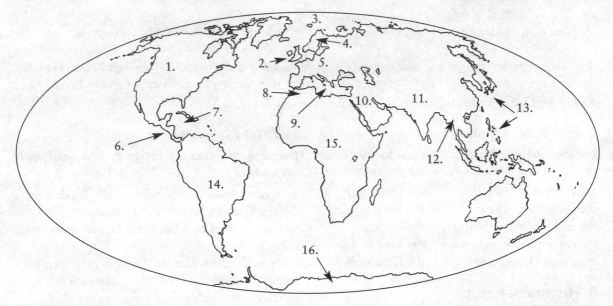

2   Countries

Do you know how to pronounce these countries? Check and mark the stress in any you may need. The first one has been done for you.

Algeria	Argentina	Australia	Austria	Belgium	Brazil	Canada	Chile	China
Colombia	Denmark	Egypt	Ethiopia	Finland	Germany	Hungary	India	Indonesia
Iran	Ireland	Israel	Italy	Japan	Korea	Kuwait	Lebanon	Malaysia
Mexico	Morocco	Norway	Pakistan	Peru	Poland	Portugal	Romania	Russia
Slovenia	Sri Lanka	Sweden	Taiwan	Tibet	Tunisia	Turkey	Vietnam	Zimbabwe

There are four common suffixes used to make the nationality adjective:

-ish (Spanish)   -(i)an (Albanian)   -ese (Portuguese)   -i (Saudi)

Use your dictionary if necessary to complete the lists. You may need to change the spelling.

1. -ish . . . .

. . . .

2. -(i)an . . . .

. . . .

3. -ese . . . .

4. -i . . . .

3 Exceptions

The following adjectives do not follow any of the four patterns in exercise 2. What are the countries?

1. French . . . .
2. Greek . . . .
3. Icelandic . . . .
4. Welsh . . . .
5. Thai . . . .
6. Swiss . . . .
7. Cypriot . . . .
8. Dutch . . . .

4 People

Complete the sentences with the name of the people from the country given:

1. People often say that the . . . . aren't as warm and friendly as other Europeans. *(Britain)*
2. We do quite a lot of business with the . . . . *(Japan)*
3. The . . . . and the . . . . have always been at the centre of the drive for European integration. *(France, Germany)*
4. Many people think the . . . . invented the sauna, but actually it was the . . . . *(Sweden, Finland)*
5. Some . . . . speak French, while others speak German or Italian. *(Switzerland)*
6. Lots of . . . . came to Britain before the Second World War. *(Poland)*

5 Major cities

Do you know how to pronounce the English names of these major cities? Mark the stress.

Athens	Amsterdam	Bangkok	Beijing
Berlin	Brussels	Cairo	Copenhagen
Dublin	Edinburgh	Helsinki	Lisbon
London	Madrid	Milan	Moscow
Nairobi	Naples	New York	Paris
Rejkavik	Stockholm	Tokyo	Warsaw

6 Languages

The word for a language is often the same as the adjective:

Germans speak German.

Remember, however, there are many languages which are not the name of countries, particularly those spoken in regions of a country. For many people the language they speak is a politically sensitive matter. Here are some expressions to help you talk about languages:

He speaks Swiss-German.
There's a Swedish-speaking minority in Finland.
Her first language is Catalan.
Her mother tongue is Irish Gaelic.

Some very important languages are the main or official language in certain parts of the world. Match the languages below with the places. Two of the languages are spoken in one of the countries.

1. Hebrew	a. China
2. Mandarin	b. Iran
3. Cantonese	c. Israel
4. Hindi	d. Saudi Arabia, Iraq, Egypt
5. Arabic	e. India
6. Farsi	

7 It's somewhere in Africa

Complete the sentences with in or on:

1. It's somewhere . . . Central America.
2. It's . . . the west coast of Africa.
3. I think it's . . . the Balkans.
4. It's right . . . the equator.
5. It's . . . the other side of the world.
6. It's . . . the border of Argentina and Chile.
7. It's . . . the Far East, isn't it?
8. It's right . . . the middle of Russia.
9. It's . . . the Arctic.

Add your own words and expressions

181

88   The weather

1 Basic vocabulary

The climate *refers to the general weather conditions in a place. For example:*

> *Parts of southern England have an almost Mediterranean climate for part of the year.*
> *Some people think pollution is causing* climate change *in many parts of the world.*

In countries with a tropical climate there is a dry season *and a* rainy season. *In Europe there are four seasons. Translate these into your language:*

1. spring . . . . .   2. summer . . . . . .   3. autumn . . . . . .   4. winter . . . . . .

British English autumn *= American English* fall.

2 What's the weather like?

Match the sentences on the left with the related sentences on the right:

1. It was sunny and very hot.   a. We had thunder and lightning.

2. We had a lot of rain.   b. There were a few wintry showers.

3. It snowed on and off.   c. It was quite misty.

4. It was very windy.   d. It was very overcast.

5. It was dull and cloudy.   e. There was a bit of drizzle.

6. We had some light rain.   f. There was quite a breeze.

7. It was a bit foggy.   g. We had a bit of a heatwave.

8. There was the most awful storm.   h. It was very wet.

Now put the following adjectives into the correct pattern below:

    lovely   miserable   beautiful   horrible   fabulous   glorious   terrible   foul

9. What . . . . / . . . . / . . . . / . . . . weather! It hasn't stopped raining all day.

10. What . . . . / . . . . / . . . . / . . . . weather! Let's go down to the beach.

A breeze *is a fairly strong wind. It is not as strong as a* gale.
Fog is much thicker than mist. *It's often misty in the mornings or in the mountains.*
Drizzle is very fine rain.
If it is overcast, *it is very dull.*
Wintry showers is used on weather forecasts to mean a little snow.

When would you expect to see a rainbow?

3 Weather collocations

Match each group of adjectives with one of the nouns on the right:

		Now complete these expressions with a word on the right:	
1. light, steady, heavy, torrential	a. storm	6. a gust of	f. ice
2. light, stiff	b. fog	7. a ray of	g. bad weather
3. dense, thick, patchy	c. sky	8. a sheet of	h. wind
4. severe, tropical	d. breeze	9. a blanket of	i. sunshine
5. clear, blue, grey, cloudless	e. rain	10. a spell of	j. snow

4 Temperature words

Use these words to complete the sentences:

> freezing   cool   mild
> warm   humid   chilly

1. It's absolutely . . . . . . out. I'd put a coat on if I were you.
2. We've had lovely sunshine. It's been so . . . . I've been on the beach every day.
3. I was on holiday in Thailand last month. It was so . . . . . . all the time. Thank goodness the hotel had air-conditioning.
4. It was pretty hot down at the beach but there was a lovely . . . . . . breeze.
5. It's a bit . . . . . . in here. I think I'll put the heating on.
6. We haven't had a bad winter at all. It's been very . . . . . . for the time of year.

5 Wet weather

Choose the correct ending for each sentence:

1. It's pouring . . . .
2. I'm soaked! I just got caught . . . .
3. It looks like it's going to rain. If I were you, I'd take . . . .
4. The weather's terrible. I hope it clears up . . . .
5. It suddenly started pouring down. I had to shelter . . . .
6. My feet are soaking wet. I got out of the car and stepped . . . .

a. a bit later.
b. in a doorway.
c. an umbrella.
d. in a huge puddle.
e. in that heavy shower.
f. with rain out there!

When the rain is very heavy, we say that it's pouring. It is rare for people to say that it's raining cats and dogs. This is an idiom taught by English teachers, but seldom used!

6 Weather forecasts

Use the correct form of the verbs to complete the forecast:

> rise   fall   reach   remain

Tomorrow the south will again (1) . . . . . . warm and dry. Temperatures could (2) . . . . . . 25°C during the afternoon. In the north, the day will start quite cool, but temperatures will (3) . . . . . . gradually during the day. Later in the week the weather will turn cold and night-time temperatures could (4) . . . . . . as low as 8°C.

Now use these words to complete the next forecast:

> wintry   icy   melt   sleet   frost

Tonight will be cold and most parts of the country can expect an overnight (5) . . . . . Tomorrow will also be bitterly cold with (6) . . . . . . showers in many places. Rain or (7) . . . . . . will turn to snow, especially on high ground, later in the day. Roads will be (8) . . . . . . and drivers are advised to take extra care. At the weekend daytime temperatures could fall below zero and there will be snow in most parts of the country. Monday will be a little warmer and by Tuesday morning the snow will begin to (9) . . . .

7 Vocabulary notes

Here are some notes on special expressions used to talk about the weather:

1. When a clear sky becomes cloudy, we say, "It's clouding over." When it improves, we say, "It's clearing up."
2. A long spell of unusually hot weather is called a heatwave. A cold spell is sometimes called a cold snap.
3. Another word for chilly is nippy.

Add your own words and expressions

---

89   Disasters

1   Natural disasters

Use the following words in the definitions below:

forest fire	hurricane	tornado	earthquake
flood	drought	volcano	tidal wave

1. . . . .   a long period with little or no rain

2. . . . .   a sudden violent movement of the surface of the earth, caused by the shifting of the earth's tectonic plates

3. . . . .   when huge areas of woodland are alight, often caused by someone carelessly throwing a cigarette from a car

4. . . . .   when an area of land which is usually dry becomes covered in water, often forcing people to leave their homes

5. . . . .   very strong circular winds which suck things up into them

6. . . . .   a huge wave which builds up in the sea over thousands of miles

7. . . . .   a very powerful storm, often at sea

8. . . . .   a large mountain which erupts from time to time and sends rocks up into the air and molten rock pours down the side

Now use the words in the these sentences:

9. Mount Vesuvius near Naples is one of the most famous . . . . in the world.

10. Many parts of sub-Saharan Africa suffer from . . . .

11. Many low-lying parts of England suffer from . . . . after prolonged periods of rain in the winter.

12. San Francisco and Tokyo are both situated right in the middle of dangerous . . . . zones.

2   Describing disasters

Now match each of the following descriptions with one of the disasters above:

1. This year's crop has been lost. The land here is so dry now that farmers are unable to grow anything. All the waterholes have dried up and there are dead animals everywhere.

2. The water level has been rising steadily since the river burst its banks this morning and the area is now under two metres of water.

3. Along the path of the twister cars were lifted hundreds of metres into the air. One caravan ended up half a mile from where it had been.

4. Lava poured down the side of the mountain destroying everything in its path and the village is now buried under a carpet of ash.

5. The tremor, measuring 6 on the Richter scale, only lasted for four seconds but it was enough to cause large cracks in several roads.

6. A small fishing village was the worst hit. A thirty-metre wall of water swept up the beach destroying nearly thirty houses along the seafront.

7. Helicopters are spraying the blaze from the air, and fire crews are working round the clock to set up firebreaks to prevent it spreading further.

8. Roofs were blown off buildings and trees were ripped out by their roots in winds gusting up to 120mph.

Now complete these sentences with words and phrases from above:

a. The river . . . . its banks.

b. The tremor only . . . . for four seconds.

c. The lava destroyed everything . . . .

d. Fire crews are working . . . .

e. Buildings had their roofs . . . .

f. Trees were . . . . by their roots.

3 An earthquake

Complete the text below with these words:

trapped	struck
destroyed	rubble
injured	claimed
survivors	damage

The earthquake which (1) . . . . Los Angeles yesterday is now believed to have (2) . . . . more than seventy lives. Hundreds more people have been (3) . . . .

The quake, which started at about 5am while most people were asleep, has caused extensive (4) . . . . Several large buildings collapsed and many smaller ones have been completely (5) . . . . A number of roads leading into the city are unusable.

Rescue teams are continuing to search for (6) . . . . who may be (7) . . . . in the (8) . . . .

The place where an earthquake starts is called the epicentre. *Tremors which happen after the main earthquake are called* aftershocks.

4 Floods

Use these words to complete the text:

stranded	affected	impassable
warnings	rescued	rainfall

Flooding has returned to parts of the south west after the equivalent of a month's (1) . . . . fell in just 48 hours. In parts of Avon, one of the worst (2) . . . . areas, soldiers have been called in to help evacuate homes which are waist-deep in water. Thirty children had to be (3) . . . . from a school bus after they were (4) . . . . in flood water near Bristol. Many roads in the county are (5) . . . . Weather forecasters have also issued 25 flood (6) . . . . . . in other parts of the west of England. More rain is expected tonight.

5 Drought

Use these words to complete the text below:

starvation	epidemic
refugees	contaminated
starving	supplies
aid	

The drought in East Africa will once again bring famine and (1) . . . . to the region unless desperately needed (2) . . . . arrives soon. People are drinking (3) . . . . water and there is a growing risk of an (4) . . . . Aid workers say that thousands of (5) . . . . are already flooding across the border into neighbouring countries where the situation is not much better. Families have walked up to 100 km with many parents carrying (6) . . . . children. Fifteen planes are leaving from France tomorrow morning and will drop food (7) . . . . and medicine.

6 A domestic fire

Complete this news report with the correct form of these verbs:

spread	suffer	fight	evacuate
trap	bring	start	rescue

It is now thought that the fire which destroyed the Regency Hotel in London last night (1) . . . . in the kitchen when a pan of cooking oil was left unattended. The fire quickly (2) . . . . up the stairs and through the rest of the hotel.

Most guests were able to leave the hotel before the fire got out of control but firefighters had to (3) . . . . two young children who were (4) . . . . in their bedroom on the fourth floor. Three other people were taken to hospital (5) . . . . from the effects of smoke. Surrounding buildings were (6) . . . . while firefighters (7) . . . . to (8) . . . . the blaze under control.

Add your own words and expressions

90   Wild animals

1 Animal categories

Match the following creatures with their categories highlighted in green below:

crocodile   shark   tiger   lobster   bee   ostrich

1. A large, feline mammal found in most of Asia. It has a yellow-orange coat and black stripes.
2. A large, ferocious fish with a long body, a large dorsal fin and rows of sharp teeth.
3. A large, tropical reptile with a broad head, powerful jaws and a thick covering of bony plates.
4. A fast-running, flightless African bird with dark feathers.
5. An insect with four wings that collects pollen and nectar and makes honey.
6. A large marine crustacean with eight legs and large pincers.

2 Large mammals

Match the words with the pictures:

elephant   bear   rhinoceros   camel   buffalo   giraffe
kangaroo   deer   hippopotamus   zebra   baboon   monkey

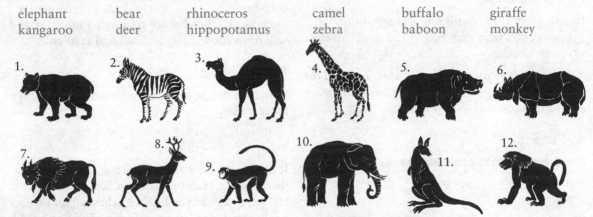

3 Small mammals

Match the words with the pictures:

fox   hedgehog   rat   squirrel   bat   mole

4 Big cats

Match the words with the pictures:

lion   tiger   leopard   panther

5 Reptiles

Match the words with the pictures:

snake   crocodile   frog   lizard   turtle

6 Animals which live in the sea

Match the words with the pictures:

whale   shark   dolphin   walrus   octopus   seal
crab   lobster   jellyfish   starfish   sea-horse   salmon

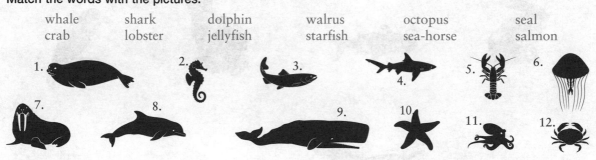

7 Birds

Match the words with the pictures:

eagle   flamingo   peacock   owl   seagull   penguin
parrot   swan   duck   wren   pigeon   swallow

8 Insects

Match the words with the pictures:

spider   bee   fly   mosquito   butterfly
grasshopper   cockroach   ladybird   ant   scorpion

Add your own words and expressions

91 Domestic and farm animals

1 Pets

Match the words with the pictures:

dog   cat   guinea pig   mouse
rabbit   goldfish   canary   tortoise

1.
2.
3.
4.
5.
6.
7.
8.

Some people keep more exotic pets like parrots, snakes, scorpions or lizards.

2 Talking about pets

Match the pets with the sentences below. The words in green will help you.

horse   dog   parrot
cat   tropical fish

1. I don't like it when I have to take him for a walk in the rain – and I hate it when he jumps all over the sofa with his muddy paws.
2. She starts purring as soon as anybody strokes her.
3. I keep him in a stable at the farm in the village. I've got to feed him early every morning.
4. I have to feed them twice a day and change the water in the tank every two weeks.
5. He's got a cage in the kitchen but sometimes I let him out to sit on my shoulder. He can say a few words.

Do you keep any pets? Did you have a pet when you were a child?

3 Riding a horse

Match the words with the pictures:

saddle   stirrups   harness
bit   whip   riding hat

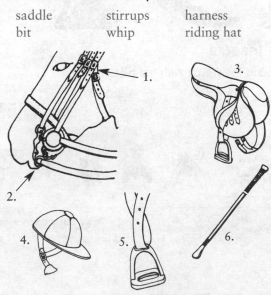

If you ride a horse, which of these verbs is fastest?

trot   gallop   canter

4 Farm animals

Match the words with the pictures:

horse	pony	donkey
cow	pig	sheep
goat	duck	hen
goose	cockerel	bull

1.

2.

3.

4.

5.

6.

5 The young of farm animals

Match the animals on the left with their young on the right:

1. hen	a. calf
2. pig	b. duckling
3. sheep	c. foal
4. horse	d. kid
5. cow	e. chicken
6. duck	f. lamb
7. goat	g. piglet

Note that the plural of calf *is* calves.

6 Farming verbs

Use the correct form of these verbs in the sentences below:

slaughter   breed   graze   milk

1. Farmers have to get up early to . . . . . . the cows.
2. If you go for a drive in the country, you'll see sheep and cows . . . . in the fields.
3. The bulls used in bullfights are . . . . specially.
4. It makes me sad to think that these lovely little lambs will soon be . . . .

7 Animals and their meat

Match up the animals and their meat. One of the animals has more than one name for its meat.

1. cow	a. venison
2. hen	b. lamb
3. pig	c. veal
4. calf	d. pork
5. deer	e. ham
6. sheep	f. chicken
	g. bacon
	h. beef

Deer are being farmed more and more and venison is becoming more common in shops.

Add your own words and expressions

92   Talking about animals

1   What do you know about animals?

Answer these questions:

1. Which one of these is not a wild animal?
   lion / elephant / goat / rhinoceros

2. Which one of these is not a domestic
   animal? *cow / fox / sheep / pig*

3. Which one of these isn't usually kept as a
   pet? *dog / cat / rabbit / camel*

4. Which one of these is not carnivorous?
   lion / bear / panda / crocodile

5. Which one of these is not a predator?
   tiger / gorilla / leopard / eagle

6. Which one of these is not an endangered
   species? *penguin / dolphin / whale / panda*

2   What animals do

Match the animals with the verbs and expressions:

1. Birds   a. hunt in a pack, howl at night.
2. Dogs   b. make honey, buzz, sting.
3. Cats   c. roar.
4. Spiders   d. hiss, slither along the ground.
5. Wolves   e. bark, wag their tails.
6. Bears   f. build nests, lay eggs.
7. Lions   g. make webs to catch flies.
8. Bees   h. hibernate during the winter.
9. Snakes   i. purr, scratch.

Now use the correct form of some of the verbs
above in the following sentences:

10. My dog . . . . his tail when he's happy.
    He's a good guard dog. He always
    . . . . when somebody comes to the door.

11. I got . . . . . . by a bee last week. It was
    really painful.

12. I looked down and there was a huge snake
    . . . . . . towards me!

13. That cat can be quite vicious sometimes. She
    . . . . . . me when I tried to pick her up just
    now.

14. Some birds have . . . . . . their nests in the
    trees outside my bedroom window. They
    make a terrible noise.

3   Parts of animals

Match the words with the numbers in the pictures:

wing	beak	feather
tail	antler	paw
claw	hoof	shell
trunk	fin	horn

4   Groups of animals

Match the words on the left with the animals on the
right to make animal groups:

1. a herd of   a. fish
2. a pack of   b. whales
3. a swarm of   c. wolves
4. a shoal of   d. birds or sheep
5. a flock of   e. cattle
6. a school of   f. bees

5 Animal proverbs and idioms

Match the following common sayings with their meanings:

1. You can't teach an old dog new tricks.
2. You can lead a horse to water but you can't make it drink.
3. Don't count your chickens (before they hatch).
4. The early bird catches the worm.

a. *It may not happen. Don't be too sure.*
b. *An old person will never change the way he or she does things.*
c. *You can't force somebody to do something they don't want to do.*
d. *The person who gets there first will get what they want.*

Use these words to complete the idioms below:

frog   bull   rat   fish   cat

5. Why do you think they haven't paid us yet? I'm a bit suspicious. I smell a . . . . !

6. It was my first time at the opera and I felt like a . . . . . . out of water.

7. I'm planning a surprise party for Kathy. You can invite whoever you like but make sure nobody lets the . . . . . . out of the bag.

8. I've got a bad cold and I've got a terrible . . . . . . in my throat so I'll stay at home today, I think. Sorry.

9. I've been having a few problems with my neighbour's dog coming in the garden. I'm just going to have to take the . . . . . . by the horns and go round and speak to her.

Do you have similar sayings in your own language?

Some words for animal noises are used idiomatically for people: He howled in pain. "Get out", he barked. She roared with laughter. "I hate you", she hissed.

6 Animal rights

Complete the text below with these words:

endangered   cruelty   habitats
extinct   skins   the wild
cosmetics   zoos   experiments

As an animal lover, I get very upset when I hear stories about (1) . . . . to animals. I am totally against using animals in laboratory (2) . . . . – especially if it's just to test (3) . . . .

I am also strongly against keeping animals in captivity. Animals should be in (4) . . . . where they belong, not in (5) . . . . or circuses.

Why is it that (6) . . . . species and beautiful animals, like leopards, are hunted for their (7) . . . . when synthetic alternatives are now available? And as we continue to cut down the rainforests, we're destroying animals' natural (8) . . . . and more and more of them are becoming rare. The giant panda, for example, is almost (9) . . . . If we're not careful, there won't be any animals left for our grandchildren to see!

Are you an animal lover? What do you think about animals being kept in zoos?

Add your own words and expressions

93   Towns and cities

1 Basic vocabulary

Translate the words in green into your own language:

1. It's about ten minutes from the town centre.
2. I wish there was a bit more nightlife in this place.
3. We live in a fairly quiet street near a park.
4. We used to live on a very busy main road.
5. My dad's moved to a house in the suburbs.
6. I live on the outskirts of Paris.
7. It's a quiet residential area.
8. She lives in a nice part of town.
9. I used to live in a really run-down area.
10. There's a large factory which employs over 1000 people.

2 Around town

Match the words on the left with those on the right:

1. city   a. precinct
2. tower   b. bins
3. pedestrian   c. lights
4. litter   d. street
5. bus / cycle   e. block
6. traffic   f. centre
7. main   g. lanes

Now use the expressions in these sentences:

8. I wish people wouldn't drop rubbish in the street. There are plenty of . . . . around town.
9. It's much safer for cyclists to get about these days with . . . . everywhere.
10. They're building a huge . . . . in the centre of town. It's going to house around a hundred families.
11. You can't drive up that street any more. They've made it into a . . . .
12. Go straight down this road and turn left at the first set of . . . .
13. The traffic system in the . . . . is impossible. It's all one-way streets.
14. The . . . . is where you'll find all the large department stores and banks.

3 Buildings and places

Put the following words into the appropriate columns below. If necessary, use a dictionary.

swimming pool   university
department store   theatre
shopping centre   museum
railway station   school
football stadium   art gallery
opera house   taxi rank
underground   college
leisure centre   mall
multi-storey car park ice rink

culture	transport	education
. . . . . .	. . . . . .	. . . . . .
. . . . . .	. . . . . .	. . . . . .
. . . . . .	. . . . . .	. . . . . .
. . . . . .	. . . . . .	

sports	shopping	
. . . . . .	. . . . . .	
. . . . . .	. . . . . .	
. . . . . .	. . . . . .	
. . . . . .		

4 Amenities

The amenities of a town or city are places which provide a service or entertainment. Match the places on the left with the ideas on the right:

1. hospital   a. gambling
2. cathedral   b. films
3. cinema   c. work and business
4. nightclub   d. borrowing books
5. casino   e. classical music
6. concert hall f. religion
7. job centre   g. healthcare
8. office block h. looking for work
9. library   i. drinking and dancing

Tick all the places you have in your town or city.

Has your town / city got a good nightlife?

5 Talking about city life

Complete the sentences with these words:

crowded   traffic   cosmopolitan
stressful   graffiti   rush hour

1. Trying to get a seat on the train during the
   . . . . is a nightmare! It's so . . . .
   Driving is even more . . . . – the
   . . . . is awful between 5 and 7.
2. The walls in the town centre are covered in
   . . . .
3. There's a real mix of people in Brighton. It
   has a very . . . . feel to it.

Now do the same with these:

efficient   suburbs   property prices
commute   convenient   public transport

4. I love it here. Everything I want is only five
   minutes away. It's so . . . .
5. Everything's a bit more expensive here and
   . . . . are extremely high. A lot of
   people have no choice but to live out in the
   . . . . and . . . . in to work.
6. It's so easy to get around. . . . . is
   excellent – it's cheap and . . . .

Now choose the correct ending for each sentence:

7. People are always so busy. Everybody's
8. The roads are terrible. I'm always getting
9. The underground system is impossible. I'm
   always
10. London's so big. It took me ages to

a. getting lost.
b. find my way round.
c. stuck in traffic.
d. rushing about all the time.

6 Problems

Do you have the following problems where you live? Check any words you don't know in your dictionary.

- homelessness
- beggars
- traffic congestion
- sub-standard housing
- unsafe areas (no-go areas)
- prostitution (red-light districts)
- vandalism
- pollution
- a high crime rate
- high unemployment
- racial tension
- overcrowding

7 Vocabulary notes

Here are extra notes on vocabulary connected with town and cities. Use the following words to complete the notes:

estate   high-rise   street
crossing   commuters   road

1. A . . . . always has buildings on one or
   both sides.
2. A . . . . may or may not have buildings
   on either side.
3. A housing . . . . is a large number of
   flats or houses built close together at the
   same time. It is part of the town, but away
   from the centre.
4. Tower blocks are also called . . . .
   blocks or . . . . flats.
5. A pedestrian . . . . is a specified place on
   the road where people can cross. It is
   sometimes called a zebra . . . .
6. People who commute to work every day are
   called . . . .

Add your own words and expressions

94   Time

1   Periods of time

Match the time periods on the left with the time periods on the right with the same meaning:

1. sixty seconds		a.	a century
2. sixty minutes		b.	a fortnight
3. seven days		c.	a minute
4. two weeks		d.	a millennium
5. twelve months		e.	a decade
6. ten years		f.	a week
7. a hundred years		g.	an hour
8. a thousand years		h.	a year

2   Past, present and future

Mark these expressions past, present or future:

1. in those days	10. right now
2. in the future	11. soon
3. in a minute	12. last week
4. in a few days	13. next week
5. a long time ago	14. ages ago
6. from now on	15. a while back
7. at the moment	16. in the past
8. the other day	17. shortly
9. for the time being	18. sooner or later

3   Time expressions

Use these expressions in the sentences below:

in those days	in a minute
straightaway	from now on
ages ago	sooner or later
the other day	for the time being

1. I saw Pam . . . . She told me she's got a new job.
2. I'm surprised you still remember that. It happened . . . .
3. We didn't have television . . . . I used to play in the garden or read.
4. He's a very good player. I'm sure he's going to win a major competition . . . .
5. Did you read that article about mad cow disease? I'm going vegetarian . . . .
6. I can't find a flat of my own so I'm staying with friends . . . .
7. Wait here. I'll be back . . . .
8. Di rang. Can you call her back . . . . ?

4   Expressions with *time*

Complete the dialogues with these phrases:

all the time	on time	next time
at the same time	just in time	by the time

1. Did you hear that I failed my driving test?
   > Oh, never mind. Better luck . . . .
2. Aren't Paul and Lynn here yet?
   > No, I'm surprised they're so late. They're usually . . . .
3. What was Buckingham Palace like?
   > It was great. We arrived . . . . to see the changing of the guard.
4. I hear they've just made you Head of Department. That must keep you busy.
   > You're not joking. I often have to do five things . . . .
5. Let's get the bus, shall we?
   > We might as well walk. . . . . the next bus comes we'll almost be home!
6. Did you find those keys?
   > Yes, they were in my pocket . . . .

Now choose the correct ending for each sentence:

7. Jane's very busy. Now is not a very
8. She isn't in a very good mood. It's probably not the
9. She's very upset. It's probably the
10. She's in a meeting. You've picked a

a. best time to discuss your salary.
b. bad time to call, I'm afraid.
c. wrong time to talk about the meeting.
d. good time to ask her for a day off.

5   When?

Today is Monday 15th June.

Match the dates on the left with the expressions on the right:

1. June 13th	a.	a week today
2. June 17th	b.	the day before yesterday
3. June 18th	c.	in three days' time
4. June 20th/21st	d.	the day after tomorrow
5. June 22nd	e.	a fortnight today
6. June 29th	f.	next weekend

6 Grammar words

Complete the sentences below with these words:

until	while	for	since
yet	just	by	during

1. I've been waiting here . . . . . . ages. Where have you been?
2. I'll try and visit you sometime . . . . the summer holidays.
3. I got annoyed because they kept talking . . . . . . I was trying to watch the film.
4. If we don't get this finished . . . . . . Friday, we'll have to work at the weekend.
5. She's always the last one to leave the office. She's here . . . . . . seven o'clock some evenings.
6. I don't want a cup of tea, thanks. I've . . . . . . had one.
7. Don't tell me what happens in the film. I haven't seen it . . . .
8. It's nearly three months . . . . . . I last saw Alison. I must give her a call.

Now do the same with these words:

finally	in the end	to begin with
recently	suddenly	so far

9. Is Jane still working here? I haven't seen her . . . .
10. The bus . . . . . . came after I'd been waiting for twenty-five minutes.
11. I waited all day for him to help me, but he forgot all about it. . . . . I had to do it myself.
12. I haven't finished the course yet, but . . . . . . I'm really enjoying it.
13. I thought Jane and I were getting on really well. Then last weekend she . . . . said she didn't want to see me any more.
14. . . . . I thought John was serious about going to Australia, but then I realised he was joking.

7 Frequency adverbs

Match the sentences:

1. I really love milk.
2. I like red wine.
3. I quite like pasta.
4. I don't like fish very much.
5. I really hate spinach.

a. I quite often have a glass with dinner.
b. I never touch it. I always refuse it.
c. I drink it all the time.
d. I have it occasionally / from time to time.
e. I rarely / hardly ever have it.

8 Time verbs

Use the correct form of these verbs to complete the sentences below:

pass	last	find
run out	spend	take

1. My daughter . . . . . . hours talking to her friends on the phone.
2. These batteries are the best you can buy. They . . . . . . for ages.
3. It'll probably . . . . . . about an hour to get from here to London by train.
4. Take something to read on the plane. It'll help . . . . . . the time.
5. We really need to get on with this job if we're going to finish it in time. Time . . . .
6. Do you think you'll be able to . . . . . . the time to help me with my homework later?

Now underline the complete expressions containing the verb. For example, find the time.

9 Notes

1. In spoken language we often say till instead of until – "Don't do anything till I say so".
2. We often say all of a sudden instead of suddenly – "All of a sudden, the lights went out."

Add your own words and expressions

95   Numbers

1 Basic vocabulary

Match the words with the examples on the right:

1. cardinal numbers   a. $\frac{1}{4}, \frac{2}{3}, \frac{40}{47}$
2. ordinal numbers   b. first, second, third, ...
3. decimals   c. 1, 2, 3, ...
4. fractions   d. 25%, 50%
5. percentages   e. 24 + 24 = 48
6. arithmetic   f. 2.5, 3.14

We say three point one four.

2 Cardinal numbers

Match the numbers with the way they are said:

1. 240
2. 2,750
3. 265,000
4. 2,500,000
5. 2,000,000,000

a. two hundred and sixty-five thousand
b. two thousand seven hundred and fifty
c. two billion
d. two hundred and forty
e. two million, five hundred thousand

2,4,6,8 etc are even numbers. *1,3,5,7 etc are* odd
numbers. We always say once *instead of one time
and usually* twice *instead of two times – "I've
been to Italy twice."*

3 Fractions, decimals and percentages

**Match these written numbers with the way they are
spoken below. Then practise saying them.**

1. 50%   5. $\frac{1}{4}$
2. $2\frac{1}{2}$ 6. 1.23
3. 2.5   7. $\frac{3}{4}$
4. 4.6%   8. $\frac{2}{3}$

a. four point six percent   e. two and a half
b. one point two three   f. three quarters
c. two point five   g. a quarter
d. two thirds   h. fifty percent

*After fractions and percentages we use of – "A
third of all marriages end in divorce" or "33% of
all marriages ..."*

More than half is a majority. *Less than half is a*
minority.

4 Saying '0'

**'0' is said in different ways depending on the
context. Match the spoken phrases with the
situations below:**

1. It's four two nine three two oh.
2. In nineteen oh three.
3. It's three degrees below zero.
4. They won two nil.
5. She's winning two sets to love.

a. the result of a football match
b. the temperature
c. a telephone number
d. the score in a tennis match
e. the year somebody was born

5 Arithmetic

**Put these words and phrases into the sentences
below:**

   times   divided by   minus   plus

1. Six . . . . six equals **twelve.**
2. Ten . . . . six equals **four.**
3. Ten . . . . six equals **sixty.**
4. Ten . . . . two equals **five.**

**Now match the following words with the four
patterns above:**

multiplication   addition   division   subtraction

6 Dates

**Dates are more difficult to say than to write. You
can write** February 26th **or** 26th February. **You can
say either** February the twenty-sixth **or** the twenty-
sixth of February. **Match these important days with
the spoken dates and then practise saying them:**

1. American Independence Day
2. Christmas Day
3. New Year's Day
4. Valentine's Day

a. February the 14th / the 14th of February
b. December the 25th / the 25th of December
c. July the 4th / the 4th of July
d. January the 1st / the 1st of January

*Abbreviations for the months are: Jan, Feb, Mar,
Apr, May, Jun, Jul, Aug, Sept, Oct, Nov, Dec.*

7 Ordinal numbers

To form ordinal numbers we usually add 'th' to the cardinal number – fourth, sixth, seventh, etc. You have to change the spelling with twentieth, thirtieth, fortieth etc but this is usually spoken language anyway – "It's their fiftieth wedding anniversary next week." The exceptions are first, second, third and fifth. Notice how we write ordinal numbers: 1st, 2nd, 3rd, 4th, 10th, 25th, 100th etc.

Use these expressions which contain ordinal numbers to complete the sentences below:

third time lucky	at the eleventh hour
in seventh heaven	first class
first impressions	second-hand
sixth sense	second nature

1. I'm very lucky. My firm pays for me to fly . . . . when I travel on business.
2. I bought this jacket . . . . from a shop near the station.
3. I've got my driving test next week. I've failed it twice already.
   > Well, you know what they say – . . . . !
4. My wife seems to know exactly what I'm thinking. She's got a . . . .
5. I grew up in the mountains so skiing was . . . . to me.
6. Disneyland was fantastic. The kids were . . . .
7. I didn't like Tony much when I met him but now I really like him.
   > Well, it just shows that . . . . can be misleading.
8. They told everyone the meeting would be in London and then . . . ., they decided to change it and have it in Oxford instead.

8 Approximate numbers

We are often imprecise about numbers. Mark the sentences M (if the idea is many) or F (few):

1. Lorna's party was very dull. Only about half a dozen people turned up.
2. It wasn't a very good concert. Lots of people left before the end.
3. There are quite a few new students in the class this week.
4. There were hardly any tickets left for this concert, so I was lucky to get one.
5. There were loads of people in town this morning. I think there was some kind of demonstration.
6. I've had dozens of replies to the advert I put in the paper.

A dozen = 12.

A couple of (people) = two.

Several (people) = more than two, but not many.

Now use these words to complete the dialogues:

about	give or take	so

7. So, how many people went to Kim's party?
   > Oh, I don't know. . . . . . . thirty or thirty-five, I suppose.
8. So, Carlos, how many girlfriends did you have before me?
   > Hmm, maybe fifteen or . . . . I've never really counted!
9. So, how many tickets have we sold for this concert we're doing?
   > Around two hundred – . . . . a few.

You can say about 30 or around 30.

Approximately and roughly are more formal than about or around – "A new computer system would cost us approximately / roughly £15,000."

Add your own words and expressions

96   Similarity and difference

1 The same or different?

Which of the following descriptions of people can be used in the three situations below:

a. They're exactly the same.
b. They're completely different.
c. They're quite alike in some ways.
d. They're identical.

e. They're quite similar.
f. I can't tell the difference.
g. I can't tell them apart.
h. They're nothing like each other.

1. Jack and Ben are identical twins. At school their teachers are always mixing them up!
   Descriptions . . . .

2. Peter and Jane are twins. They both have fair hair and blue eyes.
   Descriptions . . . .

3. Bill and Matt are brothers, but you'd never guess. Bill has pale skin and red hair while Matt has dark hair and always looks tanned.
   Descriptions . . . .

2 Saying that things are the same

Choose the correct ending for these sentences:

DiCaprio's new film is	very similar	his last one.
	the same	from his last one.
	no different	to his last one.
	just like	as his last one.

3 Expressions with *same*

Complete the dialogues below with these phrases:

stay the same	the same again
the same	at the same time
the same to you	all the same

1. So, who are you going to vote for in the election?
   > Oh, I don't know. These politicians are . . . . They say one thing and then do just what they like.
2. Bye! Have a nice weekend!
   > Thanks, ...
3. I don't like change very much. I like things to basically . . . .
4. If I put all my money into this scheme, I could make a fortune.
   > Yes, but . . . . you could lose everything.

5. You look a bit stressed.
   > Oh, I just couldn't find anywhere to park again. It's . . . . every morning.
6. Would you like another drink?
   > Yes, I'll have . . . . please.

4 Adjectives

Complete the sentences with these adjectives:

equal   constant   identical   familiar

1. This watch is . . . . to the one I lost. Perhaps it's mine.
2. This place looks . . . . I'm sure I've been here before.
3. Women who are doing exactly the same jobs as their male colleagues should receive . . . . pay.
4. The number of deaths from drug abuse has remained . . . . for the last ten years.

5 Saying that things are different

Complete the dialogues below with these words and phrases:

varied   not the same   opposite   unique   incompatible   alternative

1. So, have you been to lots of Chinese restaurants since you came back from China?
   > Well, I've tried a few, but they're just . . . . as the ones in China.

2. So, does Sam's brother look like him, then?
   > No, he's the complete . . . . He's tall and thin with blond hair.

3. There's no other film maker with quite the same style, is there?
   > No, I must say he's absolutely . . . .

4. How's the new job going?
   > The one thing I really like about it is that it is so . . . . No two days are the same.

5. I hear Extrico are thinking of putting their prices up.
   > Well, if they do, we'll have to look for an . . . . supplier. We need to keep our costs under control.

6. I can't believe Kerry and Frank are getting married. They seem completely . . . .

6 Expressions with *difference*

Use these expressions to complete the sentences:

> makes all the difference
> makes no difference
> see the difference
> tell the difference
> split the difference

1. As far as I'm concerned, taking the money without asking is the same as stealing it. I really don't . . . .

2. Would you prefer butter or margarine?
   > I really don't mind. To be honest, I can't . . . .

3. We really don't mind whether we have a boy or a girl. It . . . . to us.

4. When Rivaldo isn't playing, Brazil are not the same team. He's the player that . . . .

5. I'll give you £20 for it.
   > No, I want at least £30.
   OK, let's . . . . and say £25.

7 Comparing things

Complete the sentences below with these words:

much   a lot   nowhere near   far

1. Our house is . . . . bigger than theirs.
   . . . .
   . . . .

2. Their house is . . . . as big as ours.

Now choose the correct ending for each sentence:

3. Compared to our little flat,
4. In comparison with Mexico City,
5. There's a huge contrast
6. You can't compare

a. between the north and the south.
b. life in London with life in a Welsh village.
c. London seems quite quiet.
d. his house is like a castle.

You can say compared with or compared to. You make a comparison between two things.

If we say two people are like chalk and cheese, are they very similar or very different?

Add your own words and expressions

97   Thoughts and ideas

1 Thought processes

Complete the sentences below with the following verbs:

predict   decide   imagine   remember
judge   wonder   work out   guess

1. I met a lovely girl at a party last week, but I can't even . . . . her name.

2. I can't . . . . whether to apply for this job or not. It's really well-paid, but the hours are so long.

3. I . . . . if we'll ever find a cure for the common cold.

4. Go on! . . . . how old Mark is.
   > I don't know. 40?

5. I'd love to be able to travel back in time to ancient Egypt or ancient Rome. Can you . . . . what it would be like?

6. I'm trying to . . . . how long it will take to get to Venice from Rome by car.

7. Don't ask me to . . . . who'll win the World Cup. I've got no idea.

8. I don't know why you don't like Paul. You don't really know him well enough to . . . . him.

Do you have a logical mind? Do you think logically?

Do you have a good memory? Or have you got a memory like a sieve?

If you say that someone has a good mind, you mean that they are intelligent.

2 Asking for an opinion

Choose the correct endings for these sentences:

1. What do you   a. opinion of this report?
2. What's your   b. feel if we invited Jim?
3. What are your   c. think will happen?
4. How would you   d. feelings on drugs?

If someone asks for your opinion and you'd rather not give it, you can say: I'm not sure about that or I'd need time to think about that. If you are asked to make a decision, you can say: Let me sleep on it or I'll get back to you.

3 'Thinking' verbs

In the following sentences two of the words or phrases in green are correct. Delete the wrong one.

1. Well, perhaps you should give yourself a few days to think about / consider / reckon our offer before you make a decision.

2. Let's call a taxi. Then we can all have a drink. What do you think / consider / reckon?
   > I suppose / suggest / guess we could. But won't a taxi be very expensive?
   No, I suppose not / I don't think so / I doubt it. It's only a few miles.

3. I've just had an idea / a consideration / a thought. Why don't we drive to the coast?

4. I'm sorry. I didn't realise / had no idea / didn't consider that you were waiting for me.

5. I'm amazed that Peter and Liz are going out together. I just can't realise / imagine / picture them together.

6. Don't make excuses. You hit the car in front because you weren't concentrating / were daydreaming / weren't realising.

7. I'll never finish this report. I keep losing my concentration / getting distracted / losing my mind.

8. Would you turn that music down, please? I can't imagine / can't hear myself think / can't concentrate.

4 Making decisions

Choose two correct endings for each sentence:

1. I'm not   a. decide.
2. I can't   b. sure about it.
3. I've got   c. mixed feelings about it.
                d. sure what I think.
                e. a few reservations about it.
                f. make my mind up.

You can also say, "I'm in two minds about whether to go or not."

Are you a decisive person or are you indecisive?

5 Not understanding

Use the correct form of these verbs to complete the sentences:

follow   understand   lose   make sense

1. I'm trying to set up this music system but I don't . . . . the instructions.
2. I'm trying to set up this music system, but the instructions don't . . . .
3. Sorry, I don't . . . . you. Can you explain that again?
4. I'm sorry. You . . . . me. Could you start again?

6 Intelligent or unintelligent?

Use these words to complete the following:

genius   fool   brilliant
bright   slow   stupid

1. Our Professor is considered to be one of the world's most . . . . physicists.
2. Our daughter was a very . . . . child. She was reading before she was five.
3. You drove home after drinking all night! How can you be so . . . . ?
4. I don't really understand what you're getting at. Sorry if I'm being a bit . . . .
5. Salvador Dali might have been very strange, but you have to admit the man was a . . . .
6. He lost all his money in some crazy business deal. The man's a complete . . . .

Avoid the word idiot. It can be a very strong word in some languages. If you want to say to someone "Don't be so stupid!", you can also say, "Don't be so silly!"

We often use not very + a positive word when we want to be negative: "She's not very bright." "He's not very clever."

You can also say, "He's not exactly Einstein."

7 Expressions with *mind*

Complete the expressions below with these words:

make   slipped   changed
don't   on   take

1. I've . . . . my mind.
2. I've got a lot . . . . my mind.
3. It'll . . . . your mind off it.
4. I can't . . . . up my mind.
5. I . . . . really mind.
6. It completely . . . . my mind.

Now use the whole expressions to complete these sentences:

7. I'm sorry I've been so quiet recently. . . . . at the moment.
8. I don't know whether to give her flowers or chocolates. . . . .
9. I was going to go to university but . . . . I'm going to get a job instead.
10. What do you fancy – fish or pasta? > Either, really. You choose. . . . .
11. Did you post my letter? > Oh no, sorry. . . . . ?
12. I can see you're really worried about this new job. Why don't you go away for the weekend? . . . . for a couple of days.

Add your own words and expressions

98   Size and shape

1 Size

Write the adjective beside these four basic nouns:

1. length . . . . . .   3. width . . . . . .
2. height . . . . . .   4. depth . . . .

Now match the following questions and answers:

5. How tall is John?
6. How high is Everest?
7. How long is the Channel Tunnel?
8. How wide is the Thames?
9. How deep is your swimming pool?

a. I think it's a couple of hundred yards.
b. It's 2 metres at the deep end.
c. It's over 20 miles, I think.
d. He's just over 6 foot (nearly 2 metres).
e. It's over eight and a half thousand metres.

We use tall *to talk about people and* high *to talk about mountains. We can use* tall *or* high *to talk about buildings.*

2 Big and small

Mark these adjectives B if they mean big, and S if they mean small:

large   . . .   immense   . . .
little   . . .   huge   . . .
tiny   . . .   minute   . . .
vast   . . .   enormous   . . .
massive . . .   microscopic . . .

Large is more formal than big *and you are more likely to see it in written language.* Huge, enormous, immense *and* vast *mean very big and are often used with* absolutely *– "Their new house is absolutely huge."* Vast *is usually used to talk about an area of space – "China is a vast country."*

Delete the wrong word in these sentences:

1. Have you got this shirt in a large / huge size, please?
2. There was a huge / vast dog in the park. I was terrified.
3. I want to find a bigger flat. The one I'm in now is absolutely little / tiny.
4. You can only see them through a microscope. They're absolutely small / minute.

3 Opposite adjectives

Complete the dialogues with these pairs of adjectives:

wide / narrow   low / high
short / tall   deep / shallow
long / short   thin / thick

1. Do you think Marco's good enough at basketball to become a professional?
   > He's probably a bit . . . . . . to be a top player. Some of those guys are head and shoulders bigger than him. They're so . . . . . they can just drop the ball in the basket.
2. It's quite a . . . . . . journey from my house to the college. I have to take two buses.
   > Oh really, I'm lucky. It's just a . . . . . . walk across the park for me.
3. So, what's your new house like?
   > I've got a few problems, actually. On one side of my garden the wall's too . . . . . . and the neighbours' dog keeps jumping into the garden, and on the other side they've just put up a really . . . . . . fence, which blocks out all the light.
4. Be careful if you go swimming in that lake – the water's very . . . .
   > Don't worry. It's quite . . . . . . in the part where we go.
5. One thing I noticed when I went to the US is how . . . . . . all the roads are. Where I live all the streets are really . . . . . . – just enough room for two cars to pass.
6. I'm freezing!
   > I'm not surprised with that . . . . . . jacket on. You should have brought a . . . . . . winter coat.

4 Lines

Use these adjectives to describe the lines below:

vertical   diagonal   parallel   horizontal

1.   2.   3.   4.

5 Shapes

Match the words with the shapes:

| square | rectangle | triangle | cube | circle |
| semi-circle | oval | pyramid | sphere | octagon |

1.   2.   3.   4.   5.

6.   7.   8.   9.   10.

Now match the descriptions with the pictures:

a. It's round / circular.
b. It's square.
c. It's rectangular.
d. It's triangular.
e. It's a cube.

f. It's oval.
g. It's octagonal.
h. It's semi-circular.
i. It's a pyramid.
j. It's spherical.

6 Describing shapes

Here are different ways to describe the shapes above. Match the description to the shape:

1. It's got eight sides.
2. All four sides are the same length.
3. It's a three-dimensional triangle.
4. It's egg-shaped.
5. Two of the sides are longer than the other two.
6. If you add the three angles together you get 180°.

Now use the adjectives and nouns you have learned in the following descriptions of things:

7. An A4 sheet of paper is a . . . .
8. The earth is almost . . . .
9. The Pentagon is a building with 5 . . . .
10. Trafalgar Square is not actually . . . . !
11. An egg is not a perfect . . . .

7 Other shapes

Use the following words to describe these shapes:

heart-shaped	diamond-shaped
pointed	cylindrical
star-shaped	pear-shaped

1.   2.   3.   4.   5.   6.

Add your own words and expressions

99   Distance and speed

1   Distance expressions

Here are 6 expressions. Write each one below the one of similar meaning:

> It's in the middle of nowhere.
> It's in the next street.
> It's miles away.
> It's 10 minutes by car.
> It's just across the road.
> It's not very far away.

1. It's directly opposite.

. . . .

2. It's quite near.

. . . .

3. It's miles from anywhere.

. . . .

4. It's just round the corner.

. . . .

5. It's a ten-minute drive.

. . . .

6. It's a long way away.

. . . .

Now put each of these phrases into the correct dialogue:

> It's only five minutes' walk.
> It's not far.
> It's a long way away.
> It's miles away.
> It's just round the corner.
> It's too far to walk.

7. Shall we get a taxi to the restaurant?
   > No. . . . .
   > No. . . . .
   > No. . . . .

8. Shall we walk to the restaurant?
   > No. . . . .
   > No. . . . .
   > No. . . . .

2   Expressions with prepositions

Use these prepositions in the green expressions:

in	from
on	by
to	via
into	

1. Are you flying to Paris?
   > Well, we've thought about it. It's only an hour . . . . plane. Driving isn't really any cheaper and it's much longer. It's at least a hundred miles . . . . here . . . . the Tunnel, then it takes you over an hour by the time you queue. Then when you get to the other side, it's a good two-hour drive . . . . Paris.

2. How far is it to Gothenburg?
   > . . . . . Harwich it's a 36-hour ferry crossing.

3. How far away is your office?
   > It's a fifteen-minute walk . . . . home, but the bus only takes five minutes.

4. How long is the flight to Tokyo?
   > The direct BA flight only takes about 11 hours, but we went . . . . Bangkok and it took over 24 hours. Never again!

5. Have you any idea how far it is . . . . Salisbury?
   > Well, if you go . . . . the coast road, it'll probably take you over 3 hours, but if you take the A27, then you can probably do it . . . . just under two hours.

6. I've got to change airports when I get to London. How far is Gatwick . . . . Heathrow?
   > It depends which way you go. You could either take the tube . . . . Central London, then get the train from Victoria, or you could just get the airport bus direct . . . . Heathrow. It's only about 30 miles or so and the bus takes about an hour – possibly less.

You can ask either How far is it? *or* How far away is it? *They mean the same. You can answer:* It's 7 miles *or* It's 7 miles away.

3 Near and far

Complete the sentences with these words:

> remote
> near
> nearby
> in the distance
> far
> long

1. I stayed in a really lovely hotel . . . . the railway station.
2. How . . . . is it to Pisa from here?
3. My sister and her family have moved to Northern Spain. It's a beautiful place, but it's a bit . . . . – it's about ten miles to the nearest town.
4. If you look carefully, you can just about see the sea . . . .
5. I don't take much exercise during the week, but I go for a . . . . walk every weekend.
6. I stayed in a really nice hotel and had dinner in a restaurant . . . .

If you need a noun which means 'the area near where you live', you can use in my neighbourhood.

4 Speed expressions

Complete the following expressions using these words:

> over   top   on   an   doing

a. I was only doing 30 miles . . . . . . hour.
b. I was 20 miles an hour . . . . . . the limit.
c. He must have been . . . . . . more than 100!
d. My new car's got a . . . . . . speed of 150.
e. We did about 120 miles a day . . . . . average.

Now use the above sentences in the following situations:

1. When the speed camera caught me, ... I was fined £400.

2. It's a pity the national speed limit is only 70! . . . .

3. We decided to drive to Turkey. . . . .

4. Did you see that car? . . . .

5. When I had the accident, ... in a 50-mile an hour zone.

Add your own words and expressions

100 Quantities

1 Very small quantities

Complete the following sentences with these words:

amount   stitch   drop
ounce   penny   trace

1. We've just come back from Greece. We didn't have a . . . . . . of rain all the time we were there.

2. I was robbed in the centre of town. The guy grabbed my bag with all my money. I wasn't left with a . . . . . . !

3. You won't believe what happened when the Prime Minister was in the middle of his speech. A guy ran onto the platform. He was stark naked! He wasn't wearing a . . . . . . !

4. When the police arrived at the flat, they couldn't find even the slightest . . . . . . of drugs.

5. Jill is very fit. There's not an . . . . . . of spare flesh on her!

6. If you're going to use curry powder in this recipe, just use a tiny . . . . Otherwise, it'll ruin the taste.

Although the UK has changed to the metric system of weights, some of the words from the older system are still common in the language: ounce, pound, pint, gallon.

2 Very large quantities and numbers

Complete the following sentences with these words:

calls   money   detail
people   books   times

1. That car must have cost Mel at least £50,000! He must have loads of . . . . . . to be able to afford it.

2. When we visited my grandfather, he was surrounded by piles of . . . . . . and old newspapers.

3. There must have been thousands of . . . . . . at the demonstration against nuclear weapons.

4. I'm not going to tell you again to lock the back door! I must have told you hundreds of . . . . . . !

5. It'll take you a couple of days to read through the contract. It's a mass of . . . . . . , and we can't afford to get anything wrong.

6. After I put an advert in the paper trying to sell my car, I had dozens of . . . . . . in the first couple of days.

Now go back and underline the complete expression, for example: loads of money.

3 Collocations

Add the following words to the group of nouns they go with:

set   crowd   group   slice   piece
sheet   bunch   pair   game   lump

1. a . . . . of flowers, grapes, bananas, roses
2. a . . . . of paper, cardboard, metal
3. a . . . . of tennis, cards, chess, golf
4. a . . . . of people, demonstrators, football fans
5. a . . . . of friends, scientists, boys, schoolchildren
6. a . . . . of bacon, bread, ham, cold meat, cake
7. a . . . . of shoes, glasses, socks, gloves, slippers
8. a . . . . of wood, metal, advice, chicken, cloth
9. a . . . . of golf clubs, conditions, brakes, false teeth, tools
10. a . . . . of cheese, coal, rock, ice

4 Containers

Use the following words to complete the phrases:

can   bottle   tub   slice
tube   box   jar   packet

1. a . . . . of toothpaste or . . . .
2. a . . . . of jam or . . . .
3. a . . . . of bread or . . . .
4. a . . . . of ice cream or . . . .
5. a . . . . of wine or . . . .
6. a . . . . of chocolates or . . . .
7. a . . . . of tea or . . . .
8. a . . . . of coke or . . . .

Now add one of the following to each of the above:

yoghurt   tissues
biscuits   tomato puree
marmalade   cake
mineral water   beer

*Very often you can use can or tin for the same
things. For example: a tin / can of beans. This is
not always true. We prefer a can of coke and a tin
of polish.*

5 Food and drink

**Here are some typical ways to buy food. Add the
following words to the expressions:**

grams   leg   steaks   loaf   bag
litre   breasts   dozen   kilo   pint

1. a . . . . of milk
2. a . . . . of lager
3. a . . . . of lamb
4. two chicken . . . .
5. a . . . . of crisps
6. 500 . . . . of cheese
7. half a . . . . rolls
8. four salmon . . . .
9. a . . . . of bread
10. a . . . . of sugar

6 Groups of animals

Do you remember these from unit 92?

herd   shoal   pack   swarm   flock

1. a . . . . of bees
2. a . . . . of cows or cattle
3. a . . . . of birds or sheep
4. a . . . . of fish
5. a . . . . of wolves

7 Rare collocations

**Some of the following expressions are less
common. Complete them with these words:**

barrel   sliver   rasher   gang   pinch
speck   sack   crate   pack   grain

1. a . . . . of bacon
2. a . . . . of lies
3. a . . . . of dirt
4. a . . . . of potatoes
5. a . . . . of glass
6. a . . . . of thieves
7. a . . . . of champagne
8. a . . . . of beer
9. a . . . . of truth
10. a . . . . of salt

8 Idiomatic uses

**Use the following words to complete the idiomatic
expressions in these sentences:**

coat   stream   mountain
sea   bags   flood

1. As I walked into the room, it was just a
   . . . . . . of faces.
2. I've got a . . . . of work at the moment.
3. This window needs a . . . . . . of paint.
4. She broke down in a . . . . . . of tears.
5. I wish I had . . . . . . of energy like you!
6. A . . . . of illegal immigrants came over
   the mountains every night.

Add your own words and expressions

Answer Key

Before you start

Exercise 1: 1d 2f 3b 4a 5c 6e
Exercise 2: 1b 2e 3f 4c 5a 6d
Exercise 3: 1. strongly 2. clearly 3. deeply 4. freely
Exercise 4: 1f 2d 3b 4a 5e 6c
Exercise 5: 1. I'm having 2. take 3. put 4. needs

Unit 1 Age

Exercise 2: 1b 2e 3a 4c 5d 6j 7h 8i 9f 10g
Exercise 3: 1. I've got an eleven-year-old son.
2. We've got a six-year-old daughter. 3. They've got a two-month-old baby. 4. I teach seven- and eight-year-olds. 5. They were mostly sixteen-year-olds. 6. He was only a nine-year-old.
Exercise 4: 1. same 2. your 3. all 4. get 5. of
6. look 7. child 8. at
a. at your age b. When I was your age c. at the age of 43 d. child of his age e. people of all ages f. the same age as g. You don't look your age h. When you get to my age
Exercise 5: 1. the younger generation 2. the age difference 3. of my generation 4. the generation gap
Exercise 6: 1. bright 2. tall 3. fit 4. great 5. grown-up 6. remarkable
Exercise 7: 1. dog 2. wrong 3. over 4. getting
a. You can't teach an old dog new tricks. b. over the hill c. getting on a bit d. the wrong side of 50
Exercise 8: 1. feel 2. forty 3. age, income

Unit 2 Stages of life

Exercise 1: 1. birth 2. childhood 3. puberty
4. Adolescence 5. marriage 6. middle age
7. retirement 8. old age
Exercise 2: a. teens, childhood, twenties b. child, teenager, student, kid c. growing up, at university, young, single, at school
1. spent 2. brought up 3. grew up 4. had
Exercise 3: 1c 2d 3b 4e 5a
Exercise 4: 1e 2d 3b 4c 5f 6a
7. leave school 8. get divorced 9. change schools
10. losing his wife 11. leave home 12. moving house
Exercise 5: 1. the best day of my life 2. turning-point
3. my lucky break 4. the lowest point
Exercise 6: a. all b. new c. way d. whole e. my
f. full
1. spent his whole life 2. all my life 3. in all my life
4. a very full life 5. start a new life 6. it's a way of life
Exercise 7: 1. difficult 2. right 3. wise 4. wrong
5. bad

Unit 3 Babies and children

Exercise 1: 1. born 2. pregnancy 3. birth
4. pregnant 5. newborn 6. feed 7. healthy 8. toys
Exercise 2: 1. got 2. planned 3. expecting 4. lost
Exercise 3: b g c f e a d
Exercise 4: 1. pram 2. buggy 3. cot 4. dummy
1. sleepless nights 2. nappy 3. breast-feeding
4. baby-sitter 5. maternity leave, child-minder
6. crawling 7. nursery school 8. twins
Exercise 5: 1h 2g 3e 4a 5d 6f 7b 8c
Exercise 6: being good: well-behaved, polite, behave themselves **not being good:** naughty, getting into trouble, got told off
Exercise 7: 1a,c 2b,d 3a,c 4b,d 5b,d

Unit 4 Death

Exercise 1: 1. dead 2. died 3. dying 4. death
5. deaths 6d 7e 8a 9b 10c
Exercise 2: 1. made a will, died of cancer 2. left me £2,000 in her will 3. inherited the family business
4. came to her funeral 5. was widowed
Exercise 3: a. a heart attack, old age, cancer
b. a road accident, the war, a car crash
1. burned 2. starve 3. bled 4. choked 5. froze
6. drowned 7. committed suicide, killed himself, took his own life
Exercise 4: 1. crematorium 2. cemetery 3. mourners
4. hearse 5. grave 6. gravestone (or headstone)
7. wreath 8. coffin 9. buried 10. visit 11. cremated
12. scattered
Exercise 5: 1d 2b 3e 4a 5c The headline refers to the death of Diana, Princess of Wales

Unit 5 Family

Exercise 1: 1. grandfather, grandmother 2. uncle, aunt 3. cousins 4. nephew, niece 5. grandsons, granddaughters
Exercise 2: 1. Cynthia 2. Bill 3. Kevin 4. Eve 5. Jon
6. Samantha
Exercise 3: 1a 2e 3c 4b 5d – 1e 2d 3b 4a 5c
Exercise 4: 1. a big family 2. a very close family
3. the whole family 4. a big family reunion 5. family tree
Exercise 5: a. looks b. got c. takes d. runs e. tell
1. He takes after his father. 2. She looks just like her.
3. It runs in the family. 4. She's got her father's nose.
5. You can't tell them apart.

Unit 6 Friends

Exercise 1: 1. mine 2. best 3. old 4. close 5. lifelong
6. acquaintance
Exercise 2: 1b 2e 3a 4c 5d
Exercise 3: 1h 2d 3a 4g 5c 6f 7b 8e
Exercise 4: 1f 2h 3b 4g 5c 6d 7a 8e
Exercise 5: 1. fell out 2. row 3. isn't speaking
4. lose 5. drifted apart 6. go our separate ways
Famous saying: You can choose your friends, but not
your family!

Unit 7 Love and romance

Exercise 1: 1. girlfriend 2. boyfriend 3. going out
4. date 5. romantic 6. kissed 7. in love 8. relationship
Exercise 2: 1d 2c 3b 4c 5a
6. I don't know what she sees in him 7. she's not
really interested in him 8. she fancies you 9. She's
absolutely crazy about him 10. She's always flirting
with him
Exercise 3: 1d 2c 3a 4e 5b
Exercise 4: Serious: fallen in love, madly in love,
absolutely adores **Not serious:** a casual relationship,
a holiday romance, a brief relationship
Exercise 5: 1b 2a 3a 4b 5a 6b
a. They're going out together. b. They're sleeping
together. c. They're in love. d. They've moved in
together. e. They're always kissing. f. They live
together. g. They're always holding hands.
h. They're married.
Exercise 6: 1. split up 2. finished with, weren't right
for 3. had a huge row 4. never stop fighting
Exercise 7: 1b 2a 3d 4c

Unit 8 Marriage

Exercise 2: 1. asked 2. proposed to 3. got engaged,
set a date 4. arrange
Exercise 3: 1e 2h 3g 4a 5f 6c 7d 8b
Exercise 4: The two people getting married are the
bride and the *groom*. They are being married by the
clergyman. The two little girls are the *bridesmaids*.
The man standing on the groom's right is his *best
man*. The wedding *guests* are watching the ceremony.
Exercise 5: 1. worse 2. poorer 3. health 4. death
Exercise 6: f, c, g, i, a, e, h, b, d
Exercise 7: 1. get married 2. happily married
3. silver wedding 4. golden wedding
Exercise 8: 1d 2g 3b 4h,c 5a 6f 7e

Unit 9 General appearance

Exercise 1: 1e 2a 3b 4d 5f 6c
Exercise 2: 1b 2c 3d 4a   WLTM means *would like
to meet,* GSH means *good sense of humour.*
Exercise 3: 1. big feet 2. long legs 3. thin legs
4. hairy chest 5. long nails 6. deep voice 7. lovely
complexion 8. bad skin

Exercise 4: 1. tall, good-looking man with short, fair
hair 2. tall, thin woman with long hair 3. straight,
black hair and I'm tall and very thin 4. good-looking
with a lovely tan and long blonde hair 5. tall, dark
and handsome
Exercise 5: 1d 2b 3a 4c

Unit 10 Clothes

Exercise 1: 1f 2a 3e 4c/d 5g 6b 7e 8d
Exercise 2: 1. anorak 2. coat 3. gloves 4. hat
5. scarf 6. cap
Exercise 3: 1. sandals 2. flip-flops 3. high heels
4. clogs 5. trainers 6. boots 7. slippers
Exercise 4: 1. vest 2. underpants 3. bra 4. knickers
5. boxer shorts (or boxers) 6. tights
Exercise 5: 1. hood 2. pocket 3. collar 4. sleeve
5. button 6. zip 7. cuff 8. laces 9. heel
Exercise 6: 1. umbrella 2. bracelet 3. belt 4. scarf
5. handbag 6. necklace 7. watch 8. brooch
Exercise 7: 1c 2d 3e 4a 5b 6f 7g

Unit 11 Talking about clothes

Exercise 2: 1. a cotton shirt 2. a leather jacket
3. a denim skirt 4. a fur coat 5. a woolly jumper
6. a silk blouse
Exercise 3: 1. plain 2. striped 3. checked 4. floral
Exercise 4: 1. trousers 2. skirt 3. shoes 4. shirt
Exercise 5: 1. smart 2. dress well 3. casual
4. fashionable 5. worn-out 6. scruffy
Exercise 6: 1. fit 2. suit 3. wrong 4. match 5. tight
6. go with / match
Exercise 7: 1. on 2. dressed 3. changed 4. dressed
up (got on, get dressed, get changed, get dressed up)
You do not *do up* your socks.
Exercise 8: 1d 2c 3a 4e 5b

Unit 12 Describing character

Exercise 1: 1P 2N 3N 4P 5N 6P 7N 8P
Exercise 2: 1d 2f 3a 4e 5c 6b
Exercise 3: 1. far too honest 2. much too proud
3. far too sensible 4. much too shy 5. far too modest
6. much too loyal
Exercise 4: 1d 2e 3a 4c 5b
Exercise 5: 1. selfish 2. moody 3. arrogant
4. amusing 5. silly 6. stubborn
Exercise 6: 1. nosey 2. bossy 3. sensitive 4. fussy
1c 2b 3a 4d
Exercise 7: 1. liar 2. gossip 3 extrovert 4. big-head
5. coward 6. snob 7. couch potato 8. laugh
Exercise 8: unreliable, unpleasant, impatient,
indecisive, dishonest, disloyal, immature,
unambitious, insensitive, intolerant, unfriendly,
unselfish

Unit 13 Adjectives to describe people

Exercise 1: 1. careless / silly 2. horrible / nasty
3. wise / sensible 4. strange / funny
Exercise 2: 1d 2c 3e 4a 5b
6. very rude 7. a bit clumsy 8. very kind
9. very tactful
Exercise 3: 1. optimistic 2. selfish 3. fussy
4. pessimistic 5. pushy 6. intolerant
Exercise 4: 1. generosity 2. kindness 3. carelessness
4. sympathy 5. sensitivity 6. gratitude 7. patience
8. rudeness 9. tolerance 10. wisdom
Exercise 5: 1. mean, spiteful, nasty, unkind, rude,
horrible 2. nice, sweet, kind, lovely
Exercise 6: 1. impatient 2. nosey 3. childish
4. pessimistic
1b 2d 3a 4c

Unit 14 Feelings and emotions

Exercise 1: 1d 2c 3g 4f 5a 6e 7h 8b
Exercise 2: 1g 2h 3c 4a 5d 6e 7b 8f
Exercise 3: 1. hide 2. are 3. show 4. got 5. be
The complete expressions are: don't hide your
feelings, why are you in such a bad mood, I've got
mixed feelings, be in a good mood
Exercise 4: 1. gets really jealous 2. get a bit worried.
3. getting bored 4. getting a bit tired 5. getting really
excited 6. getting embarrassed 7. getting a bit
confused 8. getting nervous
Exercise 5: 1. terrified 2. amazed 3. exhausted
4. disgusted 5. stunned 6. horrified
Exercise 6: 1. of 2. about 3. of 4. about 5. by 6. of
7. of 8. by 9. about
Exercise 7: 1d 2b 3a 4e 5c

Unit 15 Happy or sad

Exercise 1: 1b 2d 3e 4a 5c
Exercise 2: 1. moon 2. heart 3. joy 4. tears 5. world
Exercise 3: 1. Smile 2. laughing 3. crying 4. moaned
5. frowning
Exercise 4: 1. lonely 2. homesick 3. myself 4. on my
own 5. missing 6. looking
Exercise 5: 1d 2f 3c 4e 5a 6b
Exercise 6: 1H 2S 3S 4S 5H 6S 7S
1b 2e 3f 4c 5d 6a 7g
8 is similar to 6; 9 is similar to 2; 10 is similar to 7.
It's no use crying over spilt milk means there is no
point regretting a mistake you have made. There's
nothing you can do about it now.

Unit 16 Getting angry

Exercise 1: a1 b1 c2 d2 e2 f1
Exercise 2: cross and annoyed, annoying and
irritating, furious and livid, OK and calm
1. OK / calm 2. cross / annoyed 3. furious / livid
4. annoying / irritating

Exercise 3: 1e 2d 3a 4f 5b 6c
Exercise 4: 1. crazy 2. nerves 3. enough 4. straw
5. death
Exercise 5: a. more b. mean c. help d. fault e. blame
f. realise 1. didn't realise 2. it wasn't my fault 3. I
didn't mean to do it (or I couldn't help it) 4. Don't
blame me 5. I couldn't help it 6. What more can I say?
Exercise 6: 1M 2F 3M 4M 5F 6M 7F 8M

Unit 17 Liking and disliking

Exercise 1: 1. really like 2. do like 3. love
4. absolutely adore 5. absolutely mad about 6. really
look forward to
Exercise 2: very positive: wonderful, brilliant,
fantastic, excellent, great **neutral:** not bad, all right,
OK **very negative:** appalling, terrible, awful, dreadful
Exercise 3: 1e 2f 3a 4b 5c 6d
Exercise 4: 1c 2e 3a 4f 5d 6b
Exercise 5: 1. on 2. about 3. into 4. of 5. from 6. to
Exercise 6: 1b 2d 3e 4a 5c
The phrases which express very strong dislike are: I
can't stand, I can't bear, I absolutely hate, I absolutely
loathe
Exercise 7: 1b 2f 3d 4a 5e 6c
Exercise 8: 1. I like Maria's husband very much.
2. I don't like this pub at all. 3. I thought it was
absolutely brilliant. 4. I really hate people telling me
what to do.
If you *go off* something, you start to dislike it.

Unit 18 Head and face

Exercise 1: 1. moustache 2. teeth 3. lips 4. beard
5. forehead 6. nose 7. eyelashes 8. tongue
9. eyebrow 10. ear 11. eyelid 12. mouth
13. hair 14. chin 15. cheek 16. neck
Exercise 2: a. head b. hair c. teeth d. nose e. eyes
1. dyeing my hair 2. lost all his hair 3. to brush my
teeth 4. hit my head 5. ruin your eyes 6. nodding
your head, shaking it 7. blow my nose 8. scratching
your head
Exercise 3: 1. smile 2. yawning 3. winked
4. grinning 5. went bright red 6. frowning
Exercise 4: 1. lick 2. suck 3. blow out 4. chew
5. kiss 6. spit out
1. spitting 2. swallow 3. bite 4. blowing
Exercise 5: 1. ears 2. eyes 3. mouth 4. eye 5. face
6. tongue 7. ear 8. nose
Exercise 6: 1. on a tube of toothpaste 2. on a bottle
of shampoo 3. on a bottle of skin cleansing lotion
4. on a tube or tub of face cream

Unit 19 Hair and face

Exercise 1: 1. curly hair 2. shoulder-length hair
3. long hair 4. wavy hair 5. short hair 6. bald

Exercise 2: 1. shaved 2. a fringe 3. tied back 4. a centre parting 5. a side parting 6. spiky 7. a pony tail 8. dreadlocks

Exercise 3: 1. shampoo 2. conditioner 3. extensions 4. greasy 5. dandruff 6. anti-dandruff 7. implants 8. wig

Exercise 4: 1. make-up 2. wrinkles 3. pierced 4. spots 5. cheekbones 6. complexion 7. beards, unshaven 8. mole 9. scar 10. teeth, false teeth

Exercise 6: 1. She's got such lovely, clear skin. 2. She's got such beautiful, high cheekbones. 3. He's got such beautiful, white teeth. 4. She's got light brown, curly hair. 5. She's got beautiful, piercing blue eyes. 6. He's got horrible, long, greasy hair.

Exercise 7: 1. face 2. eyes 3. nose 4. teeth 5. hair 6. ears

Unit 20 Parts of the body

Exercise 1: 1. head 2. neck 3. back 4. waist 5. bottom 6. leg 7. shoulder 8. elbow 9. arm 10. wrist 11. hip 12. foot 13. ear 14. chest 15. armpit 16. breast 17. stomach 18. ankle

Exercise 2: 1. thumb 2. palm 3. finger 4. nail

Exercise 3: 1. knee 2. thigh 3. heel 4. calf 5. toes 6. big toe

Exercise 4: 1B 2O 3B 4B 5O 6O 7O 8B

Exercise 5: 1f 2c 3a 4h 5g 6b 7d 8e 9i 10l 11k 12m 13n 14o 15j

Unit 21 Body movements

Exercise 1: 1. sit down 2. stand up 3. lie down 4. lean 5. kneel 6. bow

Exercise 2: 1. walk 2. run 3. jump 4. climb 5. crawl 6. dive 7. hop 8. dance

Exercise 3: 1. push 2. pulled 3. lift 4. dragged

Exercise 4: 1. walk 2. lean 3. jump 4. climb 5. lie 6. sit

Exercise 5: 1. tripped over 2. fell down 3. fell off 4. slip 5. collapsed

Exercise 6: 1. catch 2. throw 3. wave 4. clap 5. hold 6. point 7. reach 8. punch 9. kick 1. stepped 2. slapped 3. grabbed 4. reach 5. stamped 6. waving, waved 7. shake 8. hold on

Exercise 7: Quick: rushed, dashed, leapt up, marched, raced **Slow:** tiptoed, limping, strolled, creeping, wandering

Unit 22 The senses

Exercise 1: 1. touch 2. smell 3. sight 4. taste 5. hearing

Exercise 2: 1b 2a 3d 4e 5c

Exercise 3: 1c,h 2a,g 3e,j 4b,f 5d,i

Exercise 4: 1b 2c 3d 4a 5e

Exercise 5: 1. can't see 2. can smell 3. can't hear 4. can feel 5. can really taste

Exercise 6: 1. see 2. watch 3. watch / see 4. watching

5. look 6. look 7. see

Exercise 7: 1b 2e 3d 4a 5c

Exercise 8: 1. listen carefully 2. catch, paying attention 3. overheard

Exercise 9: 1. feel 2. hear 3. touched 4. smell 5. see / hear   If you have a *sixth sense*, you are able to know what is going to happen before it happens.

Unit 23 Feeling ill

Exercise 2: 1b 2c 3d 4a

Exercise 3: 1d 2g 3f 4b 5a 6e 7c 8m 9l 10h 11i 12k 13j

Exercise 4: 1f-12, 2c-16, 3h-10, 4b-14, 5a-11, 6d-15, 7g-13, 8e-9

Exercise 5: 1f 2e 3c 4a 5d 6b

Exercise 6: 1. bronchitis 2. flu 3. an allergy 4. measles 5. food poisoning 6. hay fever

Exercise 7: feeling, get, recover, making

Unit 24 Injuries

Exercise 2: 1i 2d 3b 4f 5a 6e 7g 8c 9h

Exercise 3: 1. He's been wounded. 2. He's been injured. (*wound* normally implies a weapon, such as a knife or a gun) 1. wound 2. injury 3. wounded 4. injured a slight injury, a knife wound, an internal injury, a deep wound, a bullet wound, a back injury, a sports injury, a stab wound

Exercise 4: 1b 2a 3d 4c

Exercise 5: 1f 2b 3a 4d 5c 6e

Exercise 6: a. pain b. black c. blood d. blisters e. scratch f. agony 1. My feet are covered in blisters. 2. It's just a scratch. 3. She's in a lot of pain. 4. There was blood everywhere. 5. I was in absolute agony! 6. I'm black and blue all over this morning.

Unit 25 At the doctor's

Exercise 1: 1. appointment 2. cough 3. symptom 4. rash 5. infection 6. virus 7. medicine 8. prescription, chemist's

Exercise 2: 1D 2P 3D 4P 5P 6D 7P 8D 9D 10D 11P 12P

Exercise 3: 1e 2g 3a 4d 5c 6f 7b

Exercise 4: 1. give 2. take 3. listen to 4. take 5. take 6. give 7. give 8. take a4 b5 c2 d7 e3 f1 g8 h6

Exercise 5: a1 b3 c4 d5 e2

Exercise 6: Here are the words with the stress marked: dietician, optician, physiotherapist, psychiatrist, chiropodist, paediatrician, gynaecologist, rheumatologist 1b 2a 3h 4f 5c 6g 7d 8e

Exercise 7: 1. aromatherapy 2. hypnotism 3. massage 4. herbal remedies 5. acupuncture 6. reflexology 7. homeopathy

Unit 26 In hospital

Exercise 2: 1b 2d 3c 4f 5a 6e
Exercise 3: 1g 2e 3d 4c 5h 6f 7a 8b
Exercise 4: 1. surgeon 2. ambulance 3. nurse
4. patient 5. stretcher 6. paramedic
Exercise 5: 1. have 2. gave 3. give 4. do 5. put
6. need 7. leave 8. need
Exercise 6: seriously injured, rushed to hospital,
fighting to save his life, treated for shock
Exercise 7: 1G 2B 3G 4G 5B 6B 7G 8B
Exercise 8: 1. treated 2. cured 3. treatment 4. heal

Unit 27 A healthy lifestyle

Exercise 1: Fresh fruit, plenty of fresh air, fish, regular
exercise, salad **are all good for you.**
Smoking, lots of sugar, a lot of stress at work, too
much alcohol, too much salt **are all bad for you.**
1. keeps 2. stay 3. give up 4. cut down 5. avoid
6. keep 7. cut down 8. give up 9. avoid 10. stayed
Exercise 2: 1b,f 2a,d 3a,d 4c,g 5e,h 6e,h
(dialogue) put on, cut it out, resist, join
Exercise 3: fit and healthy: in really good shape, as fit
as a fiddle, got loads of energy
not fit: unfit, gets out of breath, out of condition
Exercise 4: 14 or 15 a's – Congratulations! You're as
fit as a fiddle. 10-13 a's – You're in pretty good
shape. Keep it up! 6-9 a's – You could be in better
condition. Perhaps you need to go on a diet or join a
gym. 0-5 a's – Oh dear! You'd better go to the doctor
for a check-up before it's too late!
Exercise 5: 1a 2d 3c 4b
Exercise 6: 1. eat between meals 2. my waist size
3. drink in moderation 4. on a regular basis 5. get
rid of spots 6. look carefully at your diet 7. eat more
healthily 8. try cutting out all sugar and butter

Unit 28 Houses and homes

Exercise 1: 1b 2d 3a 4f 5e 6c
Exercise 2: 1. the top floor 2. the first floor 3. the
ground floor 4. the basement
Exercise 3: 1. fence 2. lawn 3. hedge 4. roof
5. chimneys 6. balcony 7. front door 8. steps
9. gate 10. garage
Exercise 4: 1. ceiling 2. light switch 3. power point
4. radiator 5. wall 6. floor
Exercise 5: 1c 2f 3d 4b 5a 6e
Exercise 6: 1. share 2. furnished 3. deposit
4. advance 5. tenants 6. landlord
Exercise 7: 1c 2a 3g 4d 5f 6b 7e
Exercise 8: 1. home 2. home 3. house 4. home
5. house 6. home 7. house 8. home 9. home, house
10. home

Unit 29 The living room

Exercise 1: 1. blind 2. curtain 3. bookcase 4. stereo
system 5. television 6. cushions 7. lamp 8. picture
9. mantelpiece 10. clock 11. ornament 12. fireplace
13. dining chair 14. sofa 15. coffee table
16. armchair 17. rug 18. carpet 19. dining table
20. remote control
Exercise 2: 1c 2e 3h 4g 5f 6b 7i 8a 9d
Exercise 3: 1h 2a 3e 4c 5g 6b 7f 8d
1k 2n 3l 4p 5i 6o 7m 8j
Exercise 4: 1. napkin 2. dessert spoon 3. plate
4. wine glass 5. knife 6. coaster 7. soup spoon
8. placemat 9. fork
Exercise 5: 1a 2g 3d 4h 5e 6c 7f 8b

Unit 30 The kitchen

Exercise 1: 1. cooker 2. microwave 3. dishwasher
4. fridge 5. freezer 6. washing machine
Exercise 2: 1. tap 2. plug 3. sink 4. work surface
5. drawer 6. cupboard
Exercise 3: 1. jug 2. mug 3. dish 4. fork 5. spoon
6. bowl 7. cup 8. glass 9. plate 10. knife 11. saucer
12. teaspoon
Exercise 4: 1. casserole dish 2. kettle 3. teapot
4. grater 5. oven glove 6. corkscrew 7. tin opener
8. whisk 9. frying pan 10. wok 11. scales
12. toaster 13. large cooking pot 14. saucepan
15. food processor 16. mugs
Exercise 5: 1. open 2. boiled 3. set 4. do 5. dry
6. heat
Exercise 6: 1. a tea towel 2. a corkscrew 3. a kettle
4. in the freezer 5. a whisk 6. a tin opener 7. a
teapot 8. in the sink or in a dishwasher 9. scales
10. a grater 11. a microwave 12. an oven glove

Unit 31 The bedroom and bathroom

Exercise 1: 1. wardrobe 2. chest of drawers
3. mirror 4. lamp 5. bedside table 6. rug 7. alarm
clock 8. bed
Exercise 2: 1. pillow 2. duvet 3. sheet 4. blanket
5. mattress A *bunk-bed* is one bed above another.
Exercise 3: 1. boxer shorts 2. pyjamas 3. nightdress
4. dressing gown
Exercise 4: 1. I fell asleep 2. I felt so sleepy
3. I couldn't get to sleep 4. I woke up 5. I overslept
6. I had a nightmare
Exercise 5: 1. toilet lid 2. mirror 3. washbasin
4. towel 5. towel rail 6. tiles 7. shower 8. bath
9. shower curtain 10. toilet
1. shampoo 2. comb 3. soap 4. toothbrush 5. razor
6. shaving foam 7. toilet roll 8. toothpaste
Exercise 6: have: a shower, a bath, a shave, a quick
wash **wash:** your hair, your face, your hands
brush: your hair, your teeth

Unit 32 Jobs around the house

Exercise 1: 1. do the cooking 2. do some gardening 3. do the washing up / dishes 4. do the dusting 5. do the washing 6. do the ironing

Exercise 2: 1. bucket 2. dustpan and brush 3. mop 4. washing line 5. iron 6. vacuum cleaner / hoover 7. ironing board 8. cloth

Exercise 3: 1c 2d 3a 4b 5f 6g 7h 8e
You *polish* the table, but not the sofa. You first *clear* the table, then *wipe* it.

Exercise 4: 1f 2e 3a 4c 5b 6d

Exercise 5: 1. clean 2. clear 3. empty 4. put 5. throw out

Exercise 6: 1c 2f 3e 4a 5d 6b

Exercise 7: 1. something 2. favour 3. hand 4. mind

Unit 33 Problems around the house

Exercise 2: 1c 2d 3a 4b

Exercise 3: 1c 2a 3f 4b 5e 6d

Exercise 4: 1. knocked 2. smashed 3. dropped 4. ruined 5. stained 6. burst

Exercise 5: 1c 2a 3b 4a 5c 6b 7c 8b 9a

Exercise 6: 1. mousetrap 2. glue 3. pliers 4. needle and thread 5. spanner 6. scissors 7. hammer 8. ladder 9. torch 10. screwdriver 11. screws 12. nails 13. paintbrush 14. saw

Unit 34 Meat, fish and groceries

Exercise 1: pig: pork, ham, bacon **sheep:** lamb **poultry:** chicken, turkey, duck, guinea fowl **cow:** beef, veal **inside an animal:** liver, kidney

Exercise 2: 1. steak 2. chops 3. pork 4. burger 5. chicken

Exercise 3: 1 squid 2. tuna 3. plaice 4. sole 5. snapper 6. mussels 7. clam 8. crab 9. salmon 10. trout 11. prawn 12. lobster

Exercise 4: 1d 2e 3b 4g 5h 6c 7f 8a

Exercise 5: 1. salad 2. bread 3. soup 4. cheese 5. rice 6. oil

Exercise 6: 1. cake 2. yoghurt 3. sauce 4. chocolate 5. pie 6. ice cream

Exercise 7: 1d 2e 3b 4a 5c

Unit 35 Fruit and vegetables

Exercise 1: 1. (black)currants 2. pomegranate 3. bananas 4. orange 5. lemon 6. melon 7. pear 8. strawberries 9. peach 10. pineapple 11. raspberry 12. apple 13. cherries 14. plums 15. grapes

Exercise 2: Words that go with fruit: fresh, ripe, citrus, tropical, rotten, tinned, organic

Words that go with vegetables: fresh, rotten, frozen, raw, tinned, stir-fried, organic

Exercise 3: 1. skin 2. stones 3. bunches 4. seedless 5. pips 6. exotic 7. varieties 8. bitter

Exercise 4: 1. cauliflower 2. onion 3. cabbage 4. Brussels sprouts 5. beans 6. courgette 7. broccoli 8. potato 9. mushroom 10. sweet corn 11. leek 12. carrot 13. turnip 14. aubergine 15. peas (in a pod)

Exercise 5: 1. cucumber 2. sweet peppers 3. avocado 4. celery 5. lettuce 6. tomatoes

Exercise 6: 1. egg plants 2. zucchini 3. paprika 4. beans 5. gherkins 6. potato 7. shell 8. peel

Unit 36 Talking about food

Exercise 1: 1e 2c 3h 4a 5f 6b 7d 8g
Brunch is a large, late breakfast in mid-morning.

Exercise 2: The odd words out are: 1. easy 2. fat 3. hard 4. fit 5. fast 6. thin

Exercise 3: 1. burnt 2. fresh 3. sour 4. stale 5. rotten 6. ripe

Exercise 4: 1. off, disgusting 2. tasty, delicious 3. flavour, bland 4. wonderful, revolting 5. flavour, tender

Exercise 5: 1a 2d 3e 4c 5b 6f

Exercise 6: 1. sweet 2. hot (or spicy) 3. underdone 4. rich 5. dry, stale 6. too many bones

Exercise 7: 1d 2a 3e 4b 5c

Unit 37 Cooking

Exercise 1: 1d 2c 3b 4f 5e 6a 7i 8h 9j 10g

Exercise 2: 1. cook 2. recipe 3. delicious 4. ingredients 5. sauce 6. helping

Exercise 3: 1. beat 2. slice 3. squeeze 4. peel 5. grate 6. chop – 1b 2d 3e 4c 5a 6i 7j 8f 9h 10g

Exercise 4: 1. eggs 2. steak 3. potato 4. salmon 5. onions 6. rice

Exercise 5: 1H 2H 3G 4H 5G 6H 7G 8H 9G 10G 11G 12H 13G 14G

Exercise 6: 1. slice 2. add 3. heat the oil 4. stirring 5. cook gently 6. serve

Unit 38 Eating out

Exercise 2: 1R 2F 3R 4F 5R 6R 7R 8R 9F 10R 11R

Exercise 3: 1e 2a 3d 4f 5b 6c 7i 8g 9h

Exercise 4: a5 b4 c2 d1 e3

Exercise 5: 1d 2h 3e 4c 5b 6f 7a 8g

Exercise 6: 1a 2c 3d 4b 5e

Exercise 7: 1D 2M 3S 4M 5S 6D 7M 8D 9S

Exercise 8: 1. Italy 2. Spain 3. China 4. India 5. Scotland 6. Germany 7. Greece 8. Mexico 9. Japan 10. Korea 11. Russia (or Poland) 12. France

Unit 39 Drinks

Exercise 1: alcoholic drinks: beer, wine, cider, cava, stout, lager, rum, sherry, champagne
soft drinks: coke, juice, tonic, ginger ale, lemonade, soda, pepsi
Exercise 2: 1. lager 2. bitter 3. stout 4. cider, scrumpy
Exercise 3: 1. hops 2. distilleries 3. barley 4. malt 5. water 6. peat
Exercise 4: 1. juice 2. milk 3. water 4. wine 5. beer 6. coffee 7. tea 8. drink
Exercise 5: 1. red wine 2. lager or bitter 3. lager or bitter 4. Becks or red wine
Exercise 6: 1. What can I get you? 2. I'll have the same again 3. Can I have a soft drink, 4. I'm sorry, I'm driving 5. This is my round 6. Half or a pint? 7. Ice and lemon? 8. Cheers!
Exercise 7: 1. had 2. goes 3. open 4. stick 5. feeling 6. pour 7. mix 8. put

Unit 40 Talking about your free time

Exercise 1: 1b and e 2d and f 3a and c
Exercise 2: 1. having a party, come along, bring 2. meeting up with 3. go round 4. get together
Exercise 3: 1c 2d 3f 4a 5e 6b
7. have a very active social life 8. have a quiet night in 9. I've been stuck indoors, have some fun 10. going to a party
Exercise 4: 1. go to 2. go for 3. go 4. went shopping 5. went for a walk 6. go for a swim 7. went to the zoo 8. went for a drive in the country
Exercise 5: 1c 2f 3b 4a 5d 6e
Sentences 2, 4 and 6 answer question 7. Sentences 1, 3 and 5 answer question 8.

Unit 41 Hobbies and interests

Exercise 1: 1. collect 2. play 3. do 4. collect 5. collect 6. play 7. do 8. play 9. collect 10. collect 11. play 12. do
Exercise 2: 1. chess 2. draughts, chess 3. a pack of cards 4. dominoes 5. backgammon 6. dice
Exercise 3: 1b 2c 3d 4a
5. dominoes 6. prince 7. soldier
8. a = spades   b = hearts   c = clubs d = diamonds
Exercise 4: photography: camera, develop a film, tripod, zoom lens **painting:** brushes, oil paints, easel, watercolour **making clothes:** material, sewing machine, needle and cotton, pattern **cooking:** cake decorating, ingredients, recipe, pastry
Exercise 5: 1. in 2. on 3. with 4. of 5. into 6. in
Exercise 6: 1. learning 2. spend, joined 3. give it up 4. takes 5. gets, relax 6. took up

Unit 42 Activities and interests

Exercise 1: 1. hunting 2. skiing 3. riding 4. orienteering 5. skateboarding 6. hill-walking 7. windsurfing 8. gardening 9. camping 10. surfing 11. rollerblading 12. fishing
Exercise 2: 1. fishing 2. skateboarding 3. camping 4. hunting 5. riding 6. skiing 7. gardening 8. rollerblading 9. surfing 10. sailing 11. hill-walking 12. orienteering
Exercise 3: 1. snowboarding 2. bungee jumping 3. parachute jumping 4. paragliding 5. hang-gliding 6. water skiing 7. scuba-diving 8. climbing
Exercise 4: 1. go ten-pin bowling 2. sing in a choir 3. go to a yoga class 4. go folk dancing 5. play pool 6. play darts 7. play in a band 8. play bingo
Exercise 5: 1. often 2. used 3. times 4. time 5. other 6. twice 7. possible 8. every

Unit 43 Special occasions

Exercise 1: a. Christmas b. Hallowe'en c. Easter d. Valentine's Day e. New Year's Eve
1. Easter 2. New Year's Eve 3. Hallowe'en 4. Valentine's Day 5. Christmas
Exercise 2: 1c 2a 3b 4j 5g 6d 7i 8e 9f 10h
Exercise 3: 1. end 2. death 3. collapse 4. birth 5. landing 6. independence 7. assassination 8. discovery
Exercise 4: 1. parades 2. costumes 3. bands 4. dancing 5. festivities 6. firework
Exercise 5: 1. gave birth 2. weighing 3. was present 4. fainted 5. delighted 6. are both fine
Exercise 6: 1. dinner 2. party 3. cards 4. present 5. cake 6. candles 7. blow 8. speech
Exercise 7: 1. getting 2. passing 3. graduating 4. winning 5. having 6. reaching 7d 8a 9c 10b

Unit 44 Film and cinema

Exercise 1: 1. critic 2. star 3. review 4. director 5. scene
Exercise 2: 1. screen 2. row 3. subtitles 4. trailers 5. credits
Exercise 3: 1c 2b 3a 4d 5h 6i 7f 8e 9g
Positive: famous, classic, hilarious, epic, gripping, action-packed
Negative: predictable, dated, ridiculous
Exercise 4: 1d 2c 3e 4a 5b
Exercise 5: You should have deleted: 1. on site 2. play 3. actresses 4. the players 5. tale 6. the action 7. uniforms 8. are translated 9. the screenplay 10. special tricks
Exercise 6: 1. played, the role 2. nominated, three Oscars 3. shoot, the scene 4. given, rave reviews
Exercise 7: 1e 2d 3b 4a 5c
The film is *Jurassic Park*.

Unit 45 Books and art

Exercise 2: Part 1. fiction: ghost story, novel, thriller, classic, detective story, science fiction
non-fiction: encyclopedia, biography, atlas, textbook, dictionary, autobiography
Part 2. a. dictionary b. encyclopedia c. atlas
Part 3. 1. an autobiography 2. a cookery book
3. a children's book 4. a travel guide
Exercise 3: 1c 2e 3a 4f 5d 6b
Exercise 4: 1P 2N 3P 4N 5N 6P 7N
Exercise 5: poetry, poems, recite, poet, verses
Exercise 6: 1. portrait 2. landscapes 3. abstract
4. still life 5. oils, watercolours
Exercise 7: 1. artist 2. paintings 3. gallery
4. exhibition 5. critics 6. collectors
Exercise 8: 1. mural 2. statue 3. sculpture 4. bust
5. mosaic 6. ceramics

Unit 46 Music

Exercise 1: Section1: strings **Section 2:** brass
Section 3: woodwind **Section 4:** percussion
a. triangle b. cymbals c. clarinet d. trumpet
e. trombone f. cello g. violin h. harp
Exercise 2: 1. composer 2. conductor 3. movements, symphony 4. concerto 5. overture
Exercise 3: 1. voice, choir, solo 2. music, ear
3. lessons, practice 4. piece
Exercise 4: 1. keyboard player 2. drummer
3. backing singers 4. bass player 5. lead singer
6. guitarist
Exercise 5: 1. tour, venues, gig 2. lyrics 3. verse, chorus
Exercise 6: 1. album, track 2. solo 3. tune 4. songs, cover version 5. single, number one, charts

Unit 47 Ball and racquet sports

Exercise 1: 1. baseball 2. volleyball 3. rugby
4. basketball 5. American football 6. football
Exercise 2: 1. table tennis 2. badminton 3. squash
4. tennis
Exercise 3: *The nineteenth hole* is a way of talking about the clubhouse, where you can have a drink.
Exercise 4: 1b 2c 3a 4b 5a 6d 7b
Exercise 5: 1b 2c 3a 4a 5a 6a 7a 8b 9b
Exercise 6: 1. throw it 2. head it 3. catch it 4. hit it
5. kick it 6. pass it 7. hits the ball so hard
8. runs with the ball 9. pass the ball
Exercise 7: 1. tennis 2. golf 3. basketball 4. tennis
5. rugby 6. golf 7. rugby 8. basketball

Unit 48 Football

Exercise 1: 1. match 2. pitch 3. team 4. goal, pass
5. foul, referee, red card 6. offside 7. substitute 8. at home, Away
Exercise 2: 1c 2e 3b 4a 5d

Exercise 3: 1. post 2. crossbar 3. net 4. goal-line
1. goal 2. corner flag 3. centre circle 4. halfway line
5. touch-line 6. penalty spot 7. penalty area
8. six-yard box
Exercise 4: 1. scored 2. saved 3. committed 4. had
5. hit 6. missed 7. head 8. blocked
Exercise 5: 1. make 2. take 3. make 4. make
5. take 6. make 7. take 8. take
Exercise 6: 1. stoppage time 2. extra time 3. kick-off
4. first half 5. half-time 6. second half
Exercise 7: 1c 2d 3a 4e 5b yellow card = book a player red card = send a player off

Unit 49 Other sports

Exercise 1: 1. horse racing 2. swimming 3. show jumping 4. skiing 5. motor racing 6. ice hockey
7. ice-skating 8. weightlifting 9. gymnastics
10. cycling
Exercise 2: 1. boxing 2. swimmer 3. skier 4. ice-skating 5. gymnastics 6. athlete 7. racing driver
8. cyclist 9. horse racing 10. pentathlete
11. sailing 12. rower 13. sky diving
14. weightlifter 15. climbing
Exercise 3: 1. boxing 2. horse racing 3. motor racing
4. athletics 5. skiing 6. swimming 7. gymnastics
8. sailing/rowing
Exercise 4: 1. the shot-put 2. the long jump 3. the hurdles 4. the high jump 5. the discus
6. the javelin
Exercise 5: The world *heavyweight* champion, Lennox Lewis, successfully defended his *title* against American Evander Hollyfield last night. Right from the very start Lewis had Hollyfield in trouble and at the end of the *first round,* Hollyfield was clearly very relieved to get back to his *corner.* The *bell* went for the second round and Lewis immediately knocked his opponent down with a huge *right hand* and it seemed only a matter of time before Lewis would win by a *knock-out.* But Hollyfield recovered and as the fight went on he got increasingly stronger, causing the champion serious problems. In the end it went the full twelve rounds and Lewis was quite relieved to win on *points.*
Exercise 6: 1. boxing, wrestling, kick boxing
2. boxing, kick boxing 3. karate, judo 4. wrestling, judo
Carl Lewis – athletics
Martina Navratilova – tennis
Ayrton Senna – motor racing

Unit 50 Results and scores

Exercise 2: 1. win 2. win 3. win 4. win 5. win
6. win 7. beat 8. win 9. beat 10. beat 11. win
12. win 13. beat 14. beat 15. beat 16. win
17. champion 18. record 19. favourite 20. rival
Exercise 3: 1e 2c 3f 4a 5b 6d

Exercise 4: 1d 2c 3a 4g 5b 6e 7f
You win *silver* for coming 2nd, and *bronze* for 3rd.
Exercise 5: 1. leading 2. beating 3. winning, losing
Exercise 6: 1. won 2. beat 3. lost to 4. drew
5. scored 6. conceded
Exercise 7: 1f 2a 3c 4b 5e 6d

Unit 51 Television

Exercise 1: 1. screen 2. widescreen 3. portable TV
4. Video, DVD recorder 5. remote control
6. cable, aerial, dish 7. subscription 8. Pay-
per-view 9. channel
Exercise 2: 1. 5.15 The Hidden Planet 2. 7.30
Coronation Street 3. 4.30 Disneytime 4. 11.45 The
Jack Dee show 5. 11.00 Panorama 6. 9.30
Parkinson 7. 6.15 Pride and Prejudice 8. 8.00 Who
Wants to be a Millionaire?
Exercise 3: 1. programme 2. repeats 3. interview
4. guests 5. highlights 6. series 7. serial, episode
Exercise 4: 1. channel 2. viewers 3. live 4. adverts
5. presenter 6. contestants

Unit 52 Newspapers

Exercise 1: 1b 2c 3a 4d 5e
Exercise 2: 1. Sports news 2. Foreign news 3. Home
news 4. Readers' letters 5. Editorial 6. Classified
7. Entertainment guide 8. Business and money news
9. Obituaries 10. Weather forecast 11. Personal
12. Reviews
Exercise 3: 1b 2a 3e 4d 5c
Exercise 4: 1. article 2. front page, headlines
3. circulations 4. privacy 5. supplement
Exercise 5: 1b 2c 3a 4f 5d 6e
DIRECTOR QUITS   PLANE TRAGEDY
FESTIVAL ROW   PRIME MINISTER BACKS
PLAN   STRIKE HITS TRAVELLERS   BOMB
SCARE
Exercise 6: 1. described 2. appealed 3. demanded
4. announced 5. claimed

Unit 53 Advertising

Exercise 1: 1. a poster 2. a leaflet 3. classified ads
4. a commercial
Exercise 2: 1. influence 2. slogan 3. sponsor, logo
4. brand 5. competitors 6. agency 7. publicity
8. hype
Exercise 3: 1e 2f 3g 4a 5b 6h 7d 8c
Exercise 4: 1c 2b 3d 4a 5h 6e 7f 8g
Exercise 5: a. offer b. deal c. gifts d. loyalty e. tour
1. special offer 2. promotional tour 3. sponsorship
deal 4. free gifts 5. brand loyalty
f. prices g. magazines h. names i. points j. shot
6. brand names 7. glossy magazines
8. competitive prices 9. selling points 10. mail shot

Unit 54 Telephones

Exercise 2: 1. that, It's 2. there, take a message, call
back 3. This, ring 4. wrong, no-one 5. wrong
Exercise 3: 1. call 2. make 3. give 4. leave 5. dial
6. look it up 7. got 8. answer
Exercise 4: 1. get through 2. got the wrong number
3. was engaged 4. got cut off 5. called straight back
6. hung up
Exercise 5: The correct order is: e i d a f h b g c
Exercise 6: 1. Speaking 2. Hold the line, put you
through 3. available 4. Extension, left a message,
bear with me 5. line, hold

Unit 55 Computers

Exercise 1: 1. palmtop 2. scanner 3. keyboard
4. mousepad 5. VDU or monitor 6. computer
7. mouse 8. laptop 9. printer
Exercise 3: 1. software 2. pre-installed 3. CD-ROMs
4. hard disk 5. installation 6. helpline
Exercise 4: 1. memory 2. terminals 3. modem
4. template 5. toolbar 6. word processor
7. document 8. database 9. spreadsheets
Exercise 5: 1d 2a 3g 4e 5b 6c 7f
Exercise 6: 1. hackers 2. viruses 3. bug 4. crashed
5. lost
Exercise 7: 1. sites 2. on-line 3. download 4. chat
room 5. newsgroup 6. web page

Unit 56 Machines and equipment

Exercise 1: 1. video / DVD player 2. CD player
3. speaker 4. cassette deck 5. turntable (or record
player) 6. headphones 7. electric razor / shaver
8. electric toothbrush 9. hairdryer 10. fan 11. iron
12. video camera 13. vacuum cleaner 14. sewing
machine 15. knob 16. battery 17. extension lead
18. switch 19. socket 20. plug
Exercise 2: 1. works, press 2. runs 3. unplugged
4. went
Exercise 3: 1. out/off 2. up 3. on 4. down 5. in
Exercise 4: 1. motor 2. device 3. machinery
4. gadgets 5. appliances 6. machine
Exercise 5: 1e 2b 3f 4c 5a 6d
Exercise 6: 1. wrong 2. breaking 3. funny 4. order
5. new 6. properly

Unit 57 Money

Exercise 1: 1. notes 2. coins 3. cash 4. credit card
5. cheque 6. currency 7. money belt
Exercise 2: 1. cash 2. cheque 3. credit card
4. change
Exercise 3: 1i 2d 3e 4c 5h 6a 7f 8g 9j 10b
Exercise 4: 1. I'm getting a rise 2. earns pretty good
money 3. get £400 a week 4. make a lot more

Exercise 5: A. pay for B. pay C. pay off
1. pay bills 2. pay it off 3. pay off all my debts
4. paid the rent 5. pay off the mortgage 6. tax you have to pay
Exercise 6: 1b 2d 3a 4e 5c 6h 7f 8j 9g 10i
Exercise 7: 1. It's very good value for money.
2. What a waste of money! 3. It'll save a bit of money. 4. He's got more money than sense!
Exercise 8: 1e 2b 3d 4a 5c

Unit 58 Rich and poor

Exercise 1: Lots of money: wealthy, well-off, comfortable, they must be loaded
Little money: short of money, broke, hard up, couldn't afford
9+ 10- 11- 12- 13+ 14-
Exercise 2: 1+ 2- 3- 4- 5+ 6- 7- 8- 9+
Exercise 3: First dialogue: borrow, lending, owe, lent, pay you back **Second dialogue:** lend, borrowing, paid back, lent, get it back
Exercise 4: 1. progress 2. poverty 3. wealth
4. share 5. debt 6. poor
Exercise 5: 1. far too much, a fortune 2. hardly anything, next to nothing, peanuts
Exercise 6: 1. afford 2. belts 3. short 4. hard
5. penny 6. next 7. luxury 8. get 9. lend
10. borrow

Unit 59 At the bank

Exercise 1: 1. cash 2. account 3. loan 4. borrow
5. cheque 6. overdrawn 7. interest 8. debts
9. cashpoint 10. overdraft
Exercise 2: 1. Russia 2. Japan 3. India 4. Brazil
5. those countries which are part of the Euro-zone, for example France, Germany, etc 6. Mexico
Exercise 3: current, deposit, savings, joint **account**
credit, cash **card**
1. joint account 2. current account 3. credit card
4. cash card 5. savings account, deposit account
Exercise 4: 1. a pay-in 2. a withdrawal 3. write
4. direct debit, standing order 5. electronic
Exercise 5: 1. overdrawn 2. overdraft 3. debt
4. loan 5. interest 6. mortgage
If your account is *in the black,* it is in credit (+). If it is *in the red,* it is in debit (-).
Exercise 6: 1c 2a 3f 4c 5b 6d
7. balance 8. statement 9. transactions
Exercise 7: 1b 2d 3c 4e 5a

Unit 60 Shops and shopping

Exercise 1: 1. butcher's 2. florist's 3. baker's
4. newsagent's 5. greengrocer's 6. off-licence
7. chemist's 8. ironmonger's
Meat shop is not the correct name for a shop.
candy store = sweet shop, *drugstore* = chemist's, *liquor store* = off-licence

Exercise 2: 1. baskets, trolley 2. checkout 3. plastic
bag 4. aisle 5. organic, organic
Exercise 3: 1S 2C 3S 4S 5C 6C
Exercise 4: 1. make a list 2. pick up a bargain 3. try
this on 4. get a refund, keep the receipt 5. got this
If you're *window-shopping,* you're just looking in the shop windows with no intention of buying anything.
Exercise 5: 1. price 2. cost 3. price 4. cost 5. price
6. price 7. price 8. cost 9. the cost of living
10. half-price 11. two for the price of one
12. price list 13. price tag 14. total cost
Exercise 6: 1E 2C 3E 4E 5C 6F 7E 8E
Exercise 7: 1f 2g 3h 4c 5b 6e 7a 8d

Unit 61 Holidays

Exercise 1: 1d 2e 3b 4a 5c and f
Exercise 2: 1. holiday 2. resort 3. tour 4. trip
Exercise 3: 1g 2e 3d 4b 5c 6a 7h 8f
Exercise 4: 1. cruise 2. beach 3. safari 4. camping
5. skiing 6. adventure 7. sightseeing – The last advert is for a holiday in San Francisco.
Exercise 5: 1. travel agent's, brochures 2. break, long weekend 3. abroad 4. high season, tourists
Exercise 6: 1b 2e 3a 4c 5d
Exercise 7: 1. money 2. health 3. transport 4. food
5. shopping 6. accommodation

Unit 62 Beach holidays

Exercise 1: 1. the horizon 2. pier 3. rocks 4. cliffs
5. beach 6. sunlounger 7. waves 8. windsurfer
9. jet ski
Exercise 2: 1. inflatable dinghy 2. snorkel and mask
3. flippers 4. bikini 5. beach towel 6. swimming
costume 7. lilo 8. swimming trunks
Exercise 3: 1. crowded 2. deserted 3. golden, crystal-clear 4. unspoilt 5. rocky 6. naturist
Exercise 4: Dear Jane, Here we are in Portugal. The weather's absolutely *glorious* – the sun's been *shining* ever since we arrived. The hotel is really *luxurious* and we're only five minutes from the beach, which is *deserted* most of the time. That's where we are now. Peter's lying here next to me *soaking up* the sun and the kids are *playing* in the sea. The *tide* is coming in and we've got to move up the beach before we all get soaked! Wish you were here. Love Emma
Exercise 5: a. get b. keep c. go d. get e. go f. cool
down 1. get a lovely suntan 2. get sunburnt 3. keep out of the sun 4. cool down in the sea 5. go for a paddle 6. go for a swim
Exercise 6: 1. sunbathe 2. factor 3. sunblock
4. shade 5. exposure 6. cancer

Unit 63 Forms of transport

Exercise 1: 1. scooter 2. motorbike 3. minibus
4. bus 5. train 6. moped 7. coach 8. tram
9. bicycle 10. car 11. van 12. lorry

Exercise 2: 1. car ferry 2. speedboat 3. rowing boat
4. barge 5. submarine 6. canoe 7. fishing boat
8. lifeboat 9. yacht 10. cruise ship
Exercise 3: 1. balloon 2. airship 3. light aircraft
4. helicopter 5. jet
Exercise 4: 1. tyre 2. mudguard 3. saddle
4. crossbar 5. handlebars 6. brakes 7. spokes
8. pedal 9. chain 10 gears
Exercise 5: ship: cabin, deck, pool
bike: puncture, pump, pedalling
plane: take-off, landing, wings
train: carriages, compartment, platform
Exercise 6: 1. boat 2. car 3. train 4. bike 5. bus
6c 7d 8b 9a

Unit 64 Cars

Exercise 1: 1. hatchback 2. convertible 3. saloon
4. off-road 5. sports car 6. estate 7. limousine
Exercise 2: 1. number plate 2. headlights 3. wing
mirror 4. bonnet 5. windscreen wipers
6. windscreen 7. sunroof 8. boot 9. bumper
10. tyre 11. dashboard 12. indicator 13. steering
wheel 14. speedometer 15. accelerator 16. brake
17. clutch 18. handbrake 19. gear stick 20. heating
controls
Exercise 3: 1c 2a 3f 4e 5d 6b
Exercise 4: 1d 2b 3e 4a 5c 6. put your headlights
on 7. fasten your seatbelt 8. change gear
Exercise 5: 1. tax 2. insurance 3. comprehensive
4. servicing 5. repairs
Exercise 6: 1. park 2. reversed 3. indicate
4. overtake 5. brake 6. start, push
Exercise 7: 1. give you a lift 2. pick you up 3. drop
you off

Unit 65 Driving

Exercise 1: 1d 2c 3e 4b 5a
6. unleaded petrol, petrol station 7. double yellow
lines, parking ticket 8. traffic jam
Exercise 2: 1. roundabout 2. junction 3. steep hill
4. traffic lights 5. level crossing (trains) 6. maximum
speed limit 7. pedestrian crossing 8. wild animals
9. danger
Exercise 3: 1. No overtaking 2. No right turn 3. End
of motorway 4. No entry 5. Two-way traffic
6. Give way 7. Bend ahead 8. One-way street
Exercise 4: 1. inside lane 2. middle lane 3. outside
lane 4. hard shoulder, emergency phone 5. slip road
Exercise 5: 1c 2d 3b 4a 5. speed limit 6. head-on
collision 7. dangerous driving 8. reasonable speed
Exercise 6: 1. knocked 2. swerve 3. skidded 4. lost
5. crashed 6. damaged
Exercise 7: 1d 2b 3c 4e 5a
Exercise 8: 1S 2F 3S 4S 5F 6F

Unit 66 Public transport

Exercise 2: 1. catch 2. miss 3. leaves 4. delayed
5. running 6. cancelled
Exercise 3: 1. tube 2. line 3. change 4. stops 5. exit
Exercise 4: 1. fares 2. rush-hour 3. timetable
4. commuters 5. unreliable 6. hold-up 7. queue
8. passengers
Exercise 5: 1. arrival 2. running, delay 3. standing,
calling, change
Exercise 7: 1e 2c 3d 4a 5b 6j 7h 8g 9f 10i
Exercise 8: 1. pack 2. left 3. window, aisle
The response in number 3 is said by the passenger.
Exercise 9: 1e 2c 3b 4a 5d 6. overhead lockers
7. emergency exits, life jackets 8. upright position
9. duty-free items

Unit 67 School

Exercise 1: 1g(S) 2i(S) 3a(A) 4j(A) 5h(S) 6e(S)
7c(S) 8f(S) 9d(S) 10b(A)
Exercise 2: The verb which does not collocate with
exam is *make* – 1. passed 2. failed 3. re-sit
4. revise
Exercise 3: 1. nursery 2. primary 3. secondary
4. college 5. sat 6. passed 7. got 8. applied
9. university 10. degree 11. graduated 12. doing
Exercise 4: 1e 2g 3c 4h 5a 6b 7f 8d
Exercise 5: 1. uniform 2. rules 3. strict 4. test
5. grade 6. hour 7. period 8. discipline
Exercise 6: 1. a b e f 2. c d g
Exercise 7: 1. PE teacher 2. head of department
3. learning support assistant 4. caretaker 5. head
teacher 6. librarian 7. deputy head 8. lab technician

Unit 68 Further education

Exercise 1: 1. left 2. stayed on 3. do 4. applied
5. got in 6. entry 7. high 8. results 9. prospectus
10. college 11. course 12. diploma 13. degree
Exercise 2: fees, accommodation, expenses, grant,
loan, part-time
Exercise 3: 1. lectures, reading 2. presentation,
seminar 3. handout, notes 4. lists 5. tutor, options,
term
Exercise 4: 1. physicist 2. philosopher 3. psychologist
4. sociologist 5. architect 6. historian
7. mathematician 8. chemist 9. astronomer
10. engineer
Exercise 5: 1. academic 2. assignment 3. placement
4. qualifications 5. vocational 6. specialise
7. tutorial 8. drop out 9. qualify
Exercise 6: 1. term, coursework, deadline, dissertation
2. revising, finals, results 3. paper 4. graduation,
graduate

Unit 69 Learning a language

Exercise 1: mother-tongue, second language 2. native speaker 3. bilingual 4. strong accent
Exercise 2: 1. say 2. mean 3. difference 4. pronounce 5. spell 6. plural   1e 2c 3b 4f 5a 6d
Exercise 3: 1. say 2. made 3. studied 4. practise 5. did 6. picked up 7. improved 8. hold 10. progress 11. grammar rules 12. practise 13. a course 14. a lot of new language 15. pronunciation 16. a conversation
Exercise 4: 1. decided 2. never 3. would 4. has 5. train 6. the 7. money 8. a 9. annoyed 10. of 11. he 12. so
Exercise 5: 1. the 'to' infinitive 2. a phrasal verb 3. a gerund 4. a proverb 5. an idiom 6. a collocation
Exercise 6: 1. listen carefully 2. repeat 3. practise 4. do the exercises, hand in 5. correct 6. look it up 7. write it down 8. making mistakes 9. rub it out 10. revising

Unit 70 Jobs

Exercise 1: 1c 2a 3b
Exercise 2: 1e 2c 3f 4b 5a 6d
Exercise 3: 1c 2b 3a 4d
Exercise 4: 1d 2e 3a 4c 5b
Exercise 5: 1e 2d 3c 4a 5b
Exercise 6: 1h 2g 3e 4f 5d 6c 7a 8b
Exercise 7: 1. sailor 2. firefighter 3. paramedic 4. soldier 5. pilot 6. police officer
Exercise 8: 1e 2c 3a 4d 5b 6j 7h 8g 9f 10i
Exercise 9: 1. hairdresser 2. waiter 3. architect 4. chef 5. photographer 6. postman

Unit 71 Employment

Exercise 1: 1. section 2. qualifications 3. CV 4. application 5. interview 6. experience
Exercise 2: 1. found 2. applied for 3. go into 4. filled in, sent it off 5. offered
Exercise 3: Cleaner: requires, rates
Accounts: position, Salary
Sales Assistant: applicant, experience, training, Apply
Nurse: Temporary, leave
Exercise 4: 1P 2N 3N 4P 5P 6N 7P 8P
Exercise 5: 1f 2d 3b 4e 5a 6c
Exercise 6: 1. was sacked 2. be made redundant 3. unemployed
1. was fired 2. lose their jobs 3. out of work

Unit 72 Working life

Exercise 1: Money: isn't very well-paid, a pretty good salary, a regular pay rise, bonus **Hours:** long hours, do overtime, flexi-time, go part-time **Benefits / Perks:** a company car, pension scheme, private health insurance **Promotion:** get promoted, work your way up, career ladder **Holiday:** six weeks' paid holiday, taking a few days off
Exercise 2: 1e 2c 3a 4b 5d 6f
Exercise 3: 1N 2N 3P 4P 5P 6N 7P 8P, P
Exercise 4: 1d 2f 3a 4e 5b 6c
Exercise 5: 1. union 2. strike 3. increase 4. rejected 5. demanded 6. low pay 7. resigned 8. crisis
Exercise 6: 1. job 2. work 3. work, job 4. work 5. work 6. job 7. work 8. job Remember that *job* is countable and *work* is uncountable.
Exercise 7: 1. career 2. job 3. job 4. career 5. job 6. career 7. job

Unit 73 In the office

Exercise 1: 1. scales 2. fax machine 3. briefcase 4. wastepaper basket 5. files 6. computer 7. photocopier 8. drawers 9. filing cabinet 10. desk
Exercise 2: 1. hole punch 2. paper clip 3. envelope 4. rubber 5. in-tray 6. stapler 7. calculator 8. drawing pins 9. scissors 10. pencil sharpener 11. Sellotape
Exercise 3: 1. deal with 2. send 3. arrange 4. do 5. make
Exercise 4: 1. a client 2. a problem 3. an order 4. a meeting
Exercise 5: 1d 2a 3c 4b
Exercise 6: 1c 2e 3a 4b 5d
Exercise 7: 1. calendar 2. diary 3. scissors 4. calculator 5. filing cabinet 6. wastepaper basket 7. hole punch 8. stapler / paper clips

Unit 74 Business

Exercise 1: 1. market 2. products 3. competition 4. capital 5. facility 6. plan 7. flow 8. sales 9. expenses 10. overheads 11. investment 12. stock
Exercise 2: 1e 2d 3a 4c 5b 6f 7g
Exercise 3: 1c 2a 3d 4b 5e 6. family 7. branches 8. directors 9. firm 10. private enterprise 11. shareholders
Exercise 4: 1e 2c 3a 4b 5f 6d
Exercise 5: 1W 2W 3B 4B 5W 6B 7W 8W 9B
Exercise 6: You should have deleted: 1. do much profit, get even 2. got a huge loss 3. annual turnaround 4. expenditure 5. sales numbers 6. sales goals 7. addition 8. bottom figure
Exercise 7: 1d 2c 3a 4b 5e

Unit 75 Crime and punishment

Exercise 1: 1f/h 2b/g 3c/e 4a/d
Exercise 2: 1. crime 2. court 3. trial 4. case 5. judge 6. defence 7. evidence 8. verdict 9. sentence 10. prison (or jail) 11. fine 12. jail (or prison)
Exercise 3: 1. arrested 2. suspected 3. convicted 4. questioned 5. charged 6. heard 7. defend 8. pleaded 9. called 10. committed 11. identified 12. sentenced

Exercise 4: 1c 2a 3d 4e 5b
Exercise 5: 1. inmates 2. cells 3. recreational
4. rehabilitate 5. criminals 6. released
7. integrate 8. society
Exercise 6: 1. bring back the death penalty 2. be
behind bars 3. lock them up 4. make an example
5. get away with it

Unit 76 Serious crime

Exercise 1: 1. murder 2. terrorism 3. hijacking
4. rape 5. kidnapping 6. mugging
Exercise 2: 2. arsonist 3. blackmailer 4. hijacker
5. kidnapper 6. mugger 7. murderer 8. rapist
9. smuggler 10. terrorist
Exercise 3: 1. arson 2. smuggling 3. armed robbery
4. blackmail 5. drink-driving 6. fraud
Exercise 4: 1e 2d 3b 4a 5f 6c
The correct order is: g, i, k, l, h, j
Exercise 5: 1. set fire to 2. murdered 3. kidnapped
4. smuggle 5. robbed 6. raped 7b 8c 9a
Exercise 6: 1e 2d 3a 4f 5b 6c 7. weapon 8. killer
9. murder

Unit 77 Theft, drugs, and other crimes

Exercise 1: 1. theft 2. burglary 3. robbery
4. shoplifting 5. embezzlement 6. mugging
Criminals: thief, burglar, shoplifter
Exercise 2: 1. robbed 2. stole 3. stolen 4. stolen
5. robbed
Exercise 3: 1c 2a 3b 4e 5d 6. a forged £10 note
7. the legal limit 8. stolen goods 9. the black market
10. tax evasion
Exercise 4: 1. hooliganism 2. prostitution
3. vandalism 4. speeding
Exercise 5: 1. soft 2. pushers 3. hard 4. barons
5. decriminalise 6. possession
Exercise 6: 1. snatch 2. vandalised 3. burgled
4. mugged 5. embezzled 6. forging
Exercise 7: 1b 2c 3d 4e 5a

Unit 78 War

Exercise 2: a. weapons b. bomb c. war 1. world
2. civil 3. guerrilla 4. chemical, biological 5. petrol
6. letter
Exercise 3: The army: rifle, grenade, soldier, artillery,
tank, landmine, machine gun **The navy:** cruiser,
warship, submarine, aircraft carrier, landing craft,
destroyer, minesweeper, torpedo, sailor **The air force:**
bomber, fighter pilot, aircrew, helicopter, parachute
Exercise 4: 1. supplying 2. bombing 3. blew up
4. exploded 5. cleared 6. shot down
Exercise 5: 1. disputes, ethnic 2. attacks, deteriorates,
escalates 3. involved 4. force 5. process
Exercise 6: 1b 2e 3a 4g 5h 6c 7d 8f

Exercise 7: 1. peacekeeping 2. ceasefire 3. talks
4. deal 5. sides 6. treaty
a. peacekeeping b. temporary c. talks d. deal
e. treaty

Unit 79 Politics

Exercise 1: 1. king, queen, Prime Minister 2. dictator,
dictatorship, president 3. dictatorship, democracy
Exercise 2: You should have deleted: 1. Politics 2. an
election 3. opponents, control 4. co-operative
5. periods 6. national 7. Manager 8. cupboard
Exercise 3: 1. polling station 2. parties 3. policies
4. campaign 5. power 6. candidate 7. constituency
8. vote 9. manifesto 10. voter
a. called, held b. won c. get
Exercise 4: 1b 2c 3d 4a 5f 6e
Exercise 5: 1. capitalist 2. socialism 3. communist
4. fascism 5. nationalist 6. anarchy 7. middle
8. working-class 9. independence 10. socialists
11. right-wing 12. extreme
Exercise 6: 1. patriotic 2. extreme 3. liberal
4. politically aware, left-wing, right
5L 6R 7R 8L 9L

Unit 80 Religion

Exercise 1: 1. Christianity 2. Catholics 3. Buddhism
4. Islam 5. Jews 6. Hindus
Exercise 2: People: priest (C), vicar (C), imam (I),
bishop (C), minister (C), rabbi (J), the Pope (C), nun
(C), muezzin (I), monk (C,B) **Places:** temple (C,B,J),
chapel (C), church (C), shrine (B,C), convent (C),
minaret (I), mosque (I), synagogue (J), monastery
(C,B), cathedral (C)
Exercise 3: 1c 2b 3g 4f 5a 6e 7d
Exercise 4: 1. prayer 2. life after death 3. pilgrimage
4. for peace 5. to church
Exercise 5: 1. Christmas 2. Holy Week 3. Good
Friday 4. Lent 5. Easter 6. Advent 7. Ascension
8. All Saints
Exercise 6: 1. aisle 2. pew 3. hymn 4. pulpit,
sermon 5. service 6. altar 7. lectern 8. font
Exercise 7: religious, atheist, agnostic, devout, faith
Exercise 8: 1. angel 2. worships 3. paradise 4. faith
5. idolise 6. Bible 7. pray 8. shrine 9. Mecca

Unit 81 Social issues

Exercise 1: 1. teenage pregnancies 2. drug abuse
3. class 4. animal rights 5. homelessness 6. sexual
discrimination 7. racism 8. gay rights
a. classless b. rough c. involved d. racially
e. related f. orientation
Exercise 2: 1d 2e 3f 4c 5b 6a 7. human rights
8. race relations 9. ethnic minorities 10. inner-city
areas 11. gay community 12. single-parent families

Exercise 3: Children are on drugs. Children are taking drugs. Children are using drugs. Children are experimenting with drugs.
1. soft drugs 2. hard drugs 3. addicts
4. dealers 5. overdose
Exercise 4: 1c 2b 3d 4a
Exercise 5: A: tackle, face, address B: avoid, ignore
C: 2,4,6 – D: 1,3,5
Exercise 6: 1. abuse 2. domestic 3. housing
4. bullying 5. trap

Unit 82 The environment

Exercise 1: 1. damage 2. factory 3. pollution
4. waste, recycled 5. Environmentalists, emissions
6. protect
Exercise 2: 1. toxic waste 2. crops, pesticides
3. Emissions 4. deforestation 5. Exhaust fumes
Injure and *hurt* cannot be used with *environment*.
Exercise 3: 1b 2c 3d 4a 5. global warming
6. greenhouse effect 7. ozone layer 8. acid rain
Exercise 4: 1. gases 2. radiation 3. ice caps
4. oceans 5. sea level 6. floods 7. climate 8. deserts
Exercise 5: 1. destruction 2. natural habitats 3. in danger of extinction 4. way of life 5. indigenous people 6. long-term 7. future generations
8. natural resources 9. air quality 10. heavily polluted 11. cloud of pollution 12. uninhabitable
Exercise 6: 1f 2e 3d 4a 5b 6c 7. unleaded petrol, renewable energy 8. public transport 9. recycling point, bottle bank 10. environmentally friendly
Exercise 7: environment, environmental, environmentalist ecology, ecological, ecologist

Unit 83 The natural world

Exercise 1: 1. forest 2. waterfall 3. cave 4. cliffs
5. rocks 6. river 7. lake 8. island 9. mountains
10. valley
Exercise 2: 1e 2c 3a 4b 5d 6. flat, hilly 7. high, low 8. deep, shallow 9. low 10. steep 11. shallow
12. deep 13. fertile 14. flat 15. thick/dense 16. hilly
Exercise 3: You should have deleted: 1. nature, on the beach, follows 2. leads, on the shore 3. ends, alive, wood
Exercise 4: 1. trunk 2. branch 3. leaf 4. roots
5. fruit 6. blossom
Exercise 5: 1T 2F 3F 4T 5T 6T 7T 8F 9F 10T
11F 12F
Exercise 6: 1e 2h 3j 4f 5a 6i 7b 8d 9c 10g
Exercise 7: 1. forest 2. river 3. sea 4. ocean
5. mountain 6. tree

Unit 84 Science

Exercise 2: You should have deleted: 1. take
2. make 3. put 4. somebody's eyes 5. the evidence
6. drugs on animals 7. a conclusion

Exercise 3: 1. formulated 2. tested 3. performed
4. controlled 5 replicated 6. recorded 7. discarded
8. modified 9. ignored 10. accepted
Exercise 4: physics, physicist chemistry, chemist
astronomy, astronomer biology, biologist zoology,
zoologist botany, botanist genetics, geneticist
Exercise 5: *find* a cure for AIDS; *find* the cause of death; *discover* a way of reducing heart disease;
discover a link between smoking and heart disease;
find out why malaria is spreading; *discover* why the plane crashed; *find out* what causes infertility;
discover what causes a plant species to die out
Exercise 6: 1A 2F 3F 4F 5A 6A 7F 8A
Exercise 7: 1. breed, clone (genetic engineering)
2. test-tube baby (fertility treatment) 3. microsurgery, lasers (medical science) 4. robots (automation)

Unit 85 Materials

Exercise 1: 1. wax 2. glass 3. rubber 4. metal
5. plastic 6. wood 7. leather, leather 8. cardboard
A: wood, leather, cardboard, wax (beeswax), paper, cotton, chalk, wool
B: metal, glass, rubber, plastic, wax (if made from oil), oil, fibre glass, nylon, petrol
Exercise 2: precious stones: diamond, emerald, ruby
precious metals: gold, silver, platinum **other metals:** iron, lead, brass, copper, aluminium, steel, tin, bronze
types of wood: oak, pine, walnut, beech, mahogany, bamboo
1. steel 2. gold 3. silver, bronze 4. brass
5. steel 6. aluminium 7. emerald 8. mahogany
9. lead 10. brass, steel, bronze
Exercise 3: 1N 2S 3N 4S 5N 6N 7c 8d 9a 10b
Exercise 4: 1c 2a 3b 4e 5d 6i 7j 8g 9h 10f
Pure leather is not correct. We say *real leather*.
Exercise 5: 1. gold 2. steel 3. wood 4. silver 5. iron
6. golden 7. stone 8. lead

Unit 86 History

Exercise 1: 1. event 2. ancestors 3. Primitive
4. ancient 5. empire 6. date
Exercise 2: 1. origins 2. artefacts 3. archaeologists
4. records 5. periods 6. accounts 7. documents
8. sources
Exercise 3: 1g 2k 3a 4b 5h 6d 7i 8c 9j 10f 11l
12e 13. invasion 14. discovery 15. colonisation
16. abolition 17. invention 18. assassination
Exercise 4: 1h 2c 3b 4e 5i 6a 7d 8g 9f
Exercise 5: 1. the Ice Age 2. the Stone Age
3. the Roman Empire 4. the Middle Ages 5. the Renaissance 6. the Reformation 7. the French Revolution 8. the early nineteenth century 9. the Great Depression 10. the end of the last century
Exercise 6: 1g 2e 3d 4a 5c 6i 7f 8b 9h

Unit 87 Countries and nationalities

Exercise 1: 1. North America 2. the British Isles
3. the Arctic 4. Scandinavia 5. Central Europe
6. Central America 7. the Caribbean 8. North Africa
9. the Mediterranean 10. the Middle East 11. Asia
12. South East Asia 13. the Far East 14. South
America 15. Africa 16. Antarctica

Exercise 2:

Algeria	Argentina	Australia	Austria	Belgium
Brazil	Canada	Chile	China	Colombia
Denmark	Egypt	Ethiopia	Finland	Germany
Hungary	India	Indonesia	Iran	Ireland
Israel	Italy	Japan	Korea	Kuwait
Lebanon	Malaysia	Mexico	Morocco	Norway
Pakistan	Peru	Poland	Portugal	Romania
Russia	Slovenia	Sri Lanka	Sweden	Taiwan
Tibet	Tunisia	Turkey	Vietnam	Zimbabwe

1. (-ish) Danish, Finnish, Irish, Polish, Swedish,
Turkish
2. (-(i)an) Algerian, Argentinian, Australian, Austrian,
Belgian, Brazilian, Canadian, Chilean, Colombian,
Egyptian, Ethiopian, German, Hungarian, Indian,
Indonesian, Iranian, Italian, Korean, Malaysian,
Mexican, Moroccan, Norwegian, Peruvian,
Romanian, Russian, Slovenian, Sri Lankan, Tibetan,
Tunisian, Zimbabwean
3. (-ese) Chinese, Japanese, Lebanese, Portuguese,
Taiwanese, Vietnamese
4. (-i) Israeli, Kuwaiti, Pakistani

Exercise 3: 1. France 2. Greece 3. Iceland 4. Wales
5. Thailand 6. Switzerland 7. Cyprus 8. The
Netherlands

Exercise 4: 1. British 2. Japanese 3. French,
Germans, 4. Swedes, Finns 5. Swiss 6. Poles

Exercise 5:

Athens	Amsterdam	Bangkok	Beijing
Berlin	Brussels	Cairo	Copenhagen
Dublin	Edinburgh	Helsinki	Lisbon
London	Madrid	Milan	Moscow
Nairobi	Naples	New York	Paris
Rejkavik	Stockholm	Tokyo	Warsaw

Exercise 6: 1c 2a 3a 4e 5d 6b

Exercise 7: 1. in 2. on 3. in 4. on 5. on 6. on
7. in 8. in 9. in

Unit 88 The weather

Exercise 2: 1g 2h 3b 4f 5d 6e 7c 8a
9. miserable, horrible, terrible, foul
10. lovely, beautiful, fabulous, glorious
A *rainbow* appears when there is sunshine and rain at
the same time.

Exercise 3: 1e 2d 3b 4a 5c 6h 7i 8f 9j 10g

Exercise 4: 1. freezing 2. warm 3. humid 4. cool
5. chilly 6. mild

Exercise 5: 1f 2e 3c 4a 5b 6d

Exercise 6: 1. remain 2. reach 3. rise 4. fall 5. frost
6. wintry 7. sleet 8. icy 9. melt

Unit 89 Disasters

Exercise 1: 1. drought 2. earthquake 3. forest fire
4. flood 5. tornado 6. tidal wave 7. hurricane
8. volcano 9. volcanoes 10. droughts 11. floods
12. earthquake

Exercise 2: 1. drought 2. flood 3. tornado
4. volcano 5. earthquake 6. tidal wave 7. forest fire
8. hurricane
a. burst b. lasted c. in its path d. round the clock
e. blown off f. ripped out

Exercise 3: 1. struck 2. claimed 3. injured 4. damage
5. destroyed 6. survivors 7. trapped 8. rubble

Exercise 4: 1. rainfall 2. affected 3. rescued
4. stranded 5. impassable 6. warnings

Exercise 5: 1. starvation 2. aid 3. contaminated
4. epidemic 5. refugees 6. starving 7. supplies

Exercise 6: 1. started 2. spread 3. rescue 4. trapped
5. suffering 6. evacuated 7. fought 8. bring

Unit 90 Wild animals

Exercise 1: 1. tiger 2. shark 3. crocodile 4. ostrich
5. bee 6. lobster

Exercise 2: 1. bear 2. zebra 3. camel 4. giraffe
5. hippopotamus 6. rhinoceros 7. buffalo
8. deer 9. monkey 10. elephant 11. kangaroo
12. baboon

Exercise 3: 1. squirrel 2. bat 3. mole 4. hedgehog
5. rat 6. fox

Exercise 4: 1. panther 2. leopard 3. tiger 4. lion

Exercise 5: 1. turtle 2. frog 3. snake 4. lizard
5. crocodile

Exercise 6: 1. seal 2. sea-horse 3. salmon 4. shark
5. lobster 6. jellyfish 7. walrus 8. dolphin 9. whale
10. starfish 11. octopus 12. crab

Exercise 7: 1. seagull 2. wren 3. eagle 4. swallow
5. penguin 6. peacock 7. swan 8. duck
9. flamingo 10. parrot 11. pigeon 12. owl

Exercise 8: 1. scorpion 2. spider 3. fly 4. ladybird
5. ant 6. butterfly 7. mosquito 8. bee
9. grasshopper 10. cockroach

Unit 91 Domestic and farm animals

Exercise 1: 1. rabbit 2. goldfish 3. cat 4. canary
5. tortoise 6. dog 7. guinea pig 8. mouse

Exercise 2: 1. dog 2. cat 3. horse 4. tropical fish
5. parrot

Exercise 3: 1. harness 2. bit 3. saddle 4. riding hat
5. stirrups 6. whip
The fastest is *gallop*, then *canter*, then *trot*.

Exercise 4: 1. donkey 2. duck 3. goat 4. hen
5. horse 6. goose 7. sheep 8. pig 9. cow 10. pony
11. cockerel 12. bull

Exercise 5: 1e 2g 3f 4c 5a 6b 7d

Exercise 6: 1. milk 2. grazing 3. bred 4. slaughtered

Exercise 7: 1h 2f 3d,e,g 4c 5a 6b

Unit 92 Talking about animals

Exercise 1: 1. goat 2. fox 3. camel 4. panda
5. gorilla 6. penguin
Exercise 2: 1f 2e 3i 4g 5a 6h 7c 8b 9d
10. wags, barks 11. stung 12. slithering
13. scratched 14. built
Exercise 3: 1. antler 2. trunk 3. horn 4. tail
5. wing 6. beak 7. hoof 8. claw 9. shell
10. feather 11. fin 12. paw
Exercise 4: 1e 2c 3f 4a 5d 6b
Exercise 5: 1b 2c 3a 4d
5. rat 6. fish 7. cat 8. frog 9. bull
Exercise 6: 1. cruelty 2. experiments 3. cosmetics
4. the wild 5. zoos 6. endangered 7. skins
8. habitats 9. extinct

Unit 93 Towns and cities

Exercise 2: 1f 2e 3a 4b 5g 6c 7d
8. litter bins 9. cycle lanes 10. tower block
11. pedestrian precinct 12. traffic lights 13. city
centre 14. main street
Exercise 3: culture: opera house, theatre, museum,
art gallery **transport:** railway station, underground,
multi-storey car park, taxi rank **education:**
university, school, college **sports:** swimming pool,
football stadium, leisure centre, ice rink
shopping: department store, shopping centre, mall
Exercise 4: 1g 2f 3b 4i 5a 6e 7h 8c 9d
Exercise 5: 1. rush hour, crowded, stressful, traffic
2. graffiti 3. cosmopolitan 4. convenient
5. property prices, suburbs, commute 6. Public
transport, efficient 7d 8c 9a 10b
Exercise 7: 1. street 2. road 3. estate 4. high-rise,
high-rise 5. crossing, crossing 6. commuters

Unit 94 Time

Exercise 1: 1c 2g 3f 4b 5h 6e 7a 8d
Exercise 2: 1. past 2. future 3. future 4. future
5. past 6. future 7. present 8. past 9. present
10. present 11. future 12. past 13. future
14. past 15. past 16. past 17. future 18. future
Exercise 3: 1. the other day 2. ages ago 3. in those
days 4. sooner or later 5. from now on 6. for the
time being 7. in a minute 8. straightaway
Exercise 4: 1. next time 2. on time 3. just in time
4. at the same time 5. by the time 6. all the time
7d 8a 9c 10b
Exercise 5: 1b 2d 3c 4f 5a 6e
Exercise 6: 1. for 2. during 3. while 4. by 5. until
6. just 7. yet 8. since 9. recently 10. finally 11. In
the end 12. so far 13. suddenly 14. To begin with
Exercise 7: 1c 2a 3d 4e 5b
Exercise 8: 1. spends hours talking on the phone
2. last for ages 3. take about an hour 4. pass the
time 5. Time is running out 6. find the time

Unit 95 Numbers

Exercise 1: 1c 2b 3f 4a 5d 6e
Exercise 2: 1d 2b 3a 4e 5c
Exercise 3: 1h 2e 3c 4a 5g 6b 7f 8d
Exercise 4: 1c 2e 3b 4a 5d
Exercise 5: 1. plus (addition) 2. minus (subtraction)
3. times (multiplication) 4. divided by (division)
Exercise 6: 1c 2b 3d 4a
Exercise 7: 1. first class 2. second-hand 3. third time
lucky 4. sixth sense 5. second nature 6. in seventh
heaven 7. first impressions 8. at the eleventh hour
Exercise 8: 1F 2M 3M 4F 5M 6M
7. about 8. so 9. give or take

Unit 96 Similarity and difference

Exercise 1: 1. a,d,f,g 2. c,e 3. b,h
Exercise 2: DiCaprio's new film is: very similar to his
last one, the same as his last one, no different from
his last one, just like his last one.
Exercise 3: 1. all the same 2. the same to you 3. stay
the same 4. at the same time 5. the same 6. the
same again
Exercise 4: 1. identical 2. familiar 3. equal
4. constant
Exercise 5: 1. not the same 2. opposite 3. unique
4. varied 5. alternative 6. incompatible
Exercise 6: 1. see the difference 2. tell the difference
3. makes no difference 4. makes all the difference
5. split the difference
Exercise 7: 1. much, a lot, far 2. nowhere near
3d 4c 5a 6b
If two people are *like chalk and cheese,* they are very
different.

Unit 97 Thoughts and ideas

Exercise 1: 1. remember 2. decide 3. wonder
4. Guess 5. imagine 6. work out 7. predict 8. judge
Exercise 2: 1c 2a 3d 4b
Exercise 3: You should have deleted: 1. reckon
2. consider, suggest, I suppose not 3. a consideration
4. didn't consider 5. realise 6. weren't realising
7. losing my mind 8. can't imagine
Exercise 4: 1b and d 2a and f 3c and e
Exercise 5: 1. understand 2. make sense 3. follow
4. lost
Exercise 6: 1. brilliant 2. bright 3. stupid 4. slow
5. genius 6. fool
Exercise 7: 1. changed 2. on 3. take 4. make
5. don't 6. slipped 7. I've got a lot on my mind
8. I can't make up my mind 9. I changed my mind
10. I don't really mind 11. It completely slipped my
mind 12. It'll take your mind off it

Unit 98 Size and shape

Exercise 1: 1. long 2. high 3. wide 4. deep
5d 6e 7c 8a 9b

Exercise 2: B: large, vast, massive, immense, huge, enormous S: little, tiny, minute, microscopic
You should have deleted: 1. huge 2. vast 3. little 4. small

Exercise 3: 1. short/tall 2. long/short 3. low/high 4. deep/shallow 5. wide/narrow 6. thin/thick

Exercise 4: 1. horizontal 2. vertical 3. diagonal 4. parallel

Exercise 5: 1. circle 2. triangle 3. pyramid 4. octagon 5. rectangle 6. semi-circle 7. square 8. cube 9. sphere 10. oval
1a 2d 3i 4g 5c 6h 7b 8e 9j 10f

Exercise 6: 1. octagon 2. square 3. pyramid 4. oval 5. rectangle 6. triangle 7. rectangle 8. spherical 9. sides 10. square 11. oval

Exercise 7: 1. cylindrical 2. pointed 3. heart-shaped 4. star-shaped 5. pear-shaped 6. diamond-shaped

Unit 99 Distance and speed

Exercise 1: 1. It's just across the road. 2. It's not very far away. 3. It's in the middle of nowhere. 4. It's in the next street. 5. It's 10 minutes by car. 6. It's miles away. 7. It's only five minutes' walk. It's not far. It's just round the corner. 8. It's a long way away. It's miles away. It's too far to walk.

Exercise 2: 1. by, from, to, to 2. From 3. from

4. via 5. to, on/via, in 6. from, into, from

Exercise 3: 1. near 2. far 3. remote 4. in the distance 5. long 6. nearby

Exercise 4: a. an b. over c. doing d. top e. on
1. I was 20 miles an hour over the limit 2. My new car's got a top speed of 150. 3. We did about 120 miles a day on average. 4. He must have been doing more than 100! 5. I was only doing 30 miles an hour

Unit 100 Quantities

Exercise 1: 1. drop 2. penny 3. stitch 4. trace 5. ounce 6. amount

Exercise 2: 1. loads of money 2. piles of books 3. thousands of people 4. hundreds of times 5. a mass of detail 6. dozens of calls

Exercise 3: 1. bunch 2. sheet 3. game 4. crowd 5. group 6. slice 7. pair 8. piece 9. set 10. lump

Exercise 4: 1. tube, tomato puree 2. jar, marmalade 3. slice, cake 4. tub, yoghurt 5. bottle, mineral water 6. box, tissues 7. packet, biscuits 8. can, beer

Exercise 5: 1. litre 2. pint 3. leg 4. breasts 5. bag 6. grams 7. dozen 8. steaks 9. loaf 10. kilo

Exercise 6: 1. swarm 2. herd 3. flock 4. shoal 5. pack

Exercise 7: 1. rasher 2. pack 3. speck 4. sack 5. sliver 6. gang (or pack) 7. crate 8. barrel 9. grain 10. pinch

Exercise 8: 1. sea 2. mountain 3. coat 4. flood 5. bags 6. stream